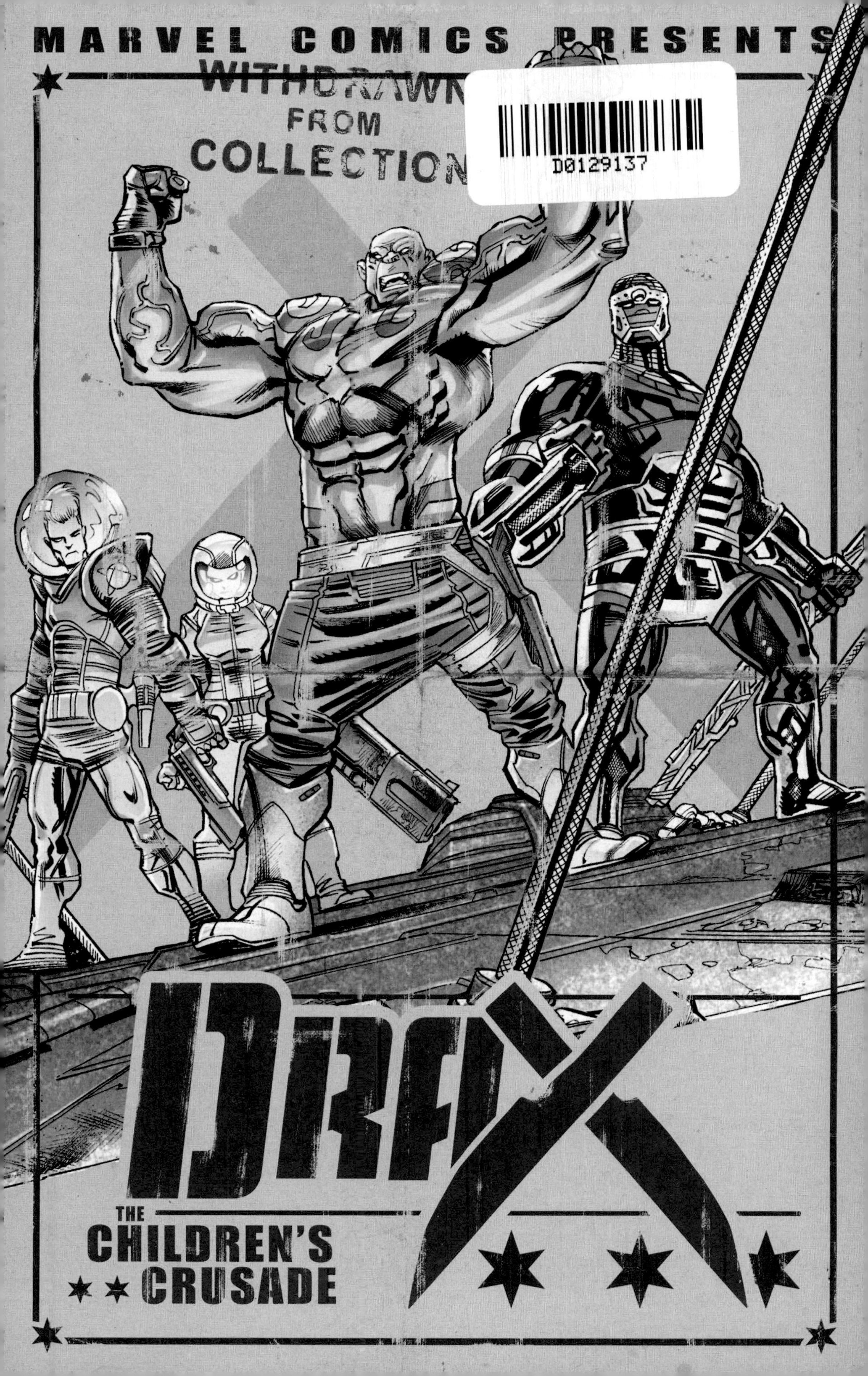
MARVEL COMICS PRESENTS
DRAX
THE CHILDREN'S CRUSADE

"THE DESTROYER" DRAX vs KILLER THRILL

COLLECTION EDITOR
SARAH BRUNSTAD

ASSOCIATE MANAGING EDITOR
KATERI WOODY

EDITOR, SPECIAL PROJECTS
MARK D. BEAZLEY

SENIOR EDITOR, SPECIAL PROJECTS
JENNIFER GRÜNWALD

VP PRODUCTION & SPECIAL PROJECTS
JEFF YOUNGQUIST

SVP PRINT, SALES & MARKETING
DAVID GABRIEL

BOOK DESIGNERS
ADAM DEL RE with **JAY BOWEN**

EDITOR IN CHIEF
AXEL ALONSO

CHIEF CREATIVE OFFICER
JOE QUESADA

PUBLISHER
DAN BUCKLEY

EXECUTIVE PRODUCER
ALAN FINE

DRAX VOL. 2: THE CHILDREN'S CRUSADE. Contains material originally published in magazine form as DRAX #6-11. First printing 2016. ISBN# 978-0-7851-9663-1. Published by MARVEL WORLDWIDE, INC., a subsidiary of MARVEL ENTERTAINMENT, LLC. OFFICE OF PUBLICATION: 135 West 50th Street, New York, NY 10020. Copyright © 2016 MARVEL No similarity between any of the names, characters, persons, and/or institutions in this magazine with those of any living or dead person or institution is intended, and any such similarity which may exist is purely coincidental. **Printed in Canada.** ALAN FINE, President, Marvel Entertainment; DAN BUCKLEY, President, TV, Publishing & Brand Management; JOE QUESADA, Chief Creative Officer; TOM BREVOORT, SVP of Publishing; DAVID BOGART, SVP of Business Affairs & Operations, Publishing & Partnership; C.B. CEBULSKI, VP of Brand Management & Development, Asia; DAVID GABRIEL, SVP of Sales & Marketing, Publishing; JEFF YOUNGQUIST, VP of Production & Special Projects; DAN CARR, Executive Director of Publishing Technology; ALEX MORALES, Director of Publishing Operations; SUSAN CRESPI, Production Manager; STAN LEE, Chairman Emeritus. For information regarding advertising in Marvel Comics or on Marvel.com, please contact Vit DeBellis, Integrated Sales Manager, at vdebellis@marvel.com. For Marvel subscription inquiries, please call 888-511-5480. **Manufactured between 9/30/2016 and 11/7/2016 by SOLISCO PRINTERS, SCOTT, QC, CANADA.**

10 9 8 7 6 5 4 3 2 1

DRAX

THE CHILDREN'S CRUSADE

WRITERS

CM PUNK
#6

CULLEN BUNN
#7-8

BREAKDOWNS
SCOTT HEPBURN
FINISHES
SCOTT HANNA
WITH SCOTT HEPBURN
COLORISTS
MATT MILLA & RACHELLE ROSENBERG

#9-11
ARTIST
SCOTT HEPBURN
COLORIST
ANTONIO FABELA

BREAKDOWNS
SCOTT HEPBURN
FINISHES
SCOTT HANNA
PENCILS, #8, PAGES 2 & 10
MARCUS TO
INKS, #8, PAGES 2 & 10
SCOTT HANNA
COLORIST
ANTONIO FABELA

COVER ART
SCOTT HEPBURN
WITH MATT MILLA
& RUTH REDMOND (#9)

ASSISTANT EDITOR
KATHLEEN WISNESKI

EDITOR
JAKE THOMAS

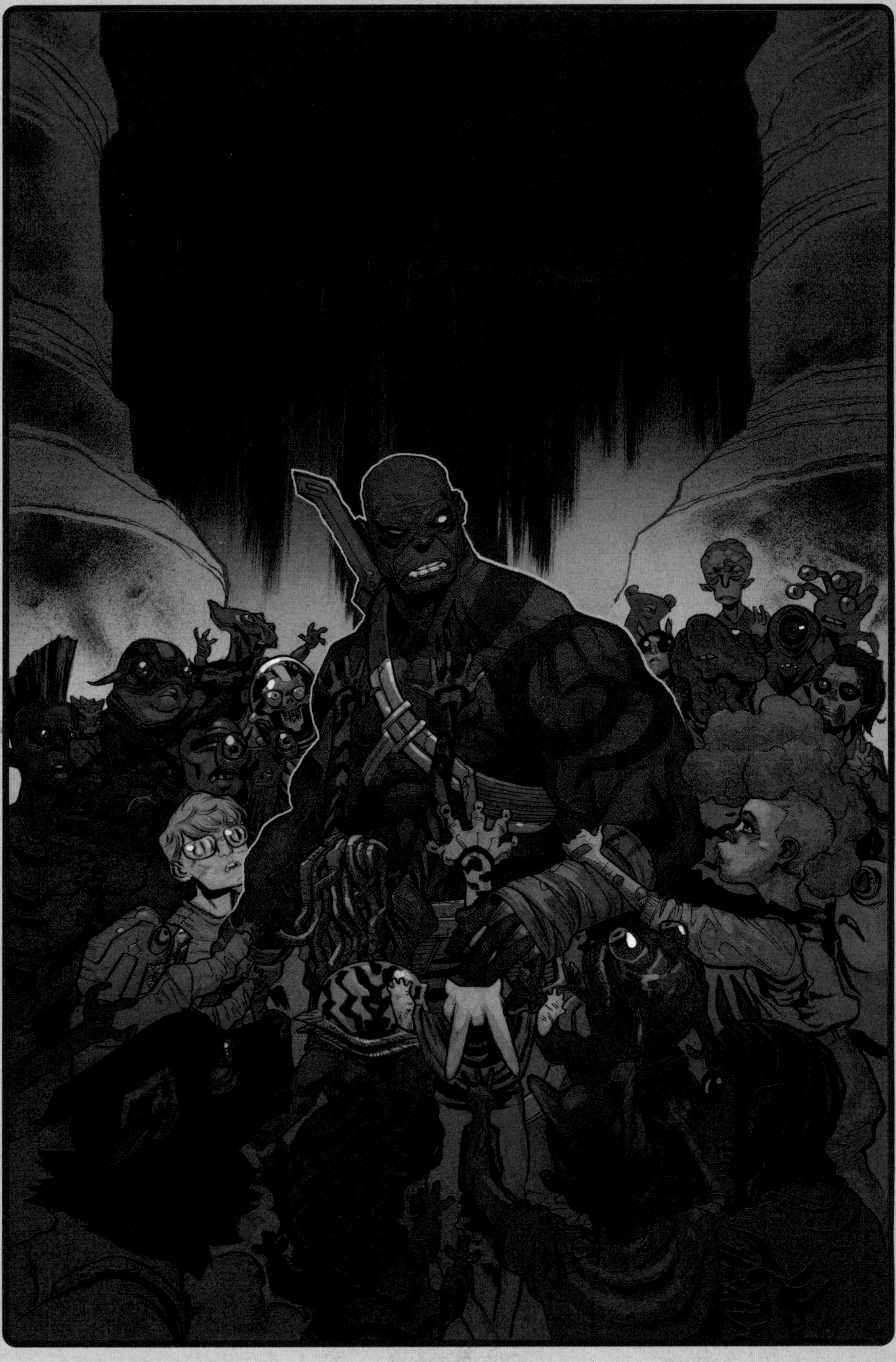

6

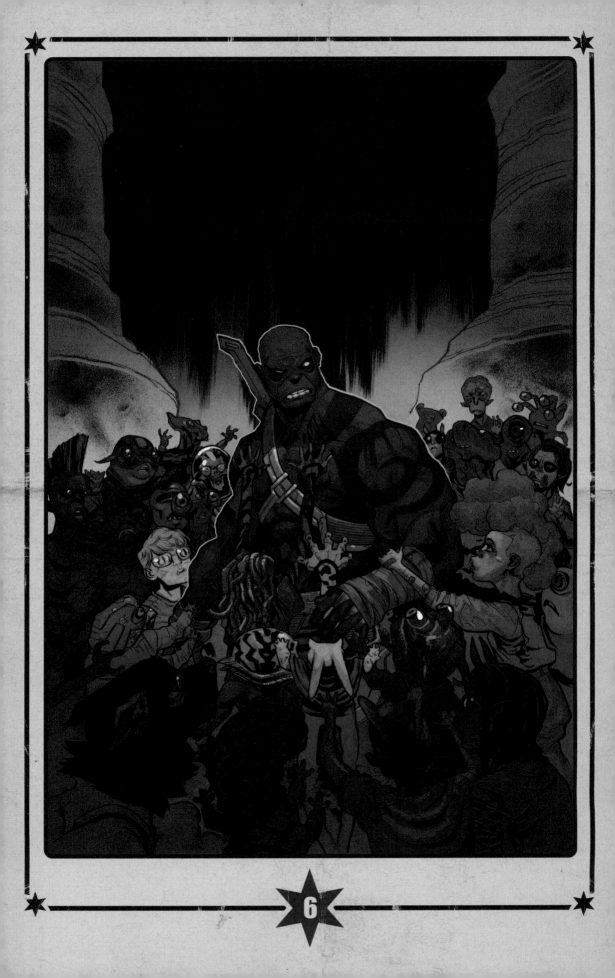

AFTER THANOS TOOK HIS FAMILY AND HIS LIFE, THE MAN NOW KNOWN AS DRAX WAS REMADE INTO A BEING OF GREAT STRENGTH WITH A THIRST FOR REVENGE. HIS PURSUIT OF JUSTICE HAS TAKEN HIM THROUGHOUT THE UNIVERSE AND SHOWN HIS INCREDIBLE COURAGE AND HEROISM, WHICH LED PETER QUILL TO INVITE HIM INTO THE GUARDIANS OF THE GALAXY. THOUGH HE FOUND A NEW HOME WITH THE GUARDIANS, TRUE PEACE REMAINS ELUSIVE FOR THE WARRIOR CALLED…

DRAX

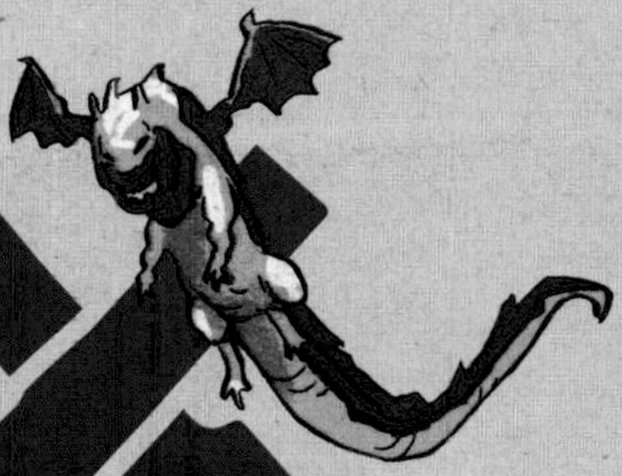

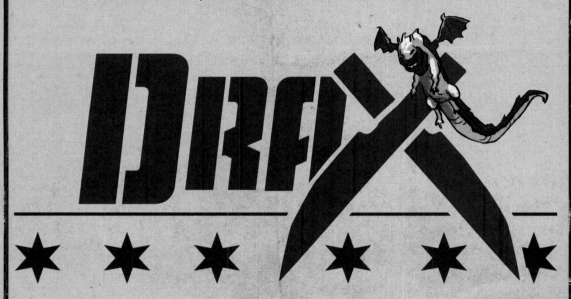

AFTER A DETOUR TO A DISTANT MOON WHERE NO ONE BUT DRAX THE DESTROYER COULD STOP FIN FANG FOOM'S RAMPAGE, DRAX IS BACK WHERE HE BELONGS: ON THE HUNT FOR THANOS!

WELL…PERHAPS DRAX HAD HELP FROM BARTENDER/GEARHEAD ORA, WARRIOR ROBOT TORGO, AND CIVILIAN ROBOT HEAD, ROBOT HEAD. AND FOOM WASN'T RAMPAGING SO MUCH AS HE WAS TAKING MACHINERY AND CHILDREN IN A FAILED ATTEMPT TO INCUBATE THE LAST OF HIS SPECIES' EGGS. AND TECHNICALLY, DRAX AND HIS ALLIES ARE NOW RETURNING THE CHILDREN RESCUED FROM FOOM TO THEIR HOME PLANETS. BUT IF YOU TAKE A VERY BROAD VIEW, DRAX IS BACK HUNTING THANOS!

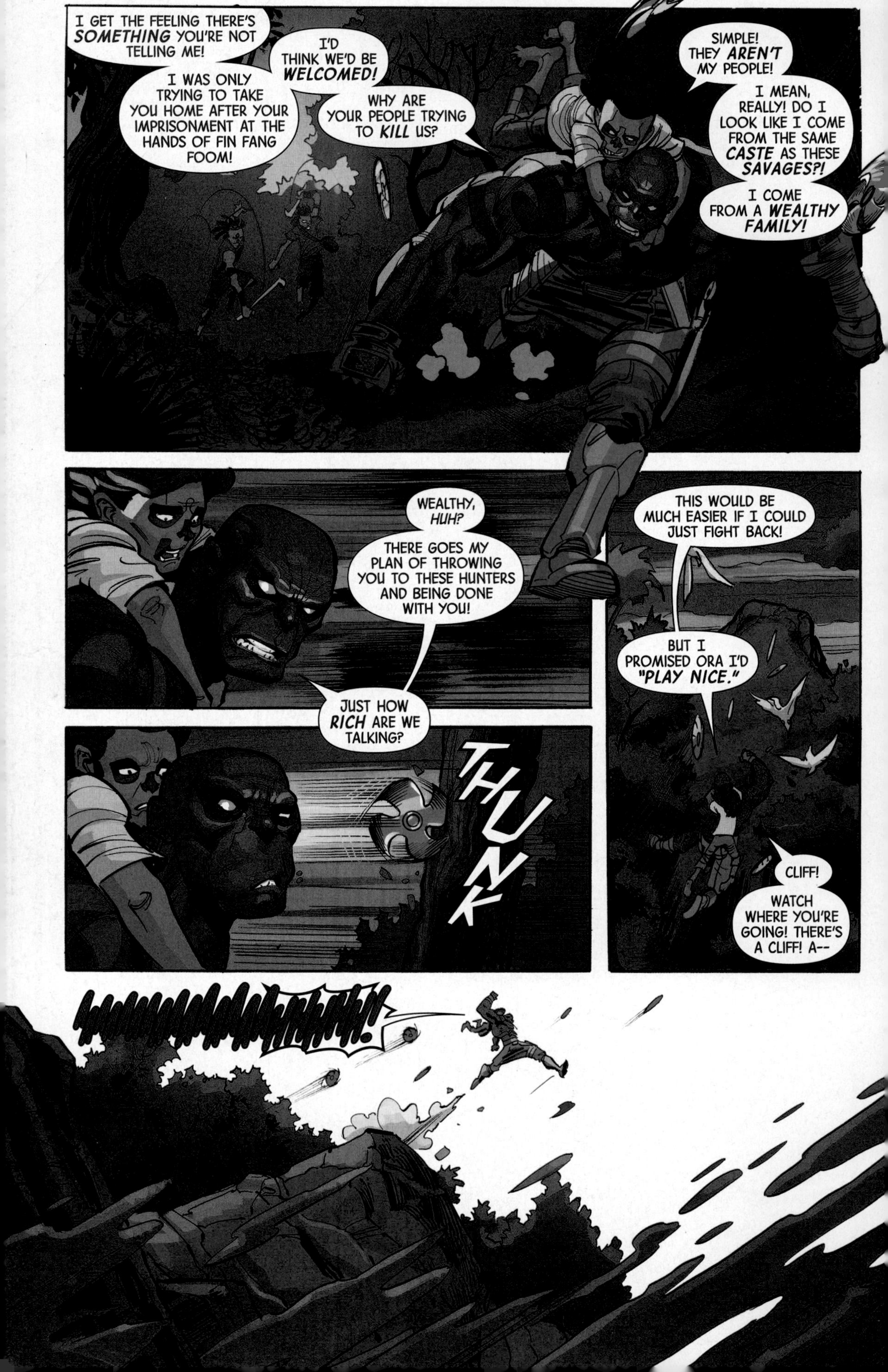
I GET THE FEELING THERE'S SOMETHING YOU'RE NOT TELLING ME!
I WAS ONLY TRYING TO TAKE YOU HOME AFTER YOUR IMPRISONMENT AT THE HANDS OF FIN FANG FOOM!
I'D THINK WE'D BE WELCOMED!
WHY ARE YOUR PEOPLE TRYING TO KILL US?
SIMPLE! THEY AREN'T MY PEOPLE!
I MEAN, REALLY! DO I LOOK LIKE I COME FROM THE SAME CASTE AS THESE SAVAGES?!
I COME FROM A WEALTHY FAMILY!
WEALTHY, HUH?
THERE GOES MY PLAN OF THROWING YOU TO THESE HUNTERS AND BEING DONE WITH YOU!
JUST HOW RICH ARE WE TALKING?
THUNK
THIS WOULD BE MUCH EASIER IF I COULD JUST FIGHT BACK!
BUT I PROMISED ORA I'D "PLAY NICE."
CLIFF!
WATCH WHERE YOU'RE GOING! THERE'S A CLIFF! A--

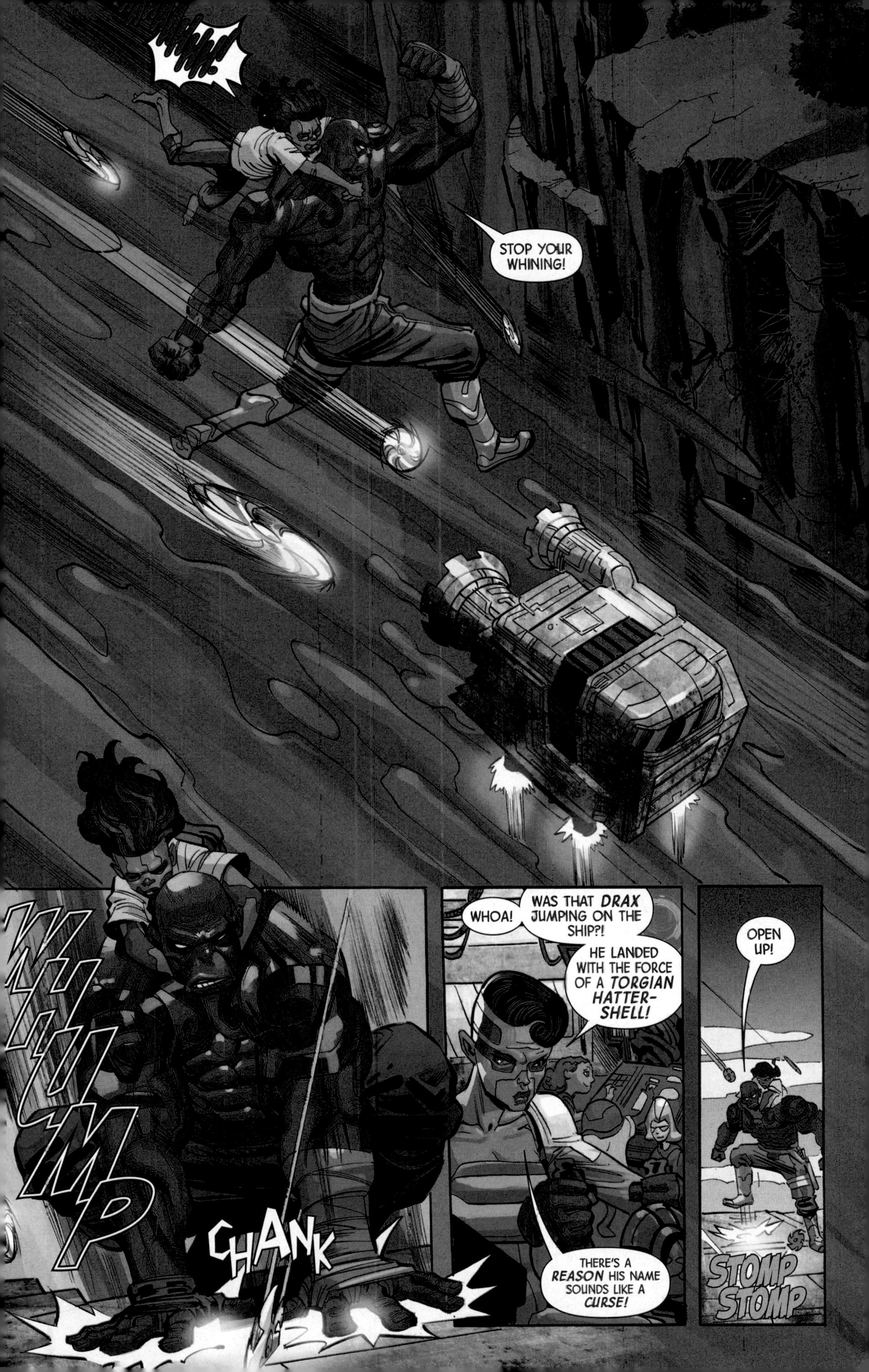
STOP YOUR WHINING!
WHUUMP
CHANK
WHOA!
WAS THAT DRAX JUMPING ON THE SHIP?!
HE LANDED WITH THE FORCE OF A TORGIAN HATTER-SHELL!
THERE'S A REASON HIS NAME SOUNDS LIKE A CURSE!
OPEN UP!
STOMP STOMP

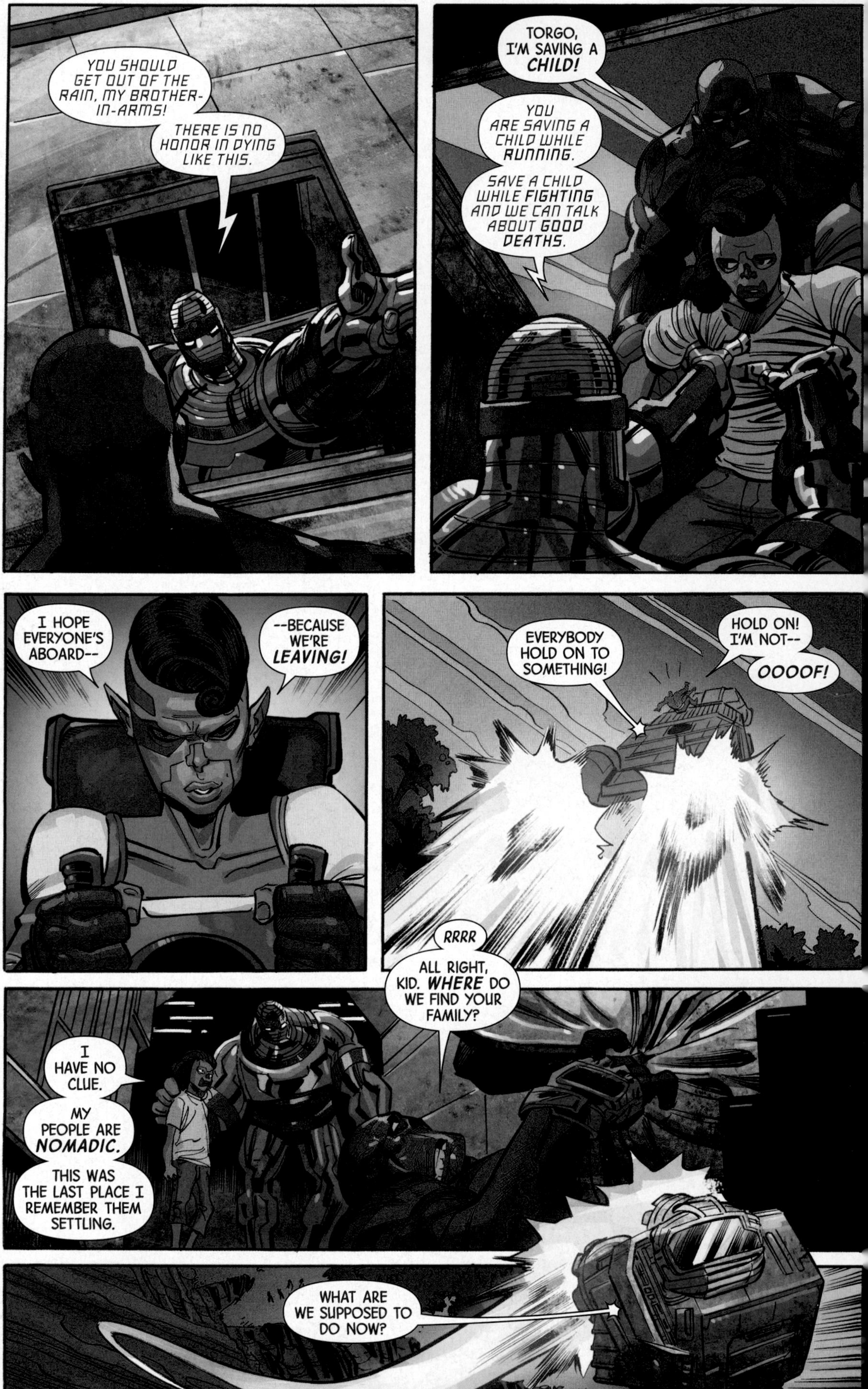
YOU SHOULD GET OUT OF THE RAIN, MY BROTHER-IN-ARMS!
THERE IS NO HONOR IN DYING LIKE THIS.
TORGO, I'M SAVING A CHILD!
YOU ARE SAVING A CHILD WHILE RUNNING.
SAVE A CHILD WHILE FIGHTING AND WE CAN TALK ABOUT GOOD DEATHS.
I HOPE EVERYONE'S ABOARD--
--BECAUSE WE'RE LEAVING!
EVERYBODY HOLD ON TO SOMETHING!
HOLD ON! I'M NOT--
OOOOF!
RRRR
ALL RIGHT, KID. WHERE DO WE FIND YOUR FAMILY?
I HAVE NO CLUE.
MY PEOPLE ARE NOMADIC.
THIS WAS THE LAST PLACE I REMEMBER THEM SETTLING.
WHAT ARE WE SUPPOSED TO DO NOW?

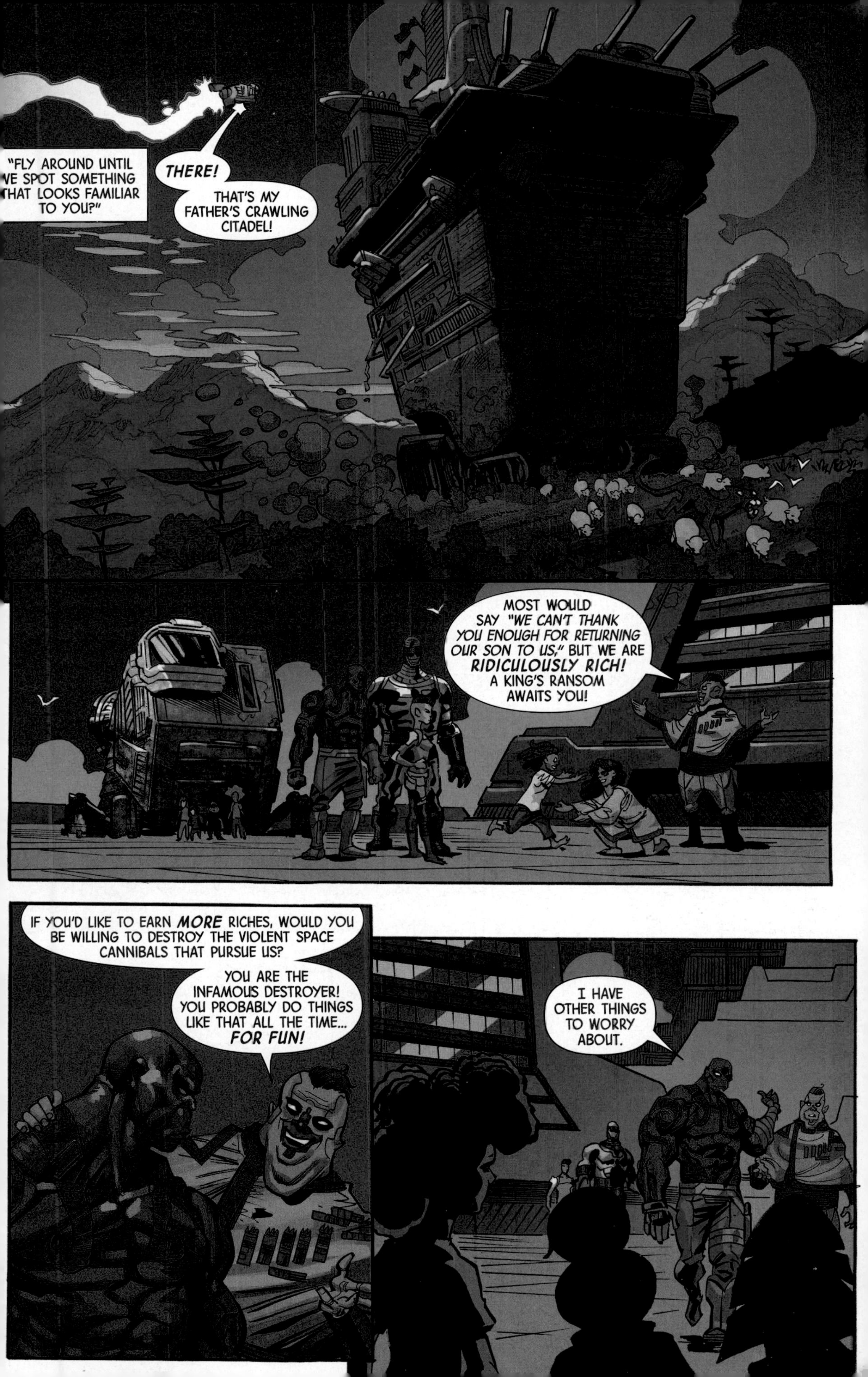
"FLY AROUND UNTIL WE SPOT SOMETHING THAT LOOKS FAMILIAR TO YOU?"
THERE!
THAT'S MY FATHER'S CRAWLING CITADEL!
MOST WOULD SAY "WE CAN'T THANK YOU ENOUGH FOR RETURNING OUR SON TO US," BUT WE ARE RIDICULOUSLY RICH! A KING'S RANSOM AWAITS YOU!
IF YOU'D LIKE TO EARN MORE RICHES, WOULD YOU BE WILLING TO DESTROY THE VIOLENT SPACE CANNIBALS THAT PURSUE US?
YOU ARE THE INFAMOUS DESTROYER! YOU PROBABLY DO THINGS LIKE THAT ALL THE TIME... FOR FUN!
I HAVE OTHER THINGS TO WORRY ABOUT.

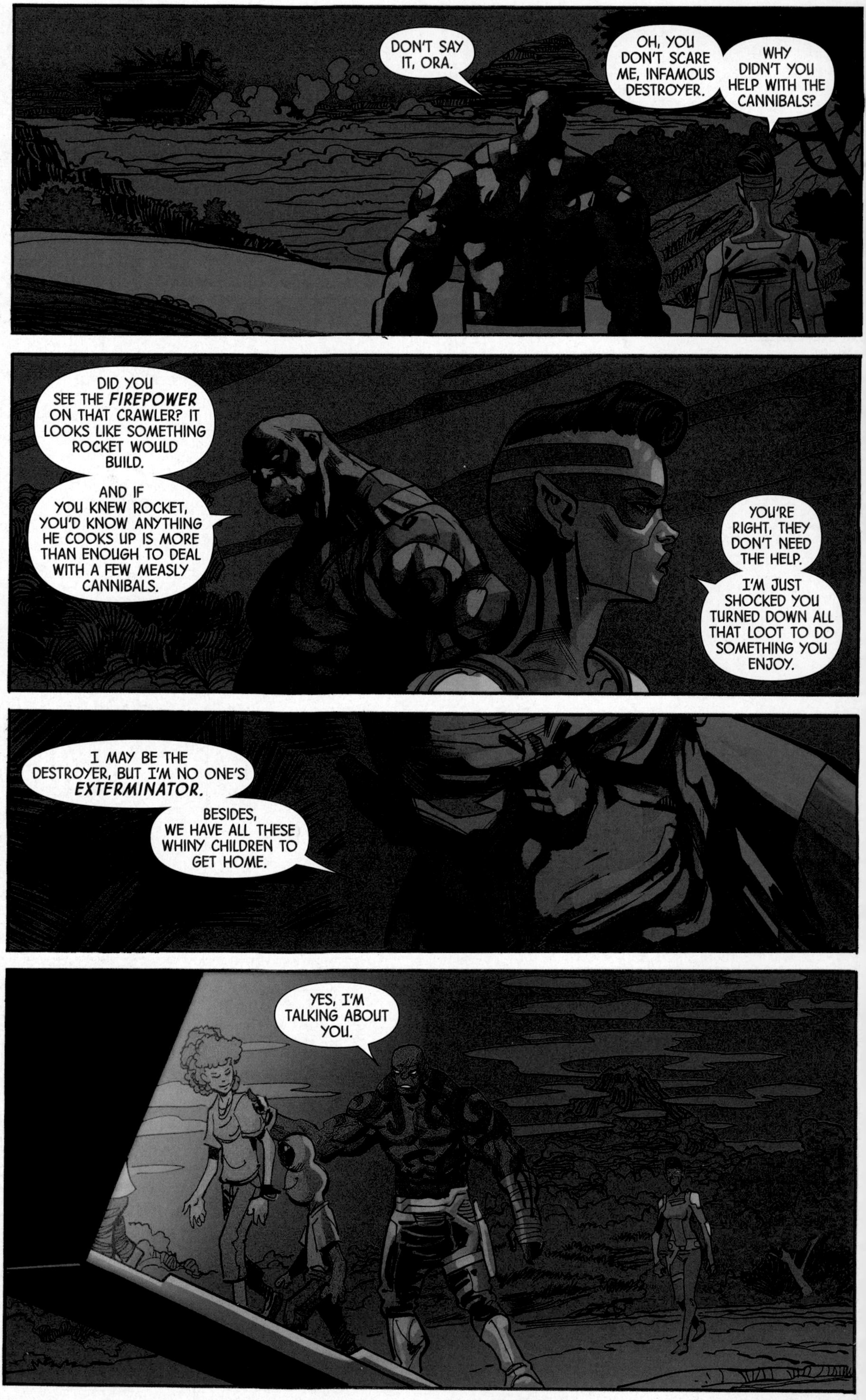
DON'T SAY IT, ORA.
OH, YOU DON'T SCARE ME, INFAMOUS DESTROYER.
WHY DIDN'T YOU HELP WITH THE CANNIBALS?
DID YOU SEE THE *FIREPOWER* ON THAT CRAWLER? IT LOOKS LIKE SOMETHING ROCKET WOULD BUILD.
AND IF YOU KNEW ROCKET, YOU'D KNOW ANYTHING HE COOKS UP IS MORE THAN ENOUGH TO DEAL WITH A FEW MEASLY CANNIBALS.
YOU'RE RIGHT, THEY DON'T NEED THE HELP.
I'M JUST SHOCKED YOU TURNED DOWN ALL THAT LOOT TO DO SOMETHING YOU ENJOY.
I MAY BE THE DESTROYER, BUT I'M NO ONE'S *EXTERMINATOR.*
BESIDES, WE HAVE ALL THESE WHINY CHILDREN TO GET HOME.
YES, I'M TALKING ABOUT YOU.

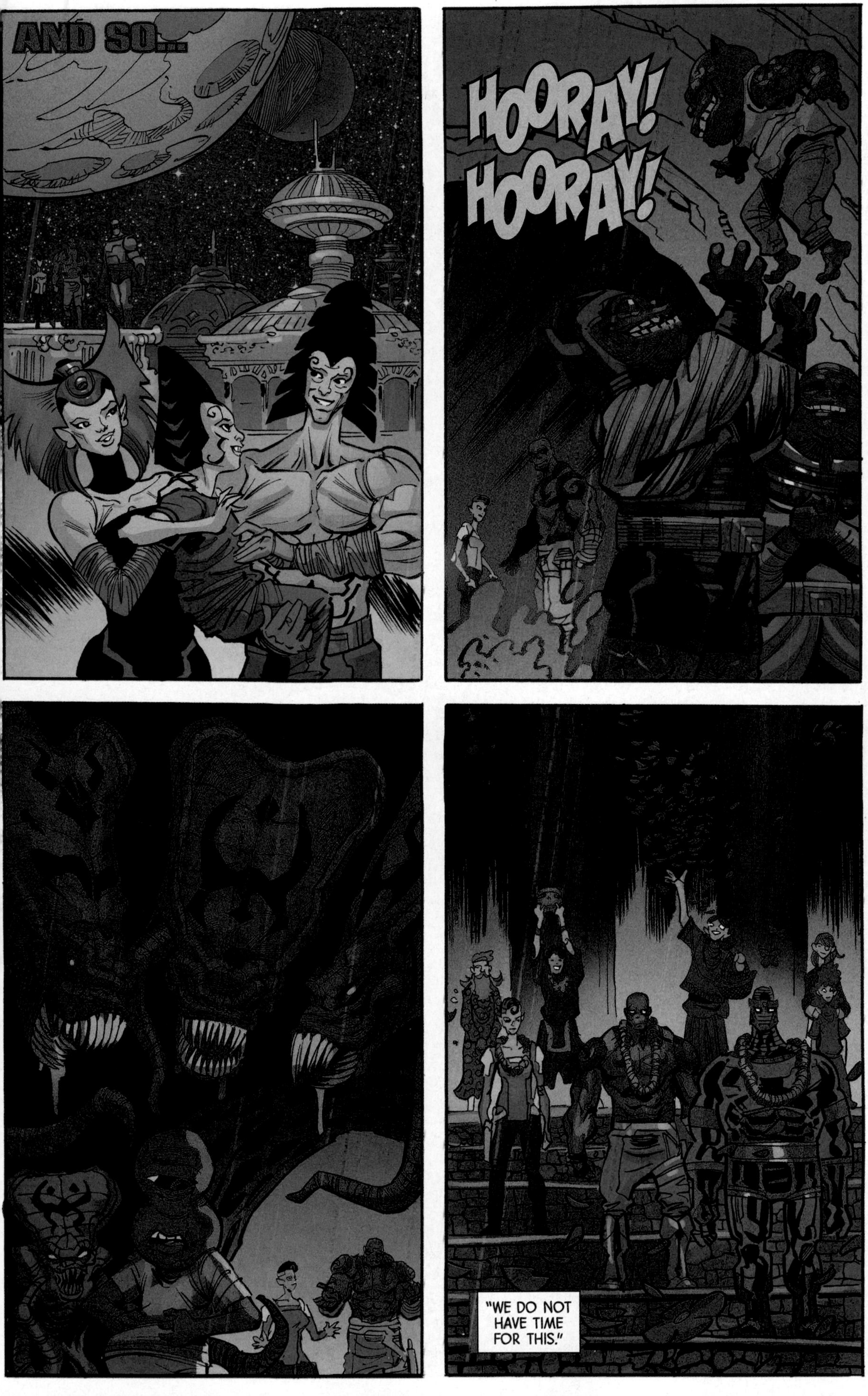
AND SO...
HOORAY! HOORAY!
"WE DO NOT HAVE TIME FOR THIS."

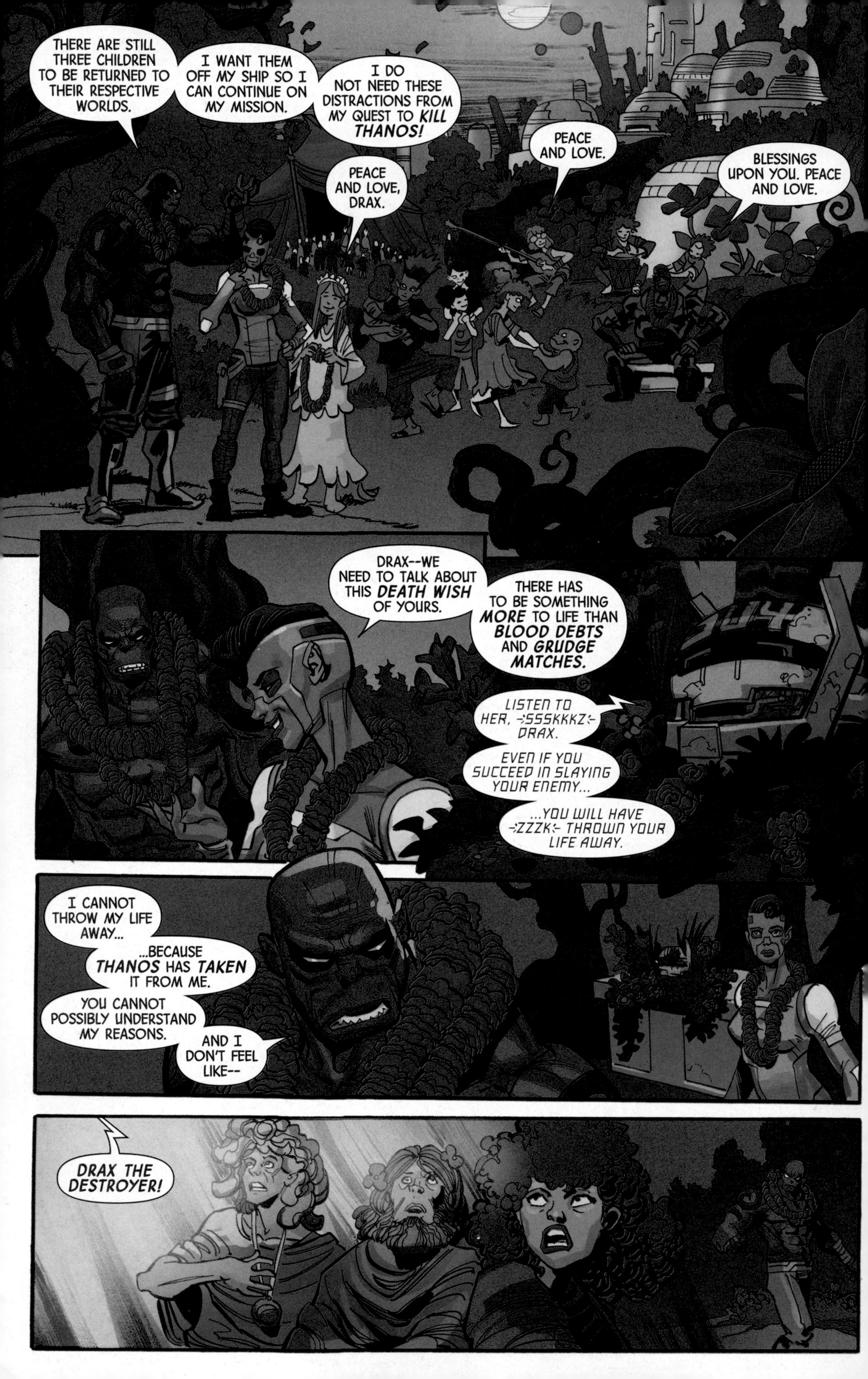
THERE ARE STILL THREE CHILDREN TO BE RETURNED TO THEIR RESPECTIVE WORLDS.
I WANT THEM OFF MY SHIP SO I CAN CONTINUE ON MY MISSION.
I DO NOT NEED THESE DISTRACTIONS FROM MY QUEST TO KILL THANOS!
PEACE AND LOVE, DRAX.
PEACE AND LOVE.
BLESSINGS UPON YOU. PEACE AND LOVE.
DRAX--WE NEED TO TALK ABOUT THIS DEATH WISH OF YOURS.
THERE HAS TO BE SOMETHING MORE TO LIFE THAN BLOOD DEBTS AND GRUDGE MATCHES.
LISTEN TO HER, -SSSKKKZ- DRAX.
EVEN IF YOU SUCCEED IN SLAYING YOUR ENEMY...
...YOU WILL HAVE -ZZZK- THROWN YOUR LIFE AWAY.
I CANNOT THROW MY LIFE AWAY...
...BECAUSE THANOS HAS TAKEN IT FROM ME.
YOU CANNOT POSSIBLY UNDERSTAND MY REASONS.
AND I DON'T FEEL LIKE--
DRAX THE DESTROYER!

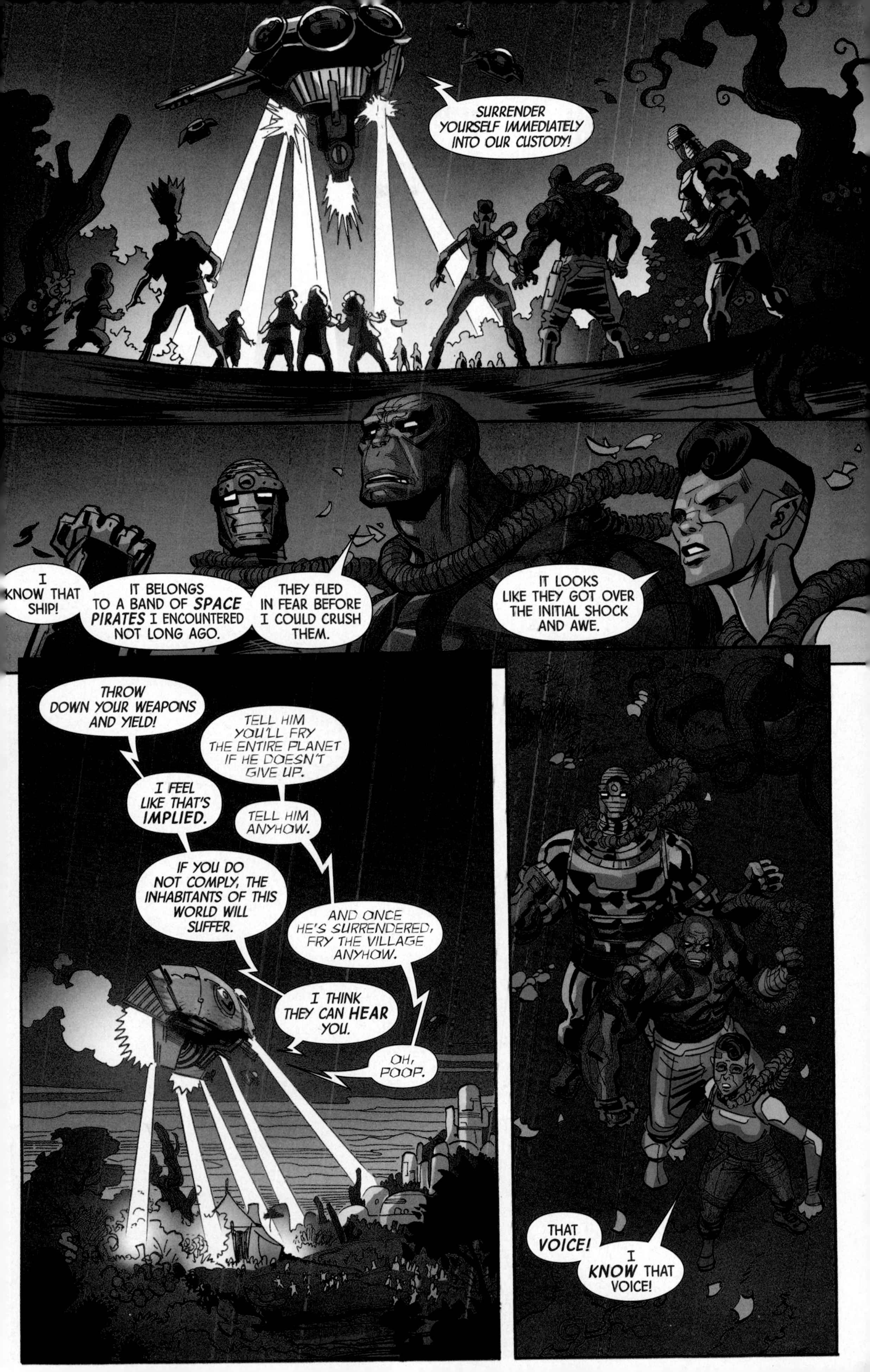
SURRENDER YOURSELF IMMEDIATELY INTO OUR CUSTODY!
I KNOW THAT SHIP!
IT BELONGS TO A BAND OF SPACE PIRATES I ENCOUNTERED NOT LONG AGO.
THEY FLED IN FEAR BEFORE I COULD CRUSH THEM.
IT LOOKS LIKE THEY GOT OVER THE INITIAL SHOCK AND AWE.
THROW DOWN YOUR WEAPONS AND YIELD!
TELL HIM YOU'LL FRY THE ENTIRE PLANET IF HE DOESN'T GIVE UP.
I FEEL LIKE THAT'S IMPLIED.
TELL HIM ANYHOW.
IF YOU DO NOT COMPLY, THE INHABITANTS OF THIS WORLD WILL SUFFER.
AND ONCE HE'S SURRENDERED, FRY THE VILLAGE ANYHOW.
I THINK THEY CAN HEAR YOU.
OH, POOP.
THAT VOICE!
I KNOW THAT VOICE!

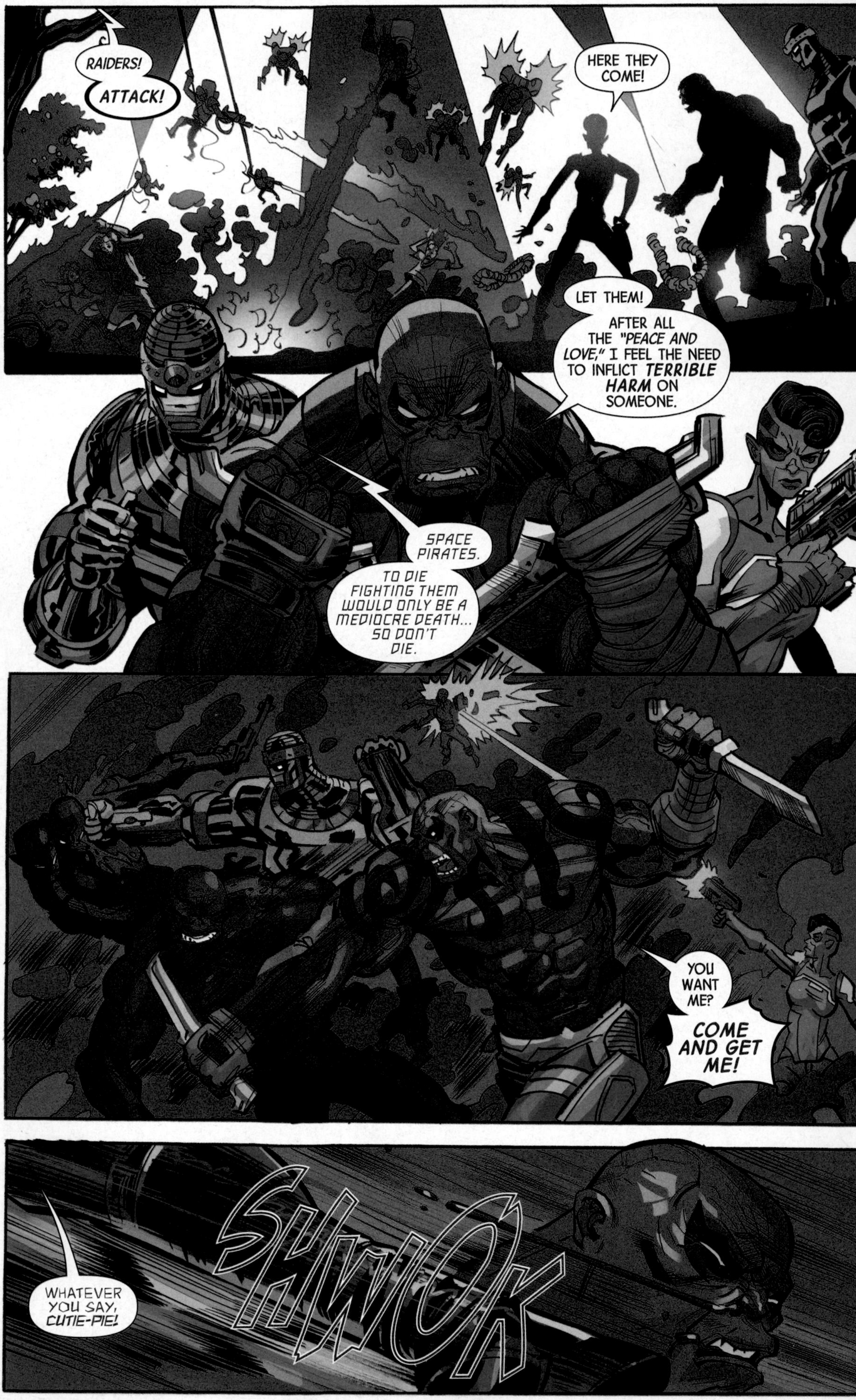
RAIDERS!
ATTACK!
HERE THEY COME!
LET THEM!
AFTER ALL THE "PEACE AND LOVE," I FEEL THE NEED TO INFLICT TERRIBLE HARM ON SOMEONE.
SPACE PIRATES.
TO DIE FIGHTING THEM WOULD ONLY BE A MEDIOCRE DEATH... SO DON'T DIE.
YOU WANT ME?
COME AND GET ME!
SHWOK
WHATEVER YOU SAY, CUTIE-PIE!

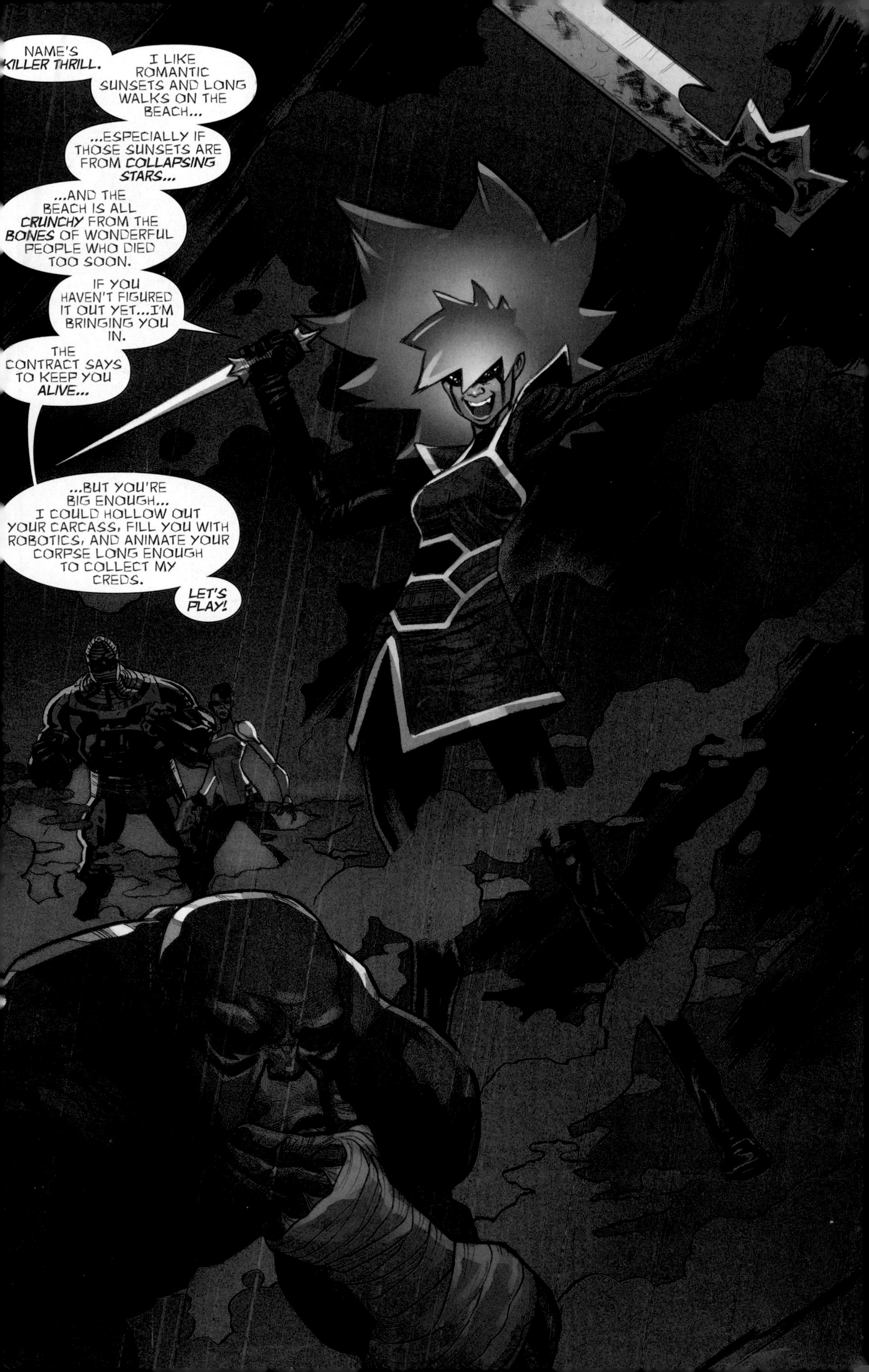
NAME'S KILLER THRILL.
I LIKE ROMANTIC SUNSETS AND LONG WALKS ON THE BEACH...
...ESPECIALLY IF THOSE SUNSETS ARE FROM COLLAPSING STARS...
...AND THE BEACH IS ALL CRUNCHY FROM THE BONES OF WONDERFUL PEOPLE WHO DIED TOO SOON.
IF YOU HAVEN'T FIGURED IT OUT YET...I'M BRINGING YOU IN.
THE CONTRACT SAYS TO KEEP YOU ALIVE...
...BUT YOU'RE BIG ENOUGH... I COULD HOLLOW OUT YOUR CARCASS, FILL YOU WITH ROBOTICS, AND ANIMATE YOUR CORPSE LONG ENOUGH TO COLLECT MY CREDS.
LET'S PLAY!

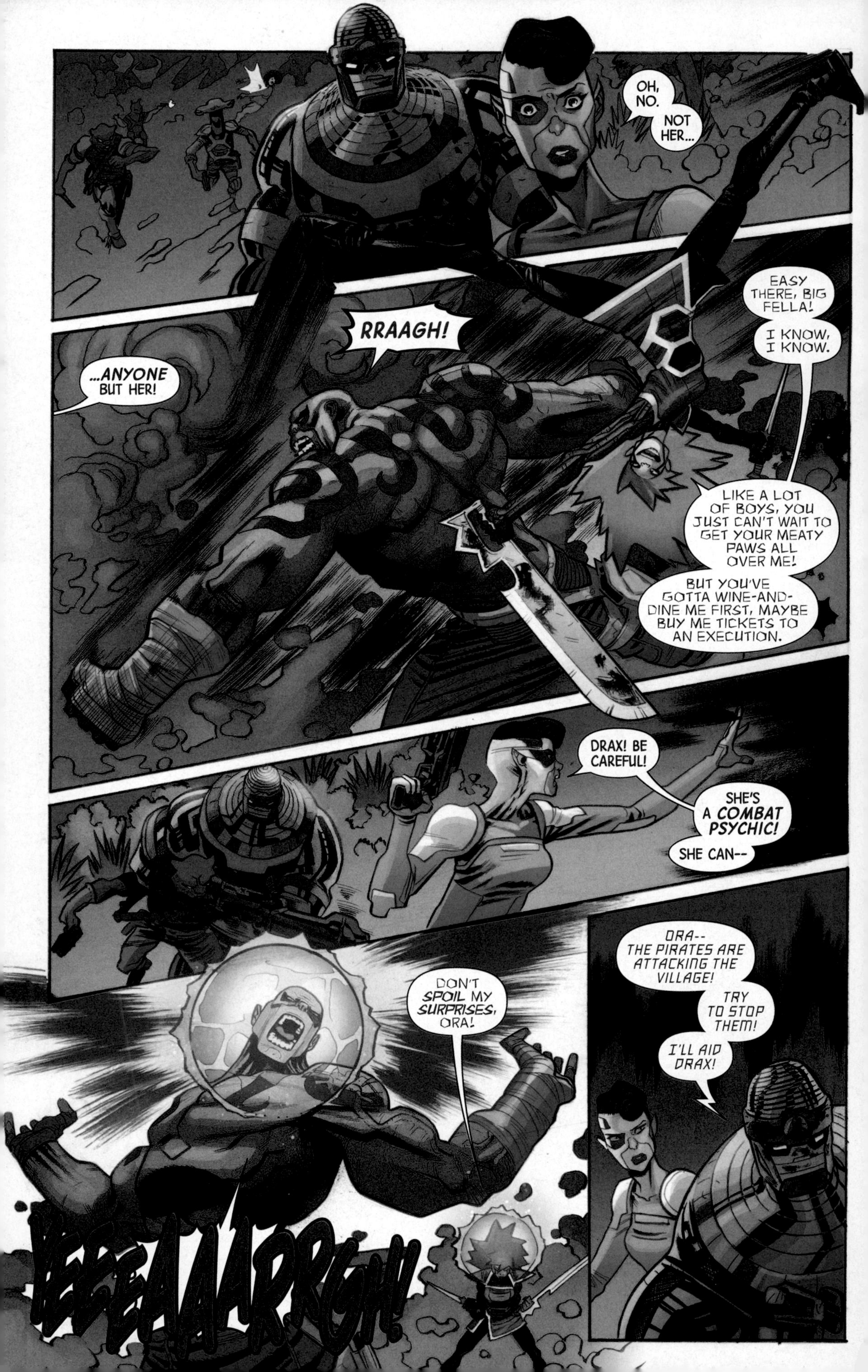
OH, NO.
NOT HER...
RRAAGH!
...ANYONE BUT HER!
EASY THERE, BIG FELLA!
I KNOW, I KNOW.
LIKE A LOT OF BOYS, YOU JUST CAN'T WAIT TO GET YOUR MEATY PAWS ALL OVER ME!
BUT YOU'VE GOTTA WINE-AND-DINE ME FIRST, MAYBE BUY ME TICKETS TO AN EXECUTION.
DRAX! BE CAREFUL!
SHE'S A COMBAT PSYCHIC!
SHE CAN--
DON'T SPOIL MY SURPRISES, ORA!
YEEEAAARRGH!
DRA--
THE PIRATES ARE ATTACKING THE VILLAGE!
TRY TO STOP THEM!
I'LL AID DRAX!

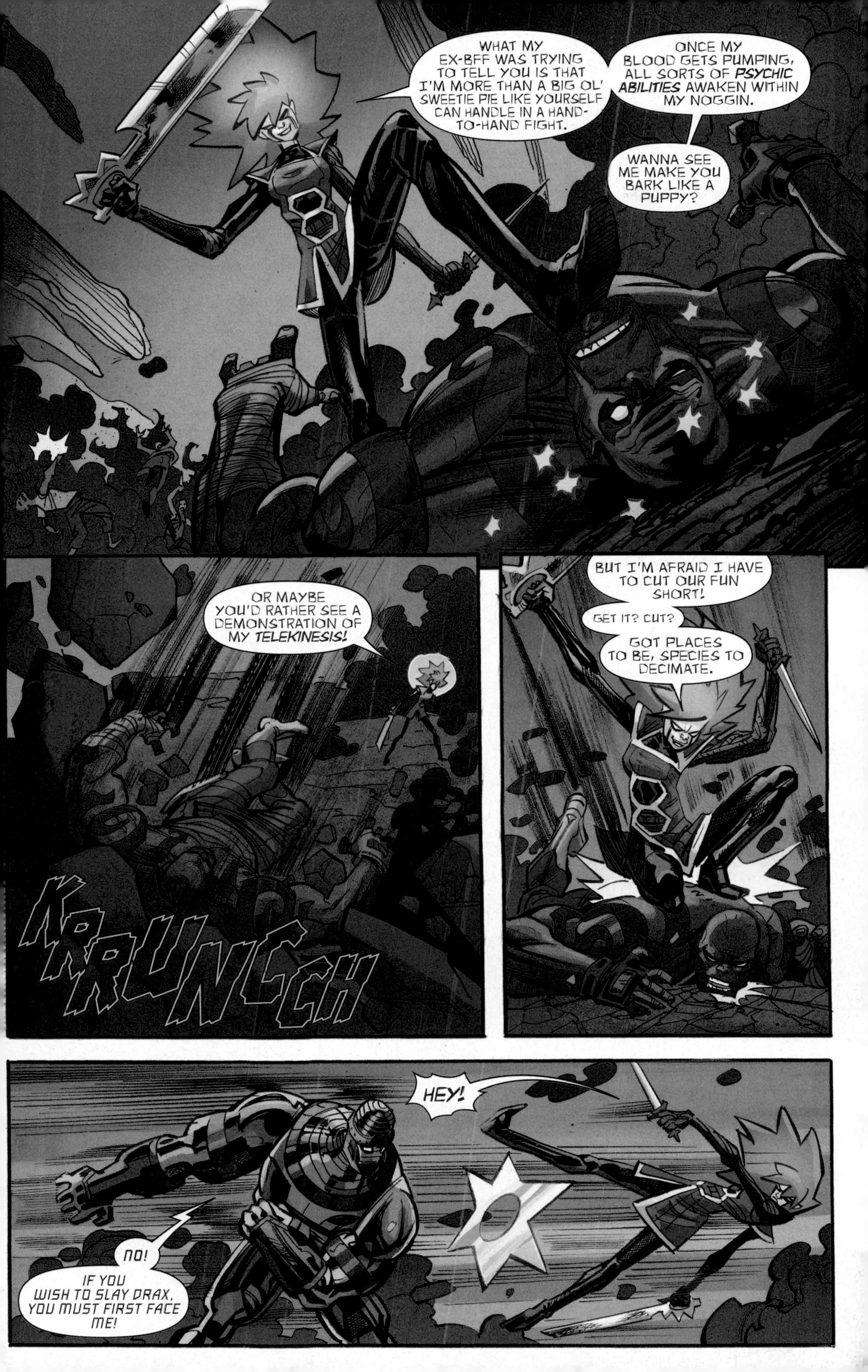
WHAT MY EX-BFF WAS TRYING TO TELL YOU IS THAT I'M MORE THAN A BIG OL' SWEETIE PIE LIKE YOURSELF CAN HANDLE IN A HAND-TO-HAND FIGHT.
ONCE MY BLOOD GETS PUMPING, ALL SORTS OF PSYCHIC ABILITIES AWAKEN WITHIN MY NOGGIN.
WANNA SEE ME MAKE YOU BARK LIKE A PUPPY?
OR MAYBE YOU'D RATHER SEE A DEMONSTRATION OF MY TELEKINESIS!
KRRUNCCH
BUT I'M AFRAID I HAVE TO CUT OUR FUN SHORT!
GET IT? CUT?
GOT PLACES TO BE, SPECIES TO DECIMATE.
HEY!
NO!
IF YOU WISH TO SLAY DRAX, YOU MUST FIRST FACE ME!

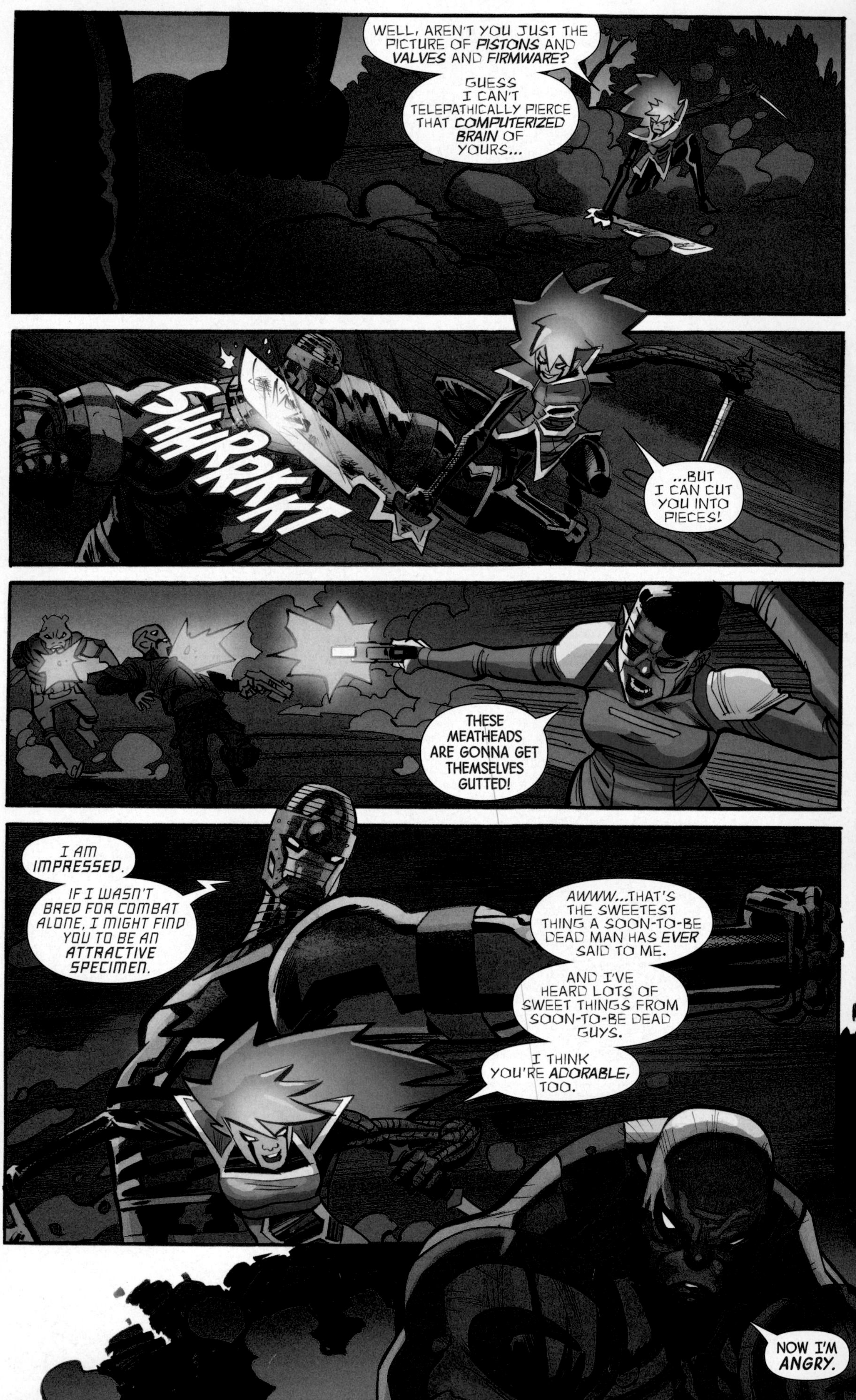
WELL, AREN'T YOU JUST THE PICTURE OF PISTONS AND VALVES AND FIRMWARE?
GUESS I CAN'T TELEPATHICALLY PIERCE THAT COMPUTERIZED BRAIN OF YOURS...
SHRRKKT
...BUT I CAN CUT YOU INTO PIECES!
THESE MEATHEADS ARE GONNA GET THEMSELVES GUTTED!
I AM IMPRESSED.
IF I WASN'T BRED FOR COMBAT ALONE, I MIGHT FIND YOU TO BE AN ATTRACTIVE SPECIMEN.
AWWW...THAT'S THE SWEETEST THING A SOON-TO-BE DEAD MAN HAS EVER SAID TO ME.
AND I'VE HEARD LOTS OF SWEET THINGS FROM SOON-TO-BE DEAD GUYS.
I THINK YOU'RE ADORABLE, TOO.
NOW I'M ANGRY.

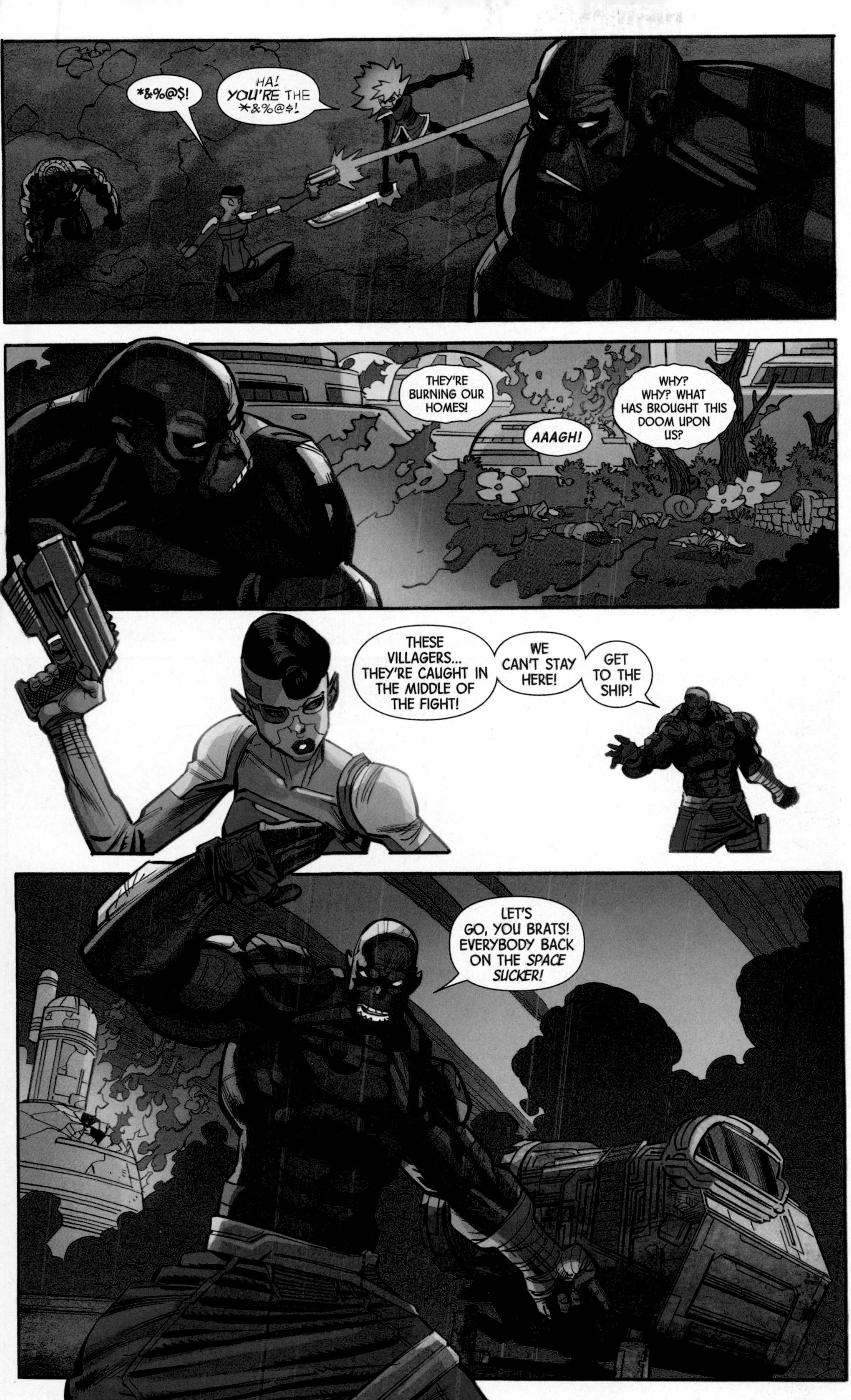
*&%@$!
HA! YOU'RE THE *&%@$!
THEY'RE BURNING OUR HOMES!
AAAGH!
WHY? WHY? WHAT HAS BROUGHT THIS DOOM UPON US?
THESE VILLAGERS... THEY'RE CAUGHT IN THE MIDDLE OF THE FIGHT!
WE CAN'T STAY HERE!
GET TO THE SHIP!
LET'S GO, YOU BRATS! EVERYBODY BACK ON THE *SPACE SUCKER!*

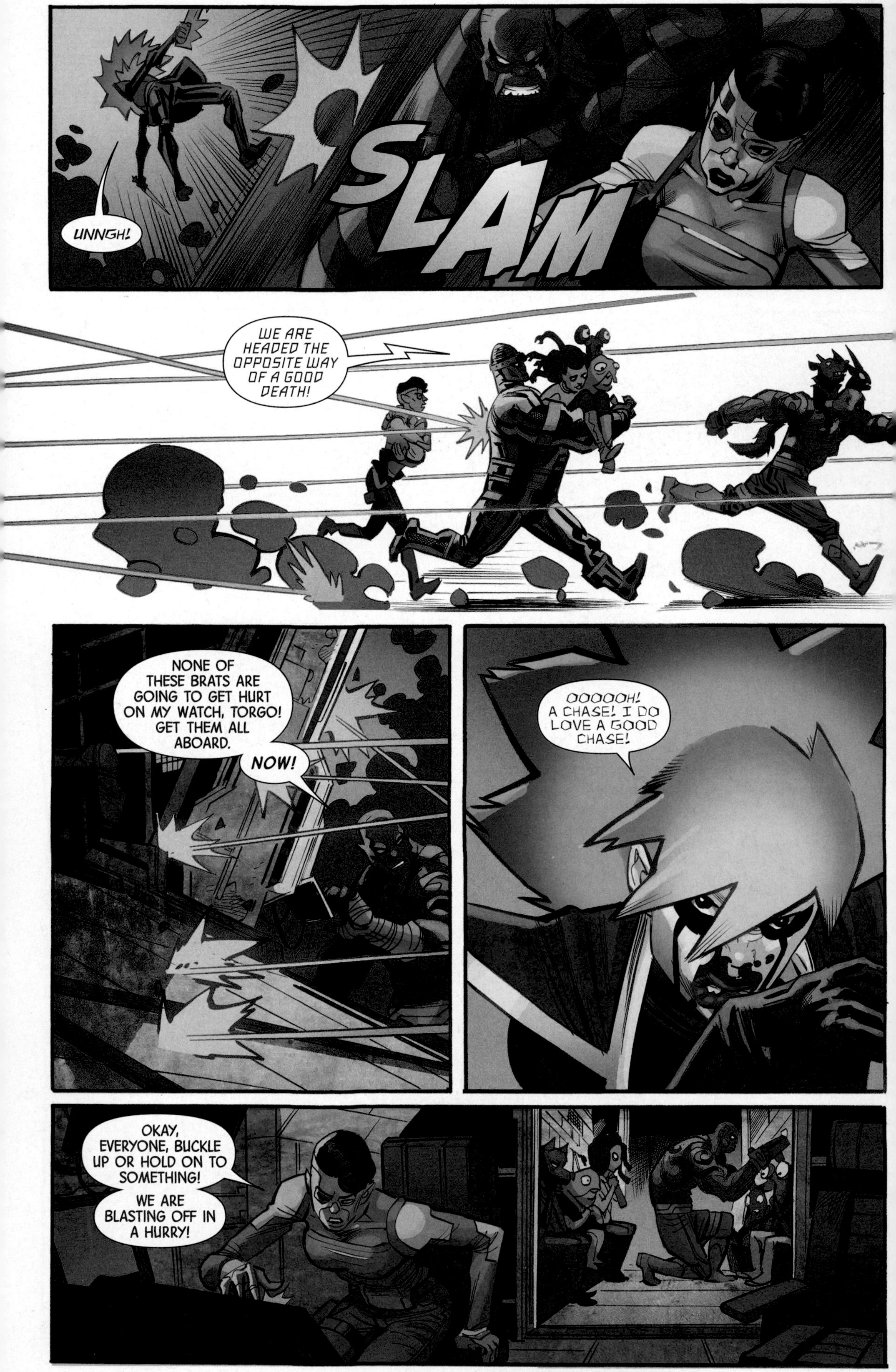
SLAM
UNNGH!
WE ARE HEADED THE OPPOSITE WAY OF A GOOD DEATH!
NONE OF THESE BRATS ARE GOING TO GET HURT ON MY WATCH, TORGO! GET THEM ALL ABOARD.
NOW!
OOOOOH! A CHASE! I DO LOVE A GOOD CHASE!
OKAY, EVERYONE, BUCKLE UP OR HOLD ON TO SOMETHING!
WE ARE BLASTING OFF IN A HURRY!

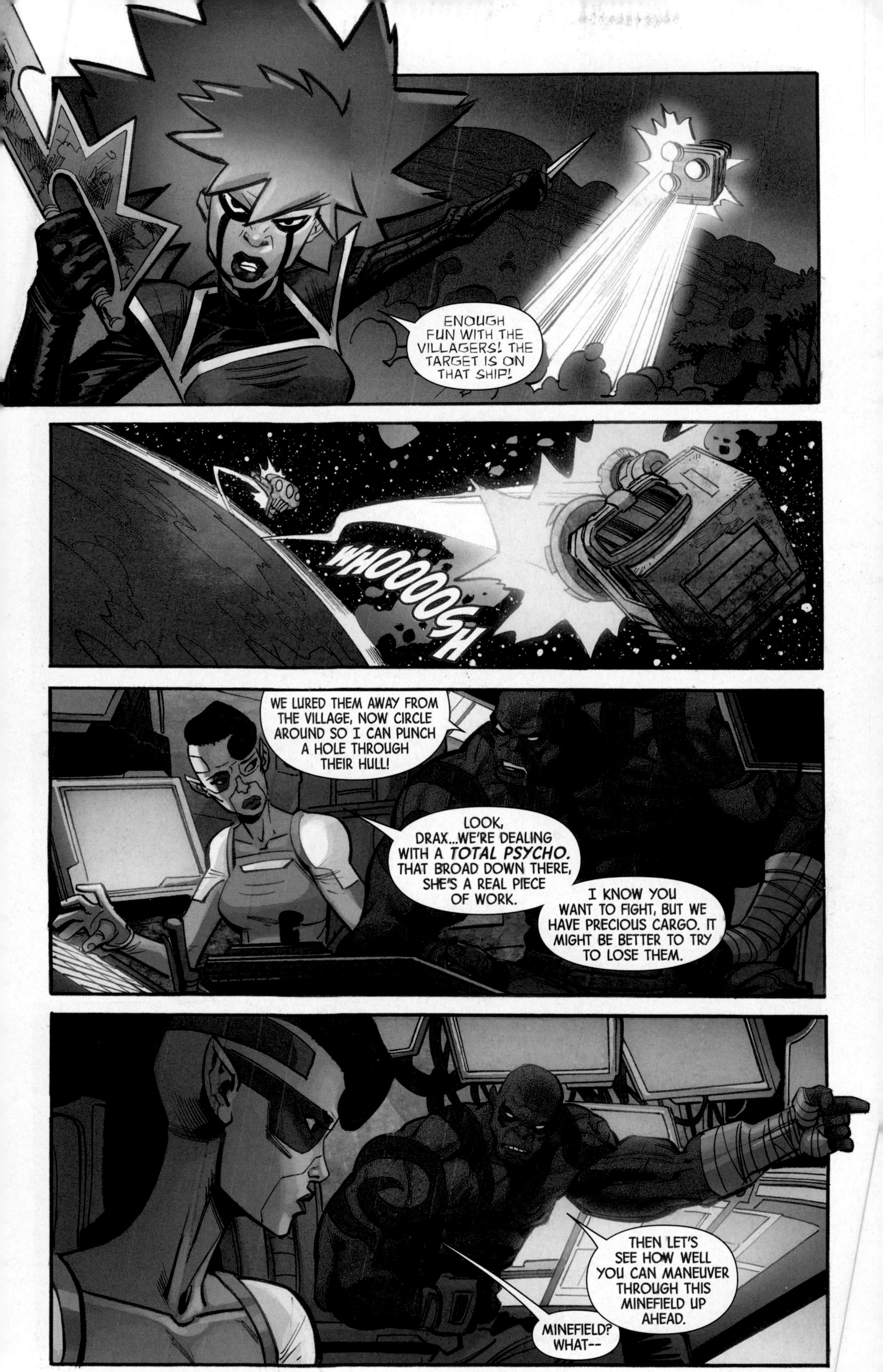
ENOUGH FUN WITH THE VILLAGERS! THE TARGET IS ON THAT SHIP!
WHOOOOSH
WE LURED THEM AWAY FROM THE VILLAGE, NOW CIRCLE AROUND SO I CAN PUNCH A HOLE THROUGH THEIR HULL!
LOOK, DRAX...WE'RE DEALING WITH A TOTAL PSYCHO. THAT BROAD DOWN THERE, SHE'S A REAL PIECE OF WORK.
I KNOW YOU WANT TO FIGHT, BUT WE HAVE PRECIOUS CARGO. IT MIGHT BE BETTER TO TRY TO LOSE THEM.
THEN LET'S SEE HOW WELL YOU CAN MANEUVER THROUGH THIS MINEFIELD UP AHEAD.
MINEFIELD? WHAT--

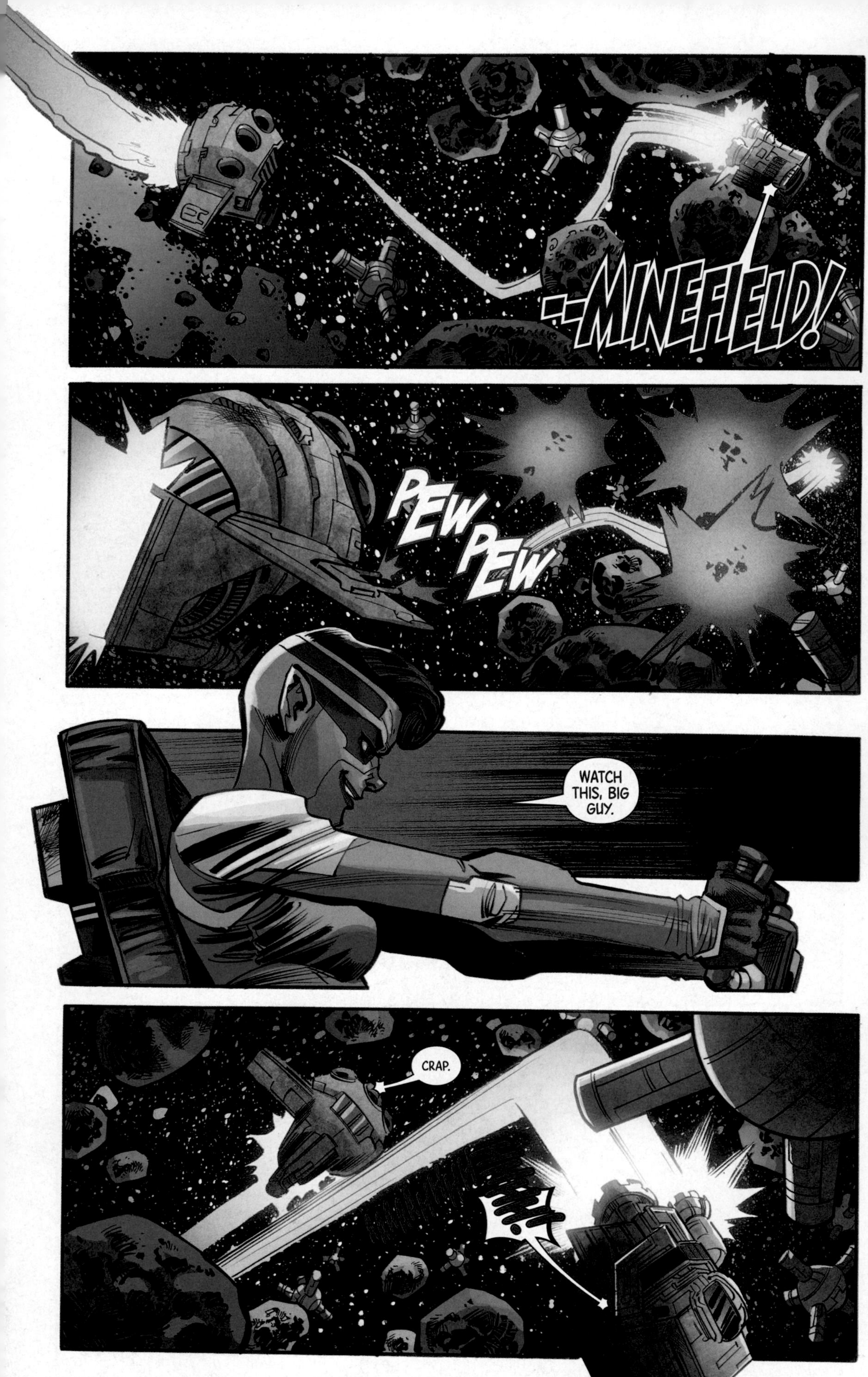
--MINEFIELD!
PEW PEW
WATCH THIS, BIG GUY.
CRAP.

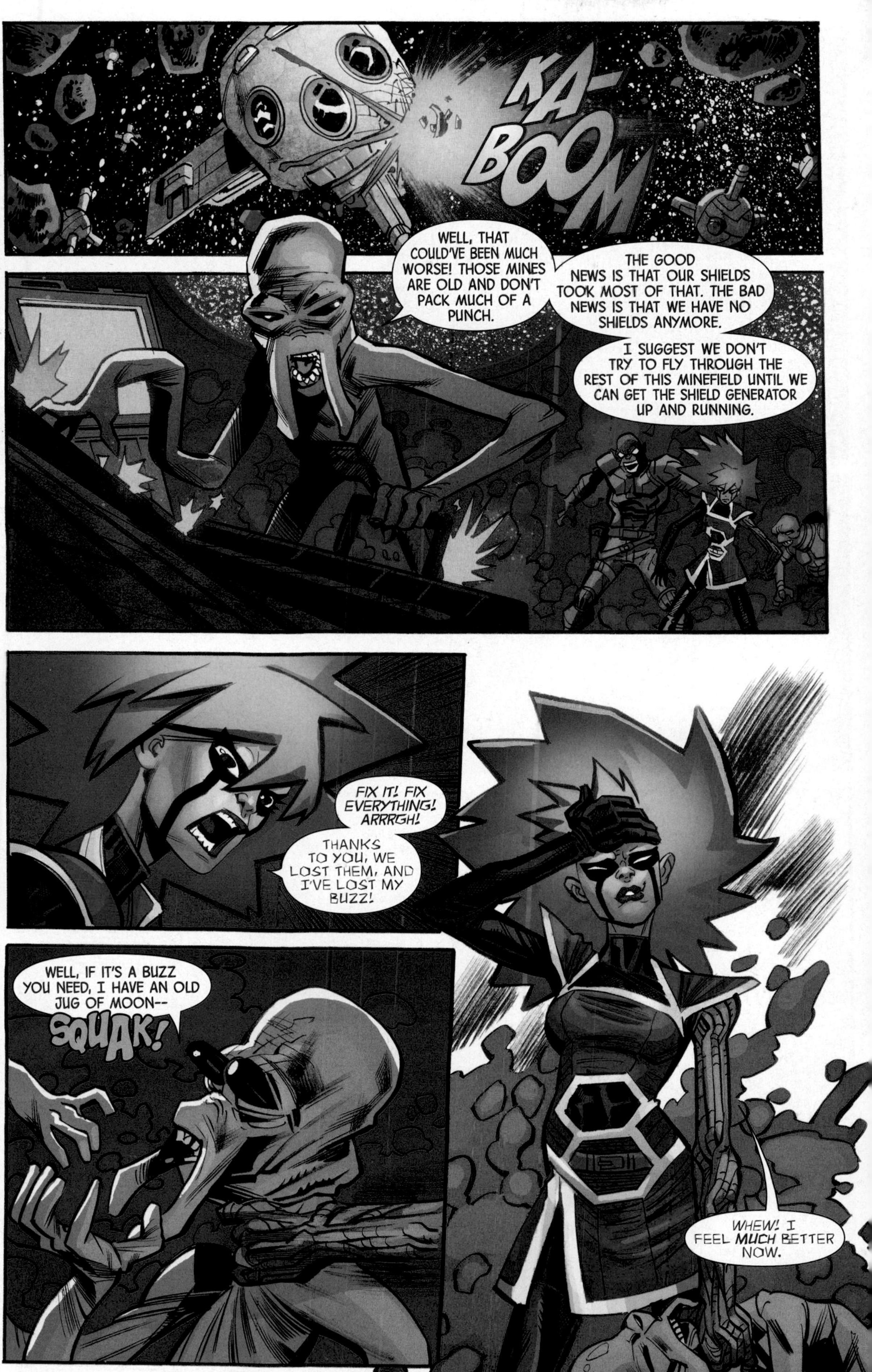
KA-BOOM
WELL, THAT COULD'VE BEEN MUCH WORSE! THOSE MINES ARE OLD AND DON'T PACK MUCH OF A PUNCH.
THE GOOD NEWS IS THAT OUR SHIELDS TOOK MOST OF THAT. THE BAD NEWS IS THAT WE HAVE NO SHIELDS ANYMORE.
I SUGGEST WE DON'T TRY TO FLY THROUGH THE REST OF THIS MINEFIELD UNTIL WE CAN GET THE SHIELD GENERATOR UP AND RUNNING.
FIX IT! FIX EVERYTHING! ARRRGH!
THANKS TO YOU, WE LOST THEM, AND I'VE LOST MY BUZZ!
WELL, IF IT'S A BUZZ YOU NEED, I HAVE AN OLD JUG OF MOON--
SQUAK!
WHEW! I FEEL MUCH BETTER NOW.

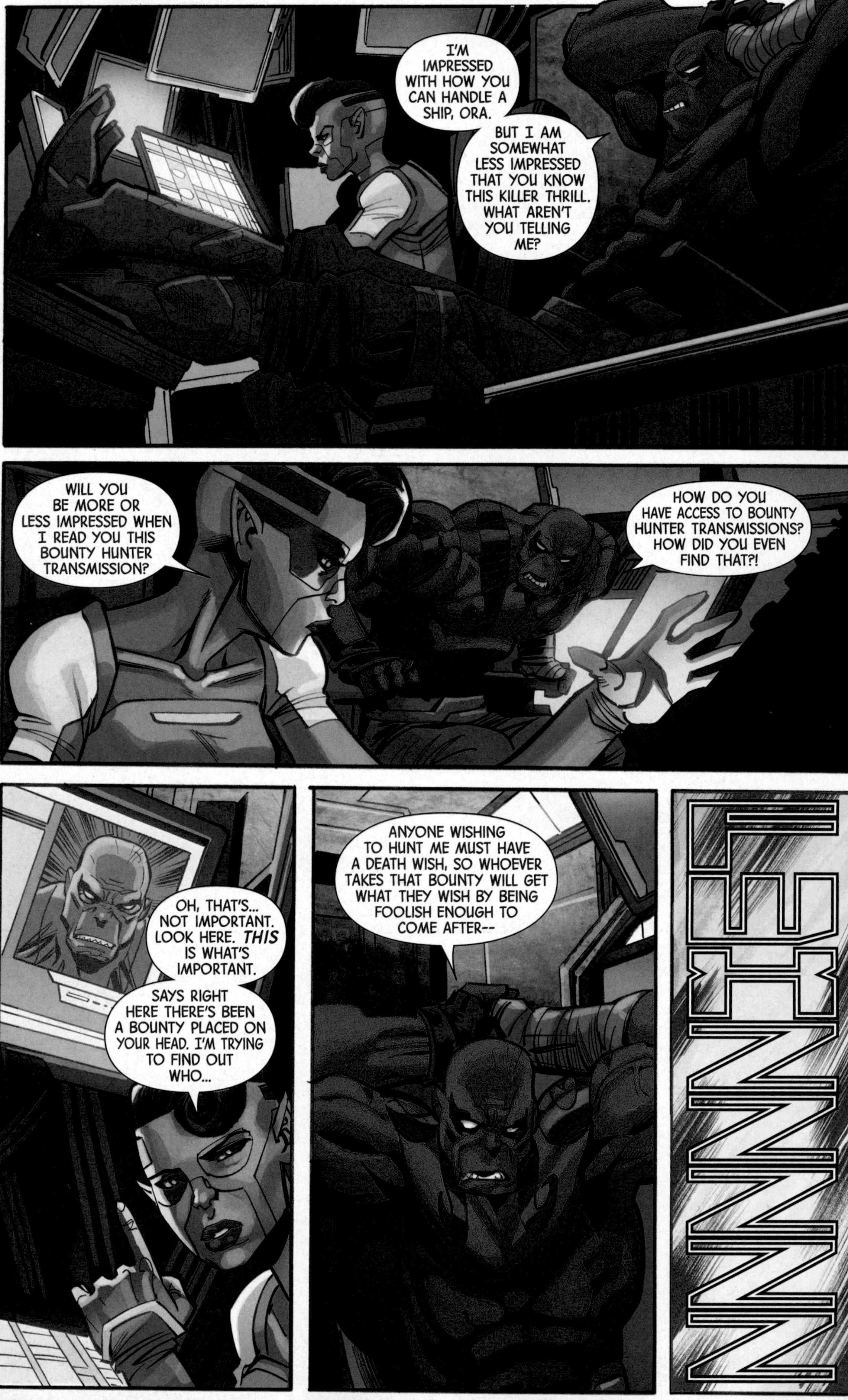
I'M IMPRESSED WITH HOW YOU CAN HANDLE A SHIP, ORA.
BUT I AM SOMEWHAT LESS IMPRESSED THAT YOU KNOW THIS KILLER THRILL. WHAT AREN'T YOU TELLING ME?
WILL YOU BE MORE OR LESS IMPRESSED WHEN I READ YOU THIS BOUNTY HUNTER TRANSMISSION?
HOW DO YOU HAVE ACCESS TO BOUNTY HUNTER TRANSMISSIONS? HOW DID YOU EVEN FIND THAT?!
OH, THAT'S... NOT IMPORTANT. LOOK HERE. *THIS* IS WHAT'S IMPORTANT.
SAYS RIGHT HERE THERE'S BEEN A BOUNTY PLACED ON YOUR HEAD. I'M TRYING TO FIND OUT WHO...
ANYONE WISHING TO HUNT ME MUST HAVE A DEATH WISH, SO WHOEVER TAKES THAT BOUNTY WILL GET WHAT THEY WISH BY BEING FOOLISH ENOUGH TO COME AFTER--

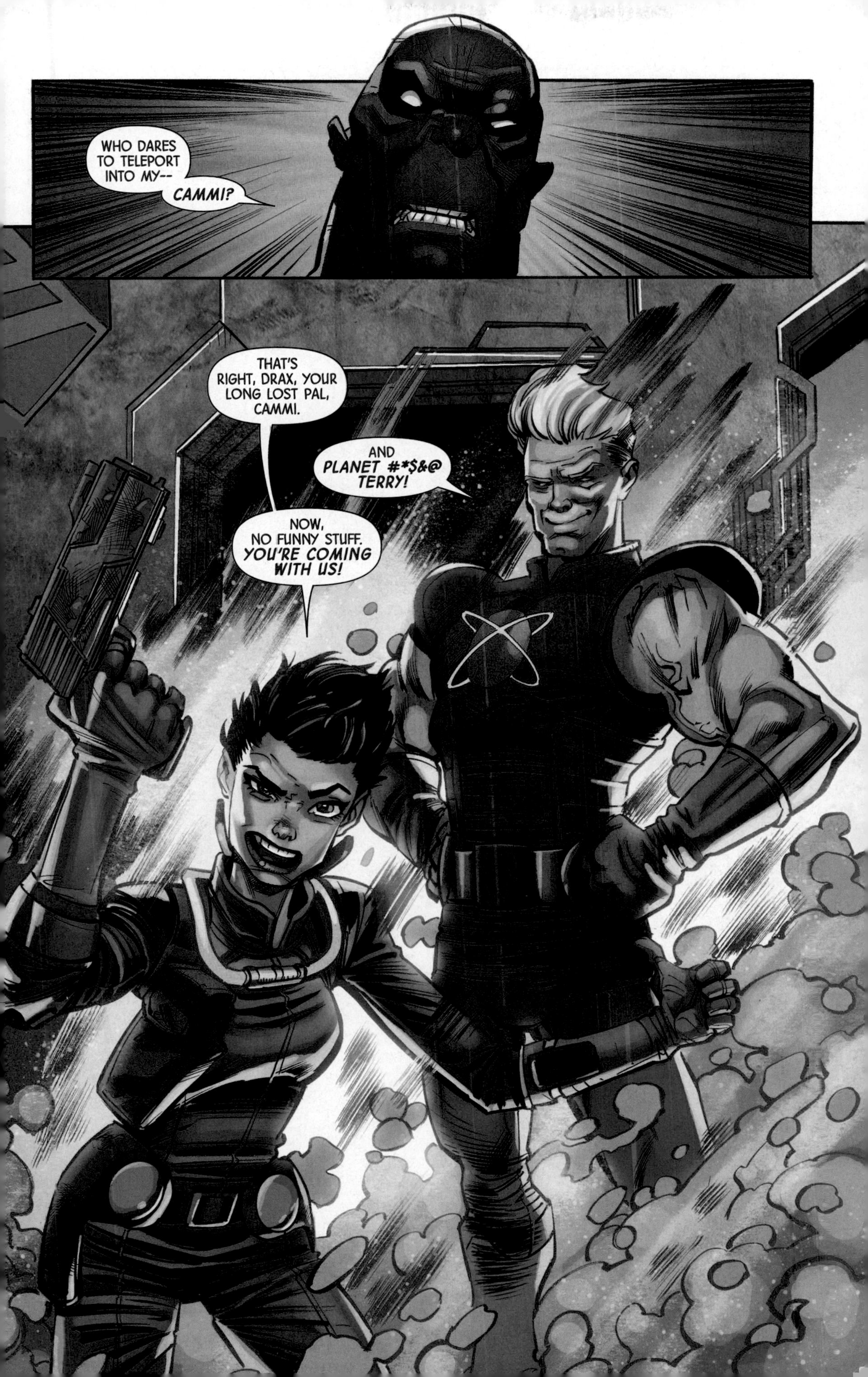
WHO DARES TO TELEPORT INTO MY--
CAMMI?
THAT'S RIGHT, DRAX, YOUR LONG LOST PAL, CAMMI.
AND PLANET #*$&@ TERRY!
NOW, NO FUNNY STUFF. YOU'RE COMING WITH US!

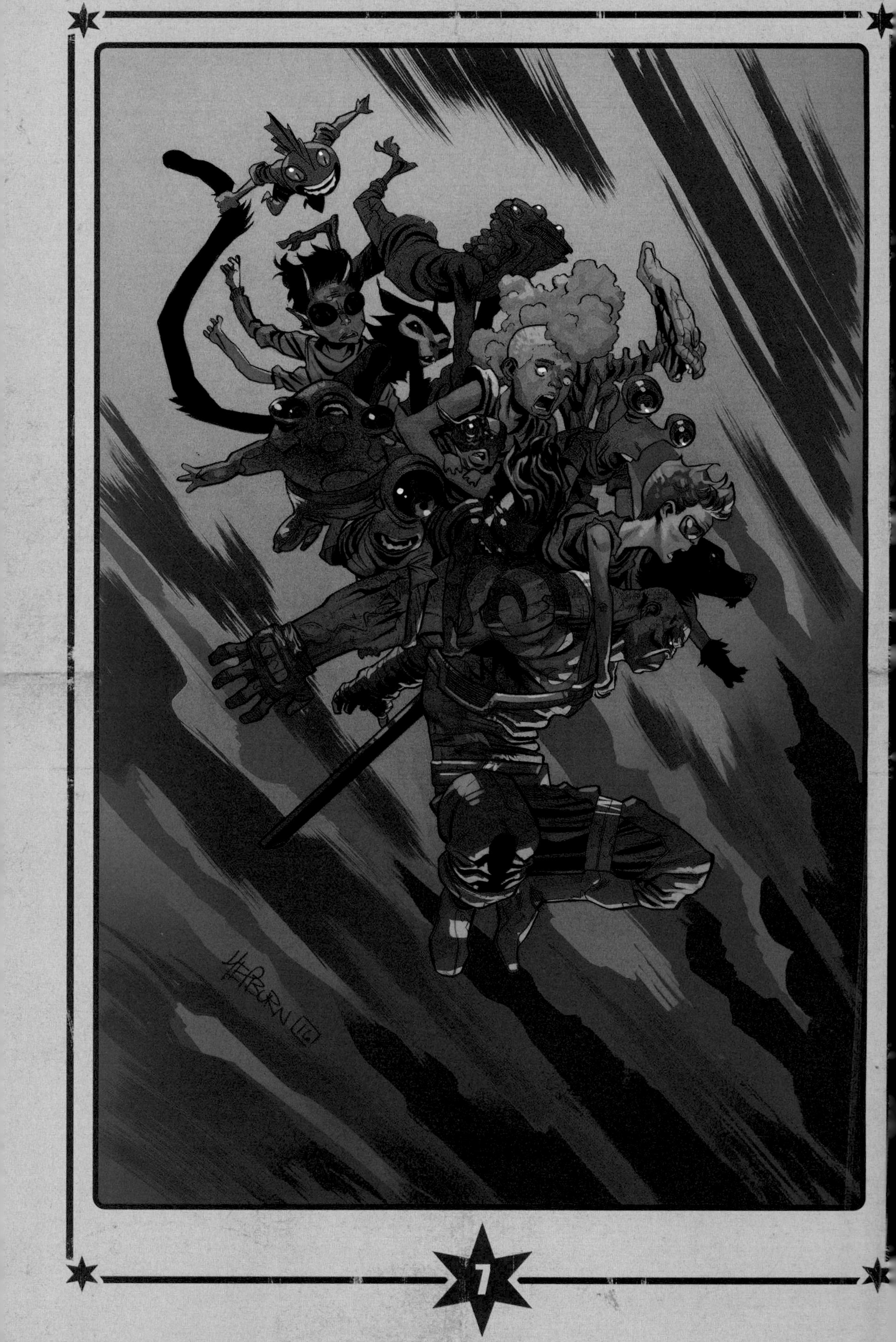

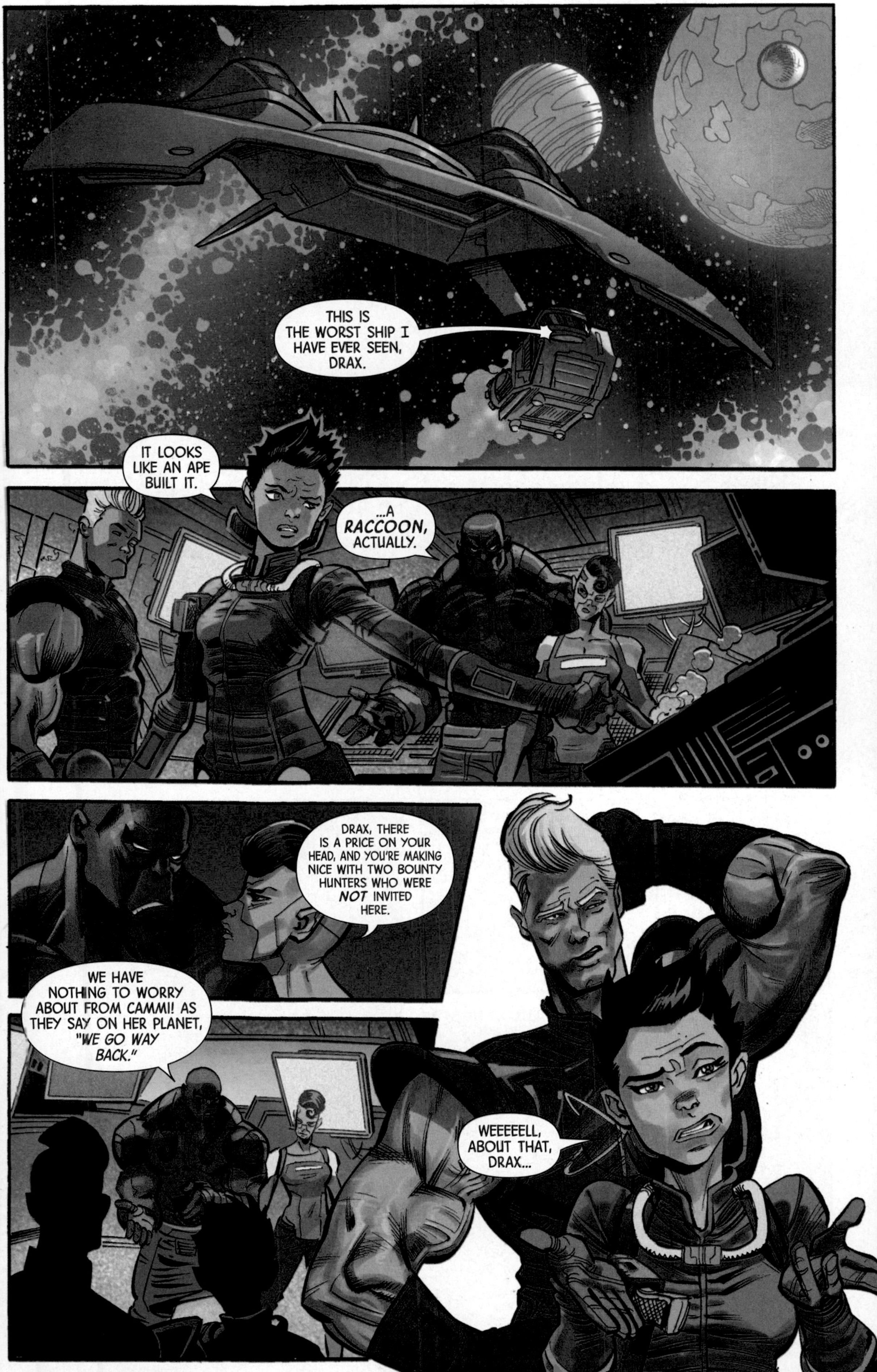
THIS IS THE WORST SHIP I HAVE EVER SEEN, DRAX.
IT LOOKS LIKE AN APE BUILT IT.
...A *RACCOON,* ACTUALLY.
DRAX, THERE IS A PRICE ON YOUR HEAD, AND YOU'RE MAKING NICE WITH TWO BOUNTY HUNTERS WHO WERE *NOT* INVITED HERE.
WE HAVE NOTHING TO WORRY ABOUT FROM CAMMI! AS THEY SAY ON HER PLANET, *"WE GO WAY BACK."*
WEEEEELL, ABOUT THAT, DRAX...

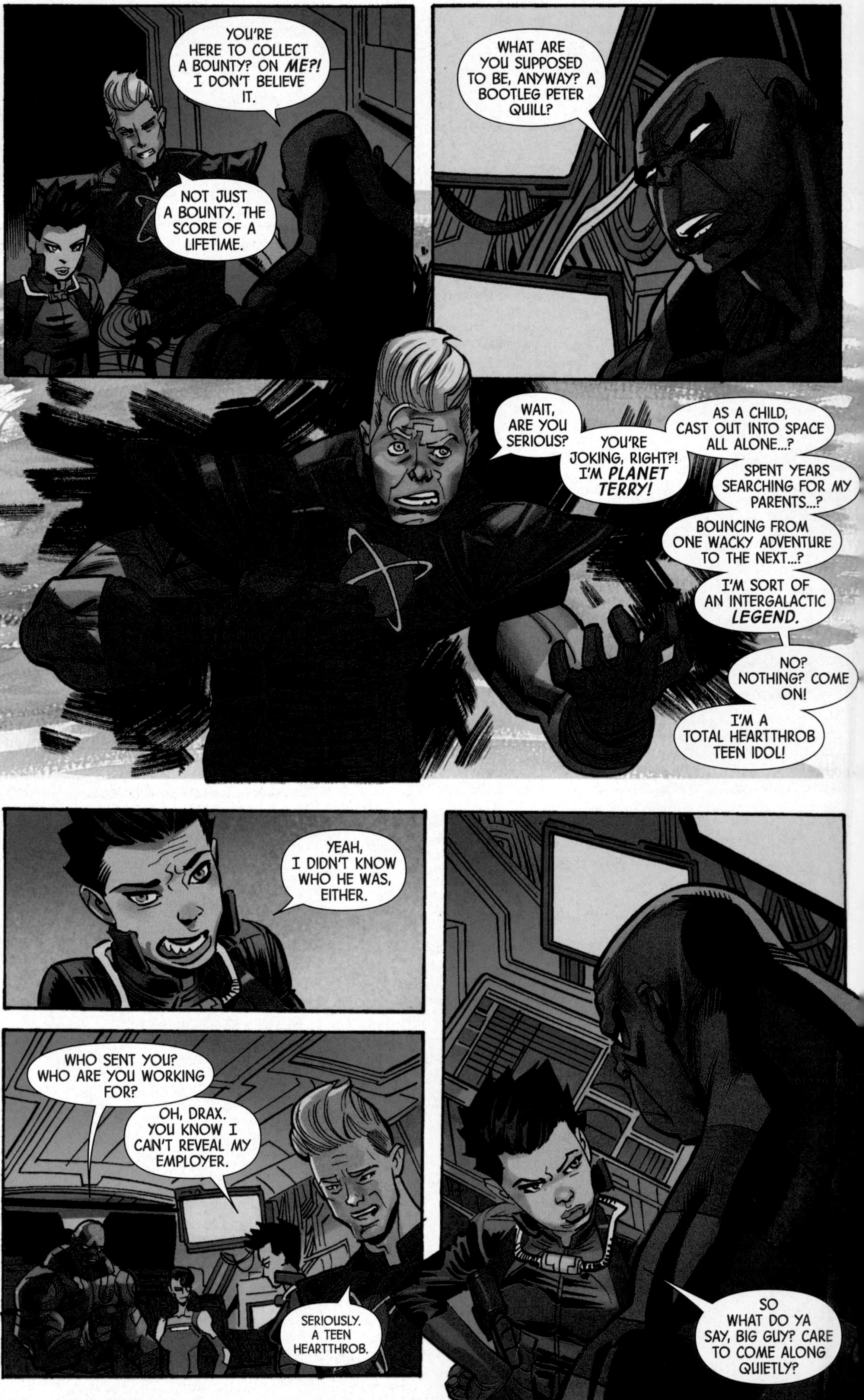
YOU'RE HERE TO COLLECT A BOUNTY? ON ME?! I DON'T BELIEVE IT.
NOT JUST A BOUNTY. THE SCORE OF A LIFETIME.
WHAT ARE YOU SUPPOSED TO BE, ANYWAY? A BOOTLEG PETER QUILL?
WAIT, ARE YOU SERIOUS?
YOU'RE JOKING, RIGHT?! I'M PLANET TERRY!
AS A CHILD, CAST OUT INTO SPACE ALL ALONE...?
SPENT YEARS SEARCHING FOR MY PARENTS...?
BOUNCING FROM ONE WACKY ADVENTURE TO THE NEXT...?
I'M SORT OF AN INTERGALACTIC LEGEND.
NO? NOTHING? COME ON!
I'M A TOTAL HEARTTHROB TEEN IDOL!
YEAH, I DIDN'T KNOW WHO HE WAS, EITHER.
WHO SENT YOU? WHO ARE YOU WORKING FOR?
OH, DRAX. YOU KNOW I CAN'T REVEAL MY EMPLOYER.
SERIOUSLY. A TEEN HEARTTHROB.
SO WHAT DO YA SAY, BIG GUY? CARE TO COME ALONG QUIETLY?

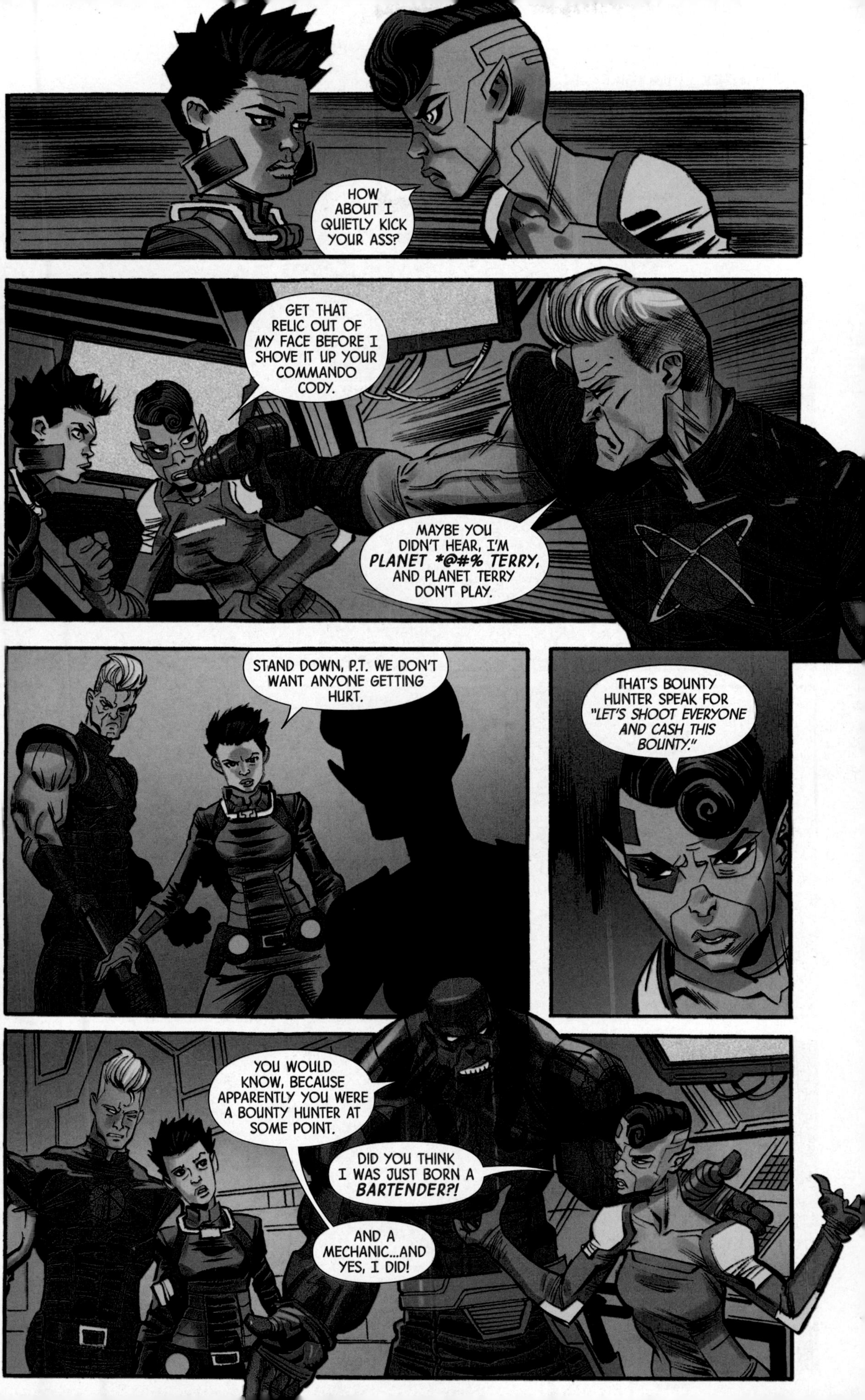
HOW ABOUT I QUIETLY KICK YOUR ASS?
GET THAT RELIC OUT OF MY FACE BEFORE I SHOVE IT UP YOUR COMMANDO CODY.
MAYBE YOU DIDN'T HEAR, I'M PLANET *@#% TERRY, AND PLANET TERRY DON'T PLAY.
STAND DOWN, P.T. WE DON'T WANT ANYONE GETTING HURT.
THAT'S BOUNTY HUNTER SPEAK FOR "LET'S SHOOT EVERYONE AND CASH THIS BOUNTY."
YOU WOULD KNOW, BECAUSE APPARENTLY YOU WERE A BOUNTY HUNTER AT SOME POINT.
DID YOU THINK I WAS JUST BORN A BARTENDER?!
AND A MECHANIC...AND YES, I DID!

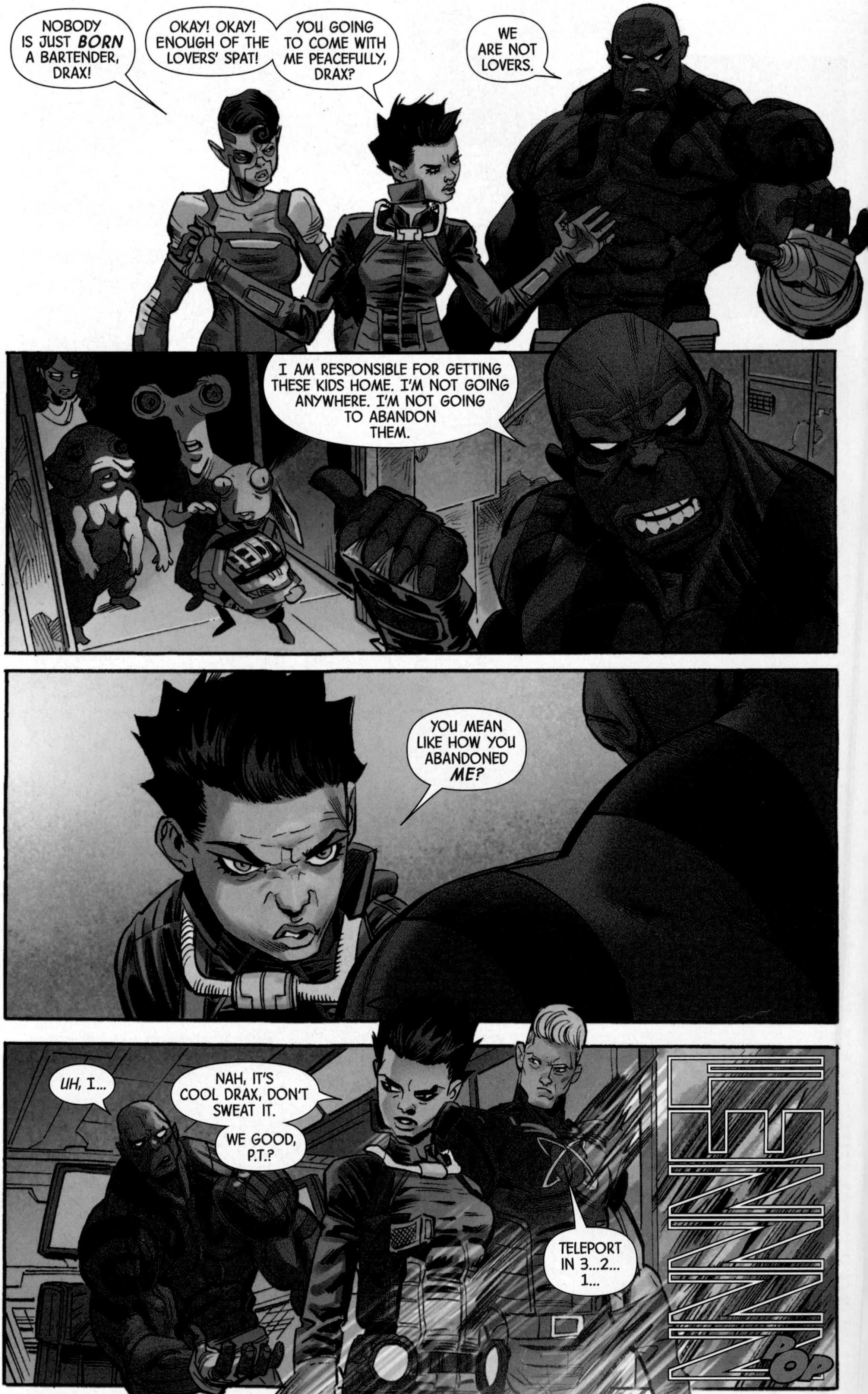
NOBODY IS JUST BORN A BARTENDER, DRAX!
OKAY! OKAY! ENOUGH OF THE LOVERS' SPAT!
YOU GOING TO COME WITH ME PEACEFULLY, DRAX?
WE ARE NOT LOVERS.
I AM RESPONSIBLE FOR GETTING THESE KIDS HOME. I'M NOT GOING ANYWHERE. I'M NOT GOING TO ABANDON THEM.
YOU MEAN LIKE HOW YOU ABANDONED ME?
UH, I...
NAH, IT'S COOL DRAX, DON'T SWEAT IT.
WE GOOD, P.T.?
TELEPORT IN 3...2... 1...
POP

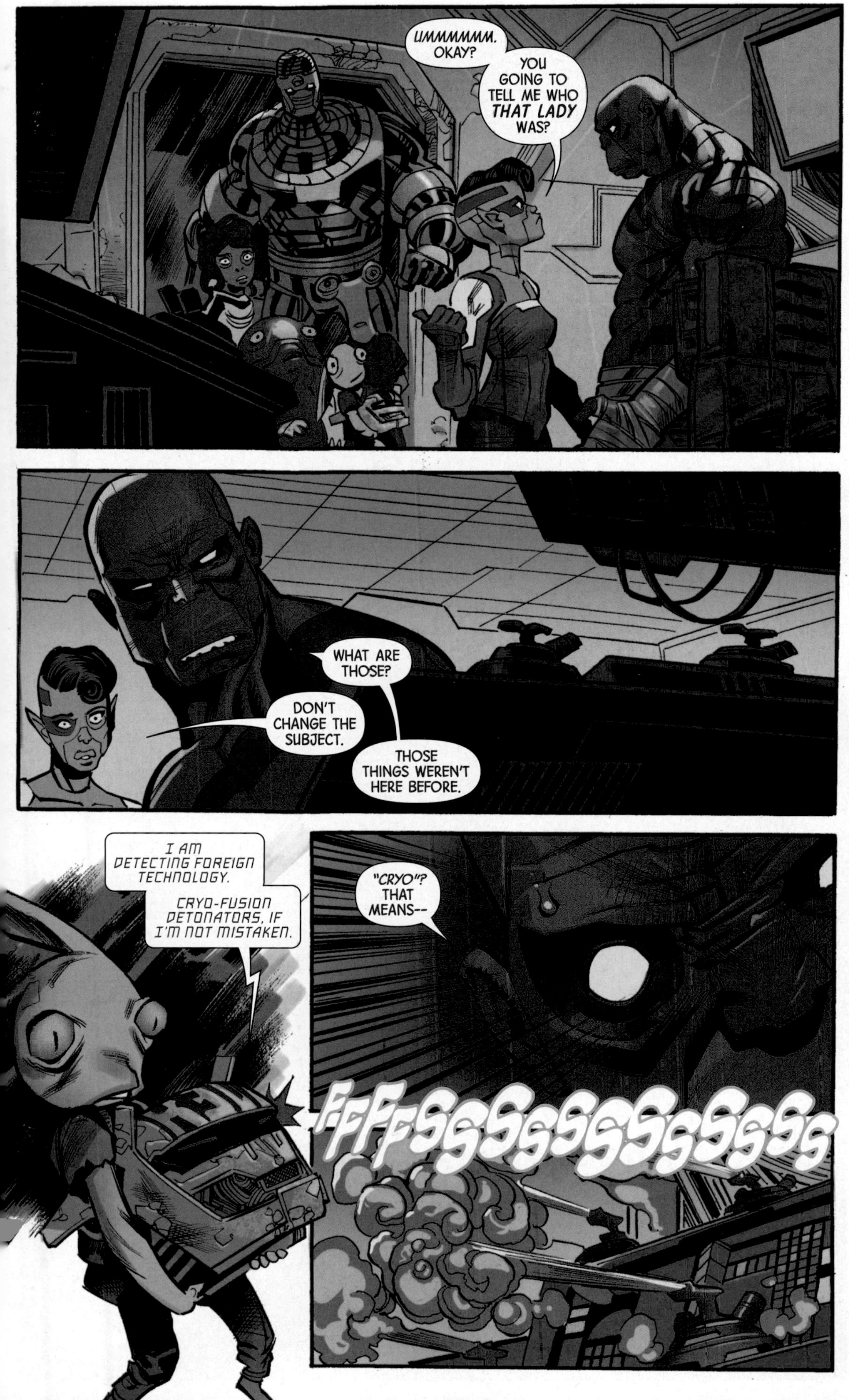
UMMMMMM. OKAY?
YOU GOING TO TELL ME WHO THAT LADY WAS?
WHAT ARE THOSE?
DON'T CHANGE THE SUBJECT.
THOSE THINGS WEREN'T HERE BEFORE.
I AM DETECTING FOREIGN TECHNOLOGY.
CRYO-FUSION DETONATORS, IF I'M NOT MISTAKEN.
"CRYO"? THAT MEANS--
FFFFSSSSSSSSSSSSSSS

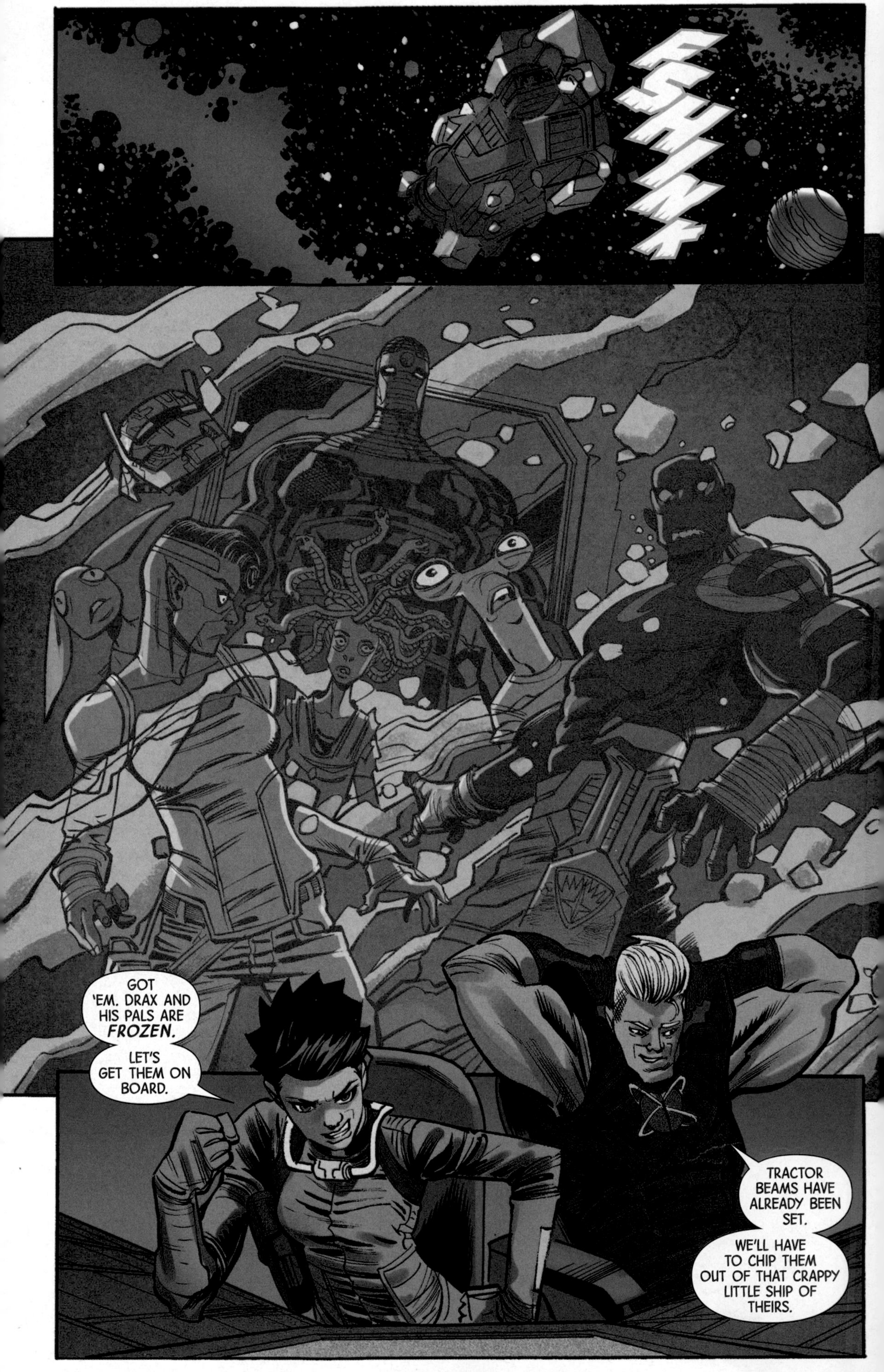
FSHHNK
GOT 'EM. DRAX AND HIS PALS ARE *FROZEN.*
LET'S GET THEM ON BOARD.
TRACTOR BEAMS HAVE ALREADY BEEN SET.
WE'LL HAVE TO CHIP THEM OUT OF THAT CRAPPY LITTLE SHIP OF THEIRS.

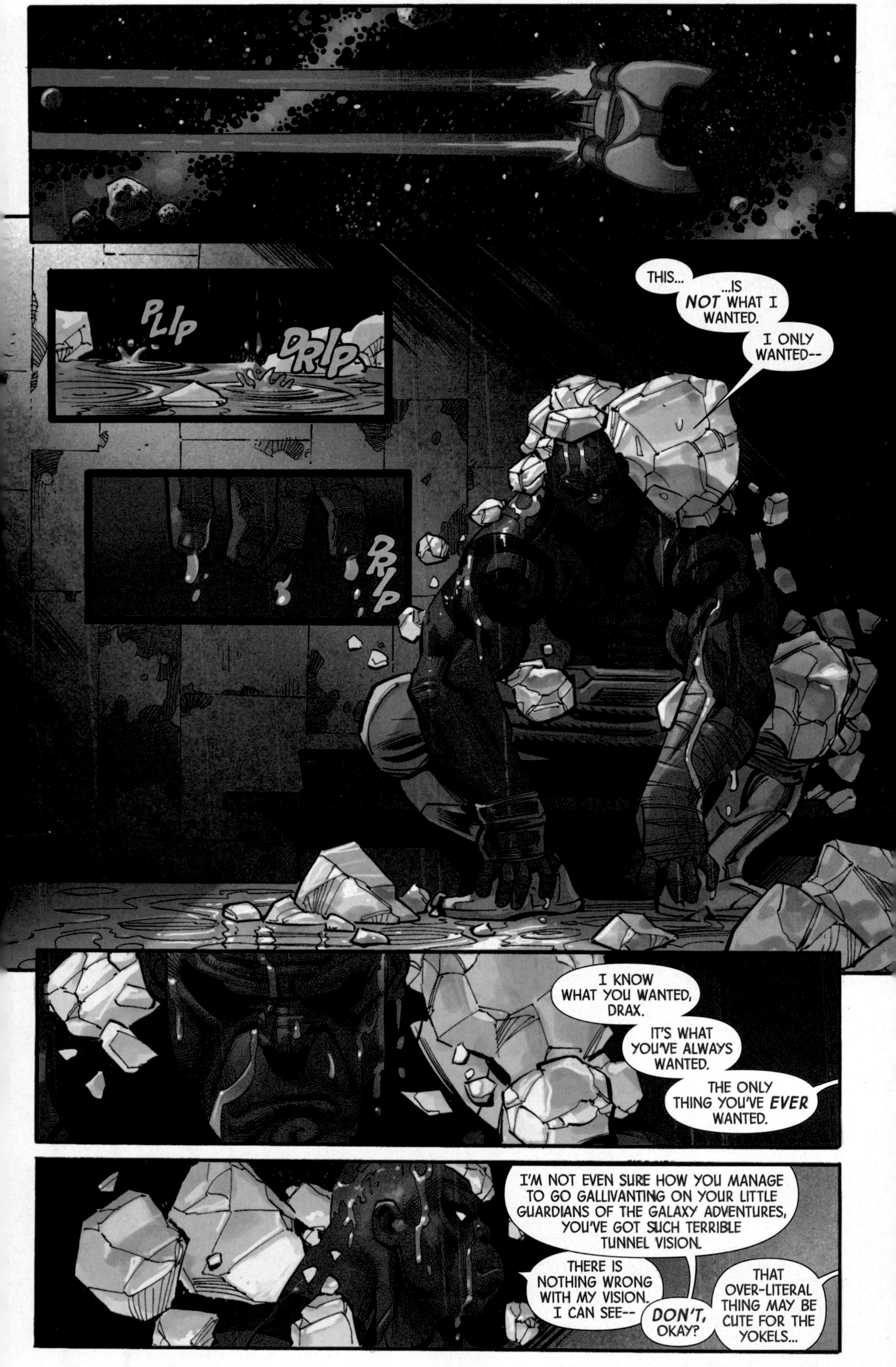
PLIP
DRIP
DRIP
THIS...
...IS NOT WHAT I WANTED.
I ONLY WANTED--
I KNOW WHAT YOU WANTED, DRAX.
IT'S WHAT YOU'VE ALWAYS WANTED.
THE ONLY THING YOU'VE EVER WANTED.
I'M NOT EVEN SURE HOW YOU MANAGE TO GO GALLIVANTING ON YOUR LITTLE GUARDIANS OF THE GALAXY ADVENTURES, YOU'VE GOT SUCH TERRIBLE TUNNEL VISION.
THERE IS NOTHING WRONG WITH MY VISION. I CAN SEE--
DON'T, OKAY?
THAT OVER-LITERAL THING MAY BE CUTE FOR THE YOKELS...

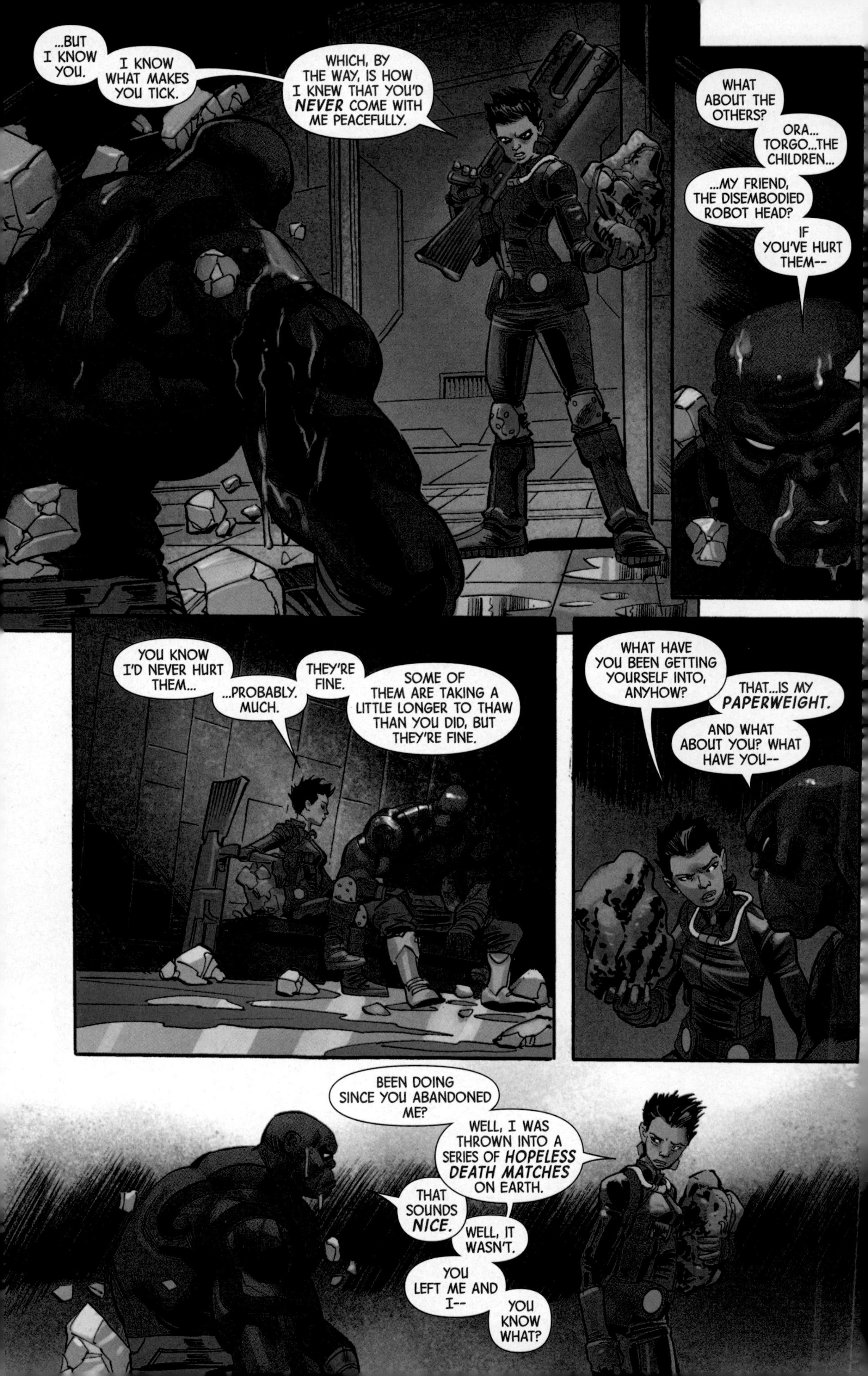
...BUT I KNOW YOU.
I KNOW WHAT MAKES YOU TICK.
WHICH, BY THE WAY, IS HOW I KNEW THAT YOU'D NEVER COME WITH ME PEACEFULLY.
WHAT ABOUT THE OTHERS?
ORA... TORGO...THE CHILDREN...
...MY FRIEND, THE DISEMBODIED ROBOT HEAD?
IF YOU'VE HURT THEM--
YOU KNOW I'D NEVER HURT THEM...
...PROBABLY. MUCH.
THEY'RE FINE.
SOME OF THEM ARE TAKING A LITTLE LONGER TO THAW THAN YOU DID, BUT THEY'RE FINE.
WHAT HAVE YOU BEEN GETTING YOURSELF INTO, ANYHOW?
THAT...IS MY PAPERWEIGHT.
AND WHAT ABOUT YOU? WHAT HAVE YOU--
BEEN DOING SINCE YOU ABANDONED ME?
WELL, I WAS THROWN INTO A SERIES OF HOPELESS DEATH MATCHES ON EARTH.
THAT SOUNDS NICE.
WELL, IT WASN'T.
YOU LEFT ME AND I--
YOU KNOW WHAT?

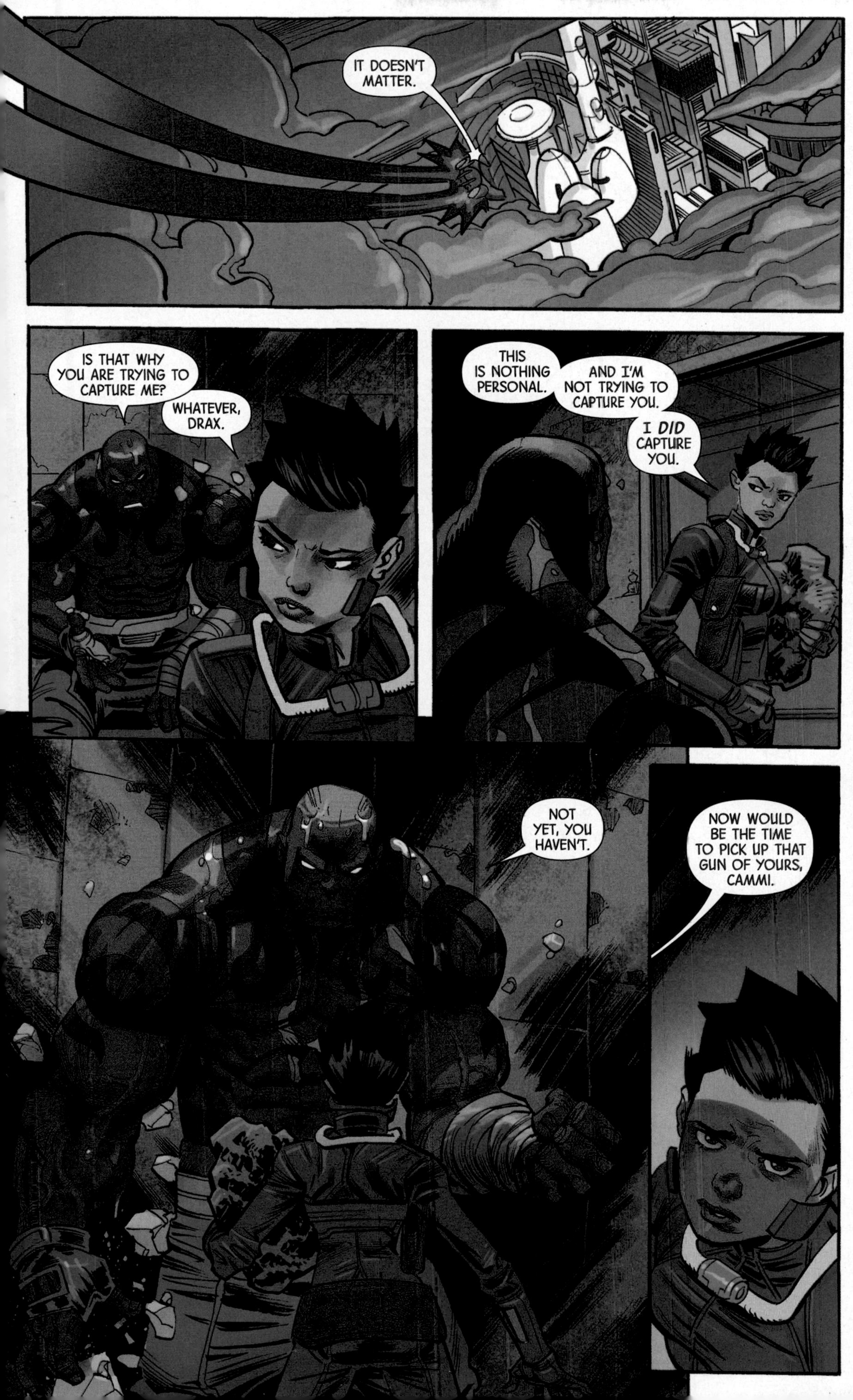
IT DOESN'T MATTER.
IS THAT WHY YOU ARE TRYING TO CAPTURE ME?
WHATEVER, DRAX.
THIS IS NOTHING PERSONAL.
AND I'M NOT TRYING TO CAPTURE YOU.
I *DID* CAPTURE YOU.
NOT YET, YOU HAVEN'T.
NOW WOULD BE THE TIME TO PICK UP THAT GUN OF YOURS, CAMMI.

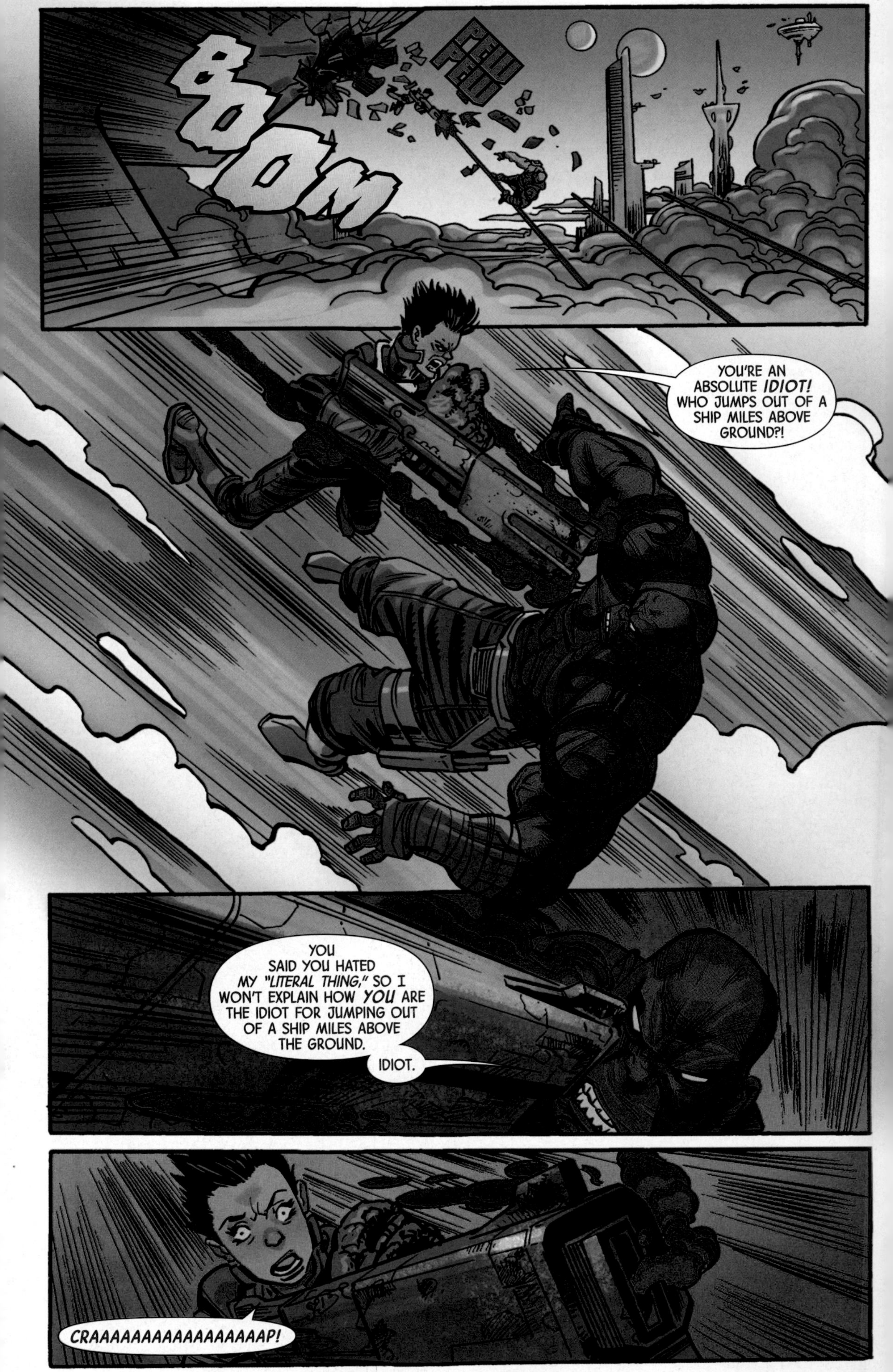
BOOM
PEW PEW
YOU'RE AN ABSOLUTE IDIOT! WHO JUMPS OUT OF A SHIP MILES ABOVE GROUND?!
YOU SAID YOU HATED MY "LITERAL THING," SO I WON'T EXPLAIN HOW YOU ARE THE IDIOT FOR JUMPING OUT OF A SHIP MILES ABOVE THE GROUND.
IDIOT.
CRAAAAAAAAAAAAAAAAAP!

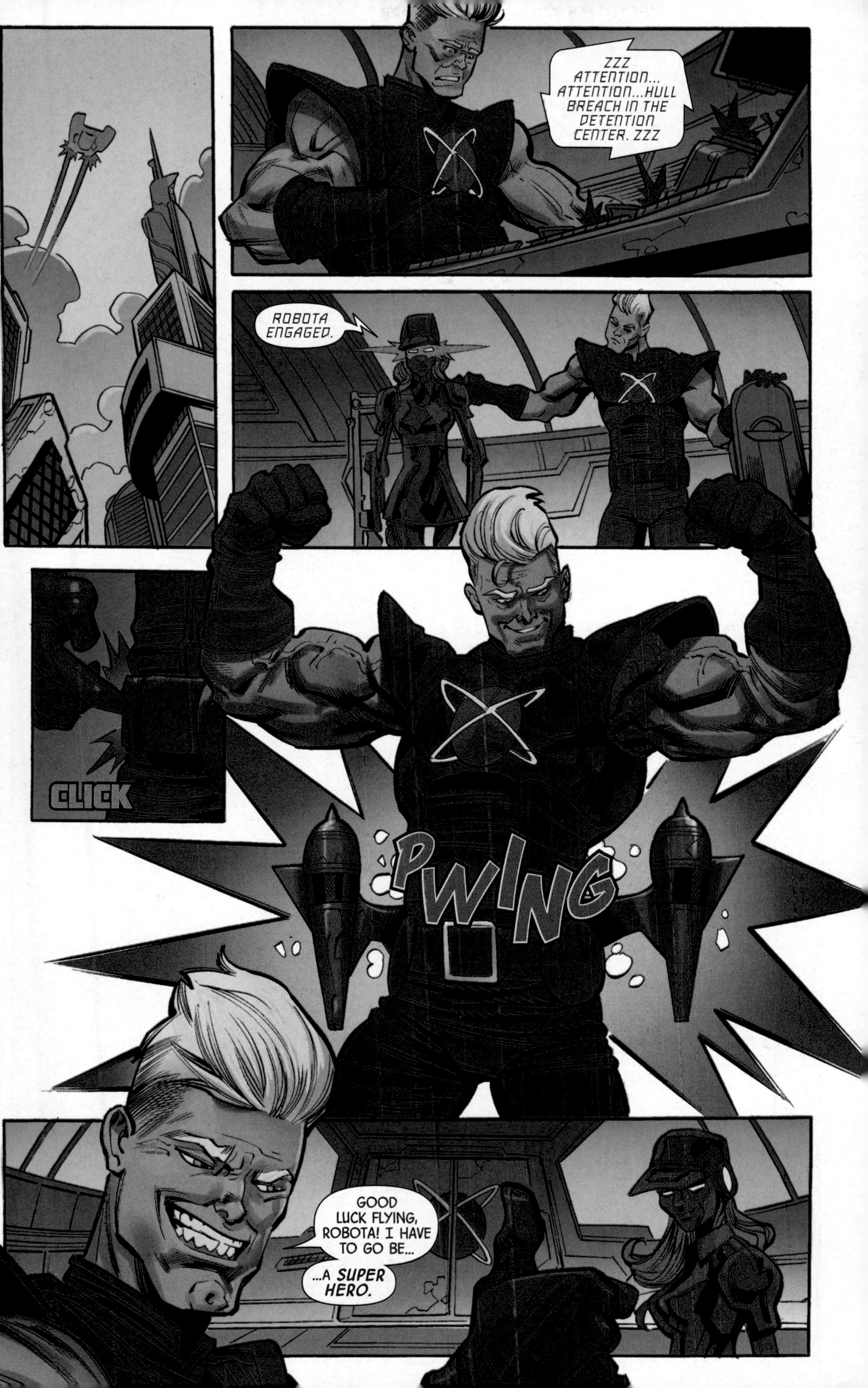
ZZZ ATTENTION... ATTENTION...HULL BREACH IN THE DETENTION CENTER. ZZZ
ROBOTA ENGAGED.
CLICK
PWING
GOOD LUCK FLYING, ROBOTA! I HAVE TO GO BE...
...A SUPER HERO.

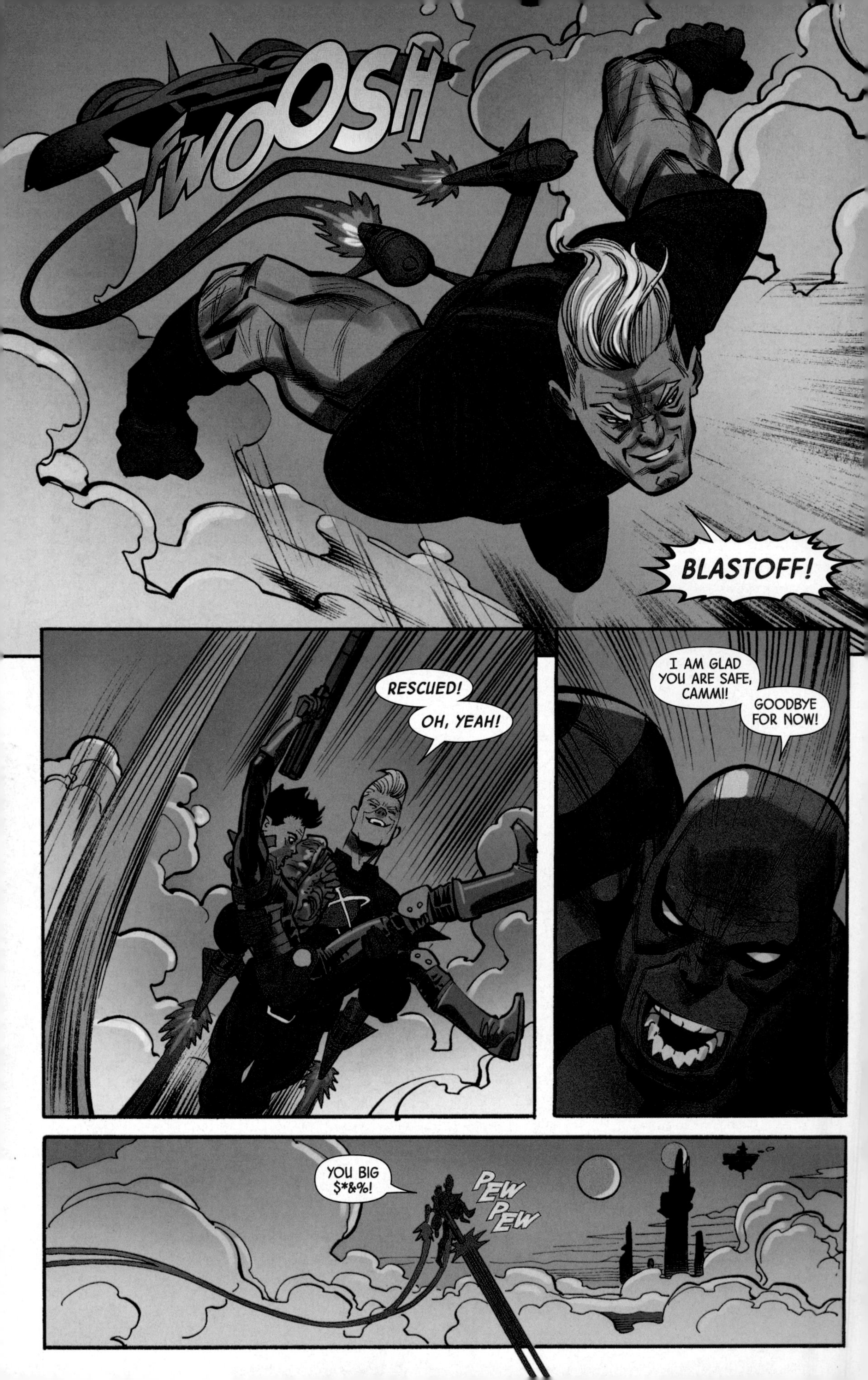
FWOOOSH!
BLASTOFF!
RESCUED!
OH, YEAH!
I AM GLAD YOU ARE SAFE, CAMMI!
GOODBYE FOR NOW!
YOU BIG $*&%!
PEW PEW

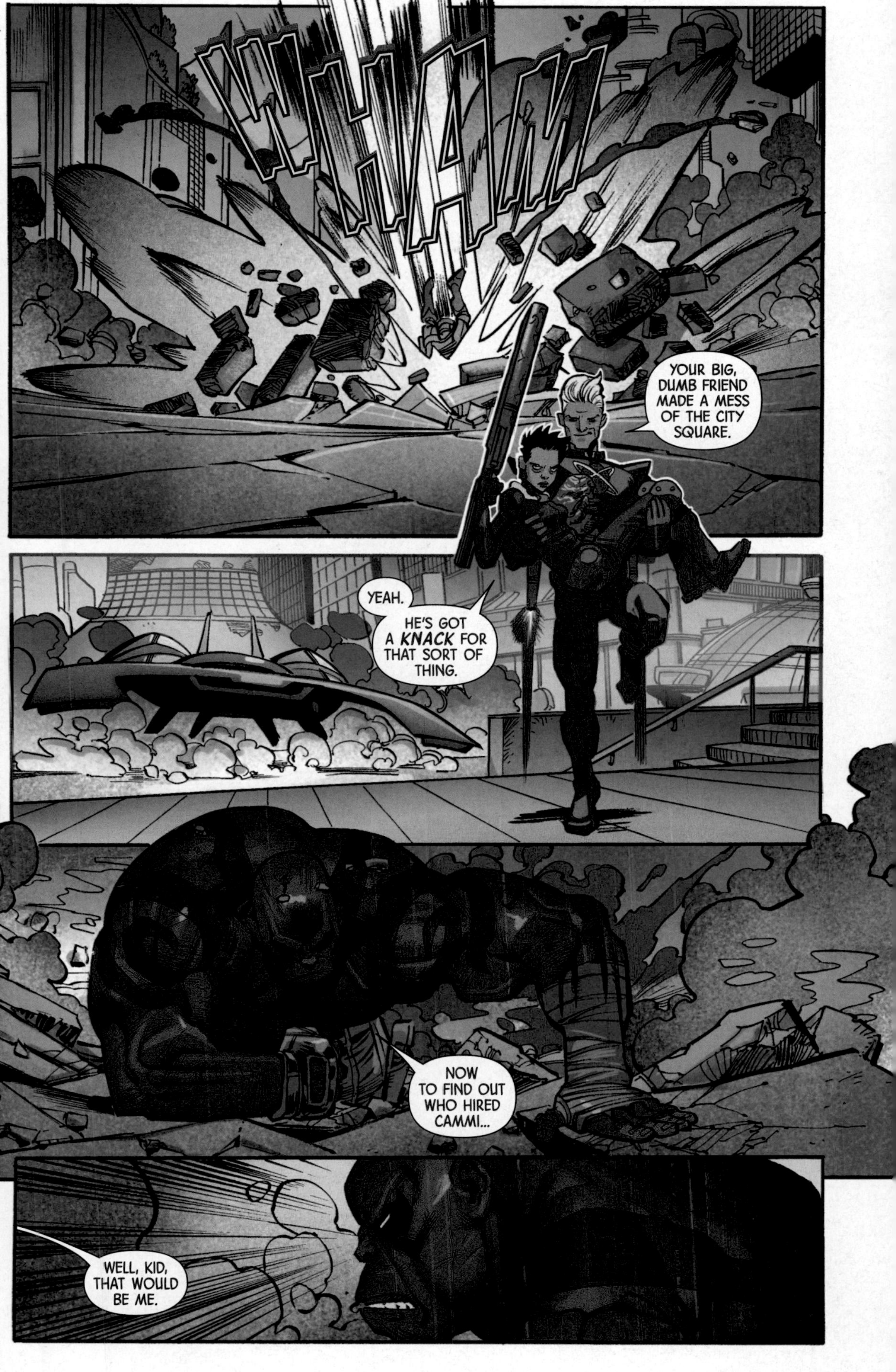
WHAM
YOUR BIG, DUMB FRIEND MADE A MESS OF THE CITY SQUARE.
YEAH.
HE'S GOT A KNACK FOR THAT SORT OF THING.
NOW TO FIND OUT WHO HIRED CAMMI...
WELL, KID, THAT WOULD BE ME.

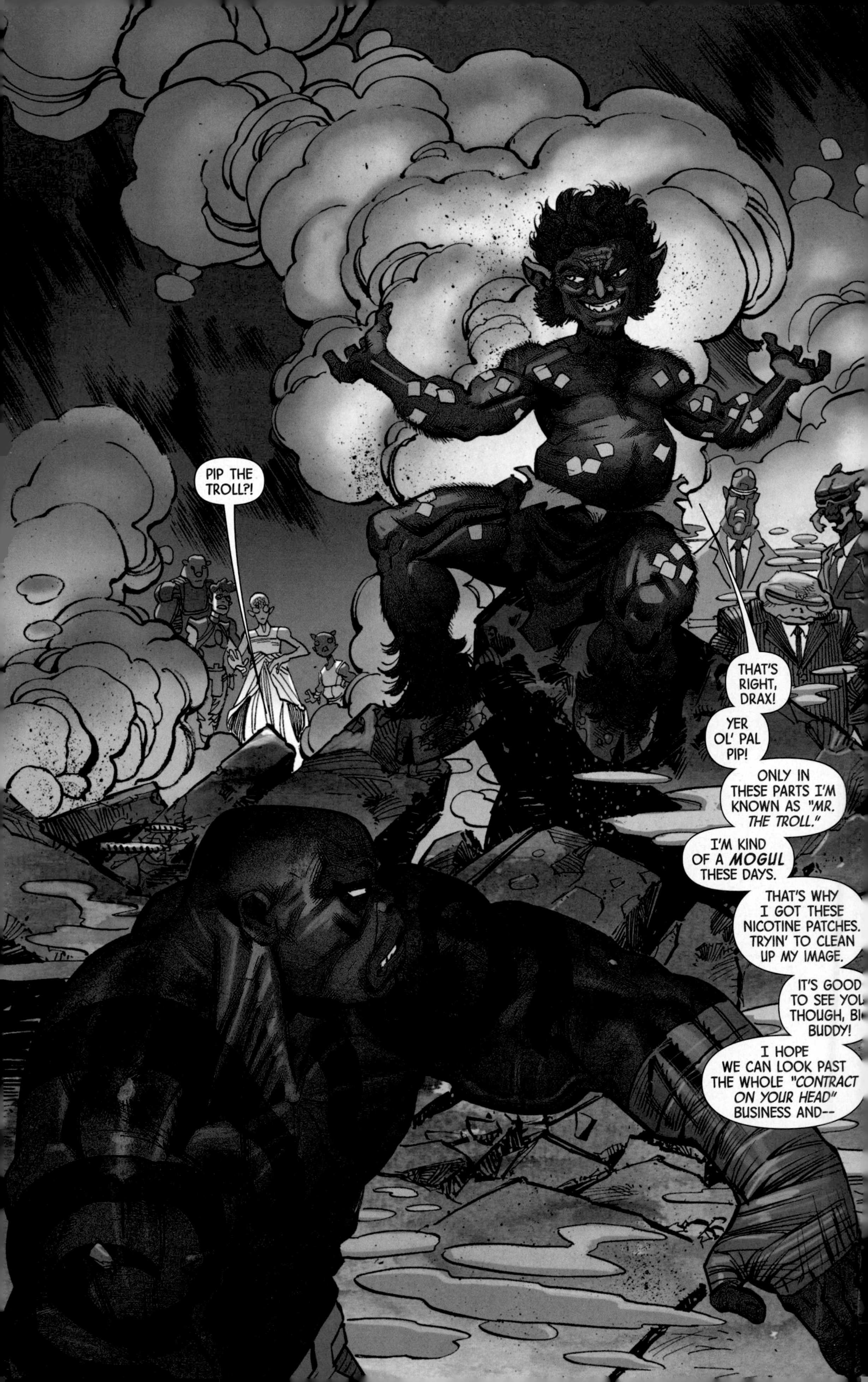
PIP THE TROLL?!
THAT'S RIGHT, DRAX!
YER OL' PAL PIP!
ONLY IN THESE PARTS I'M KNOWN AS *"MR. THE TROLL."*
I'M KIND OF A ***MOGUL*** THESE DAYS.
THAT'S WHY I GOT THESE NICOTINE PATCHES. TRYIN' TO CLEAN UP MY IMAGE.
IT'S GOOD TO SEE YOU THOUGH, BIG BUDDY!
I HOPE WE CAN LOOK PAST THE WHOLE *"CONTRACT ON YOUR HEAD"* BUSINESS AND--

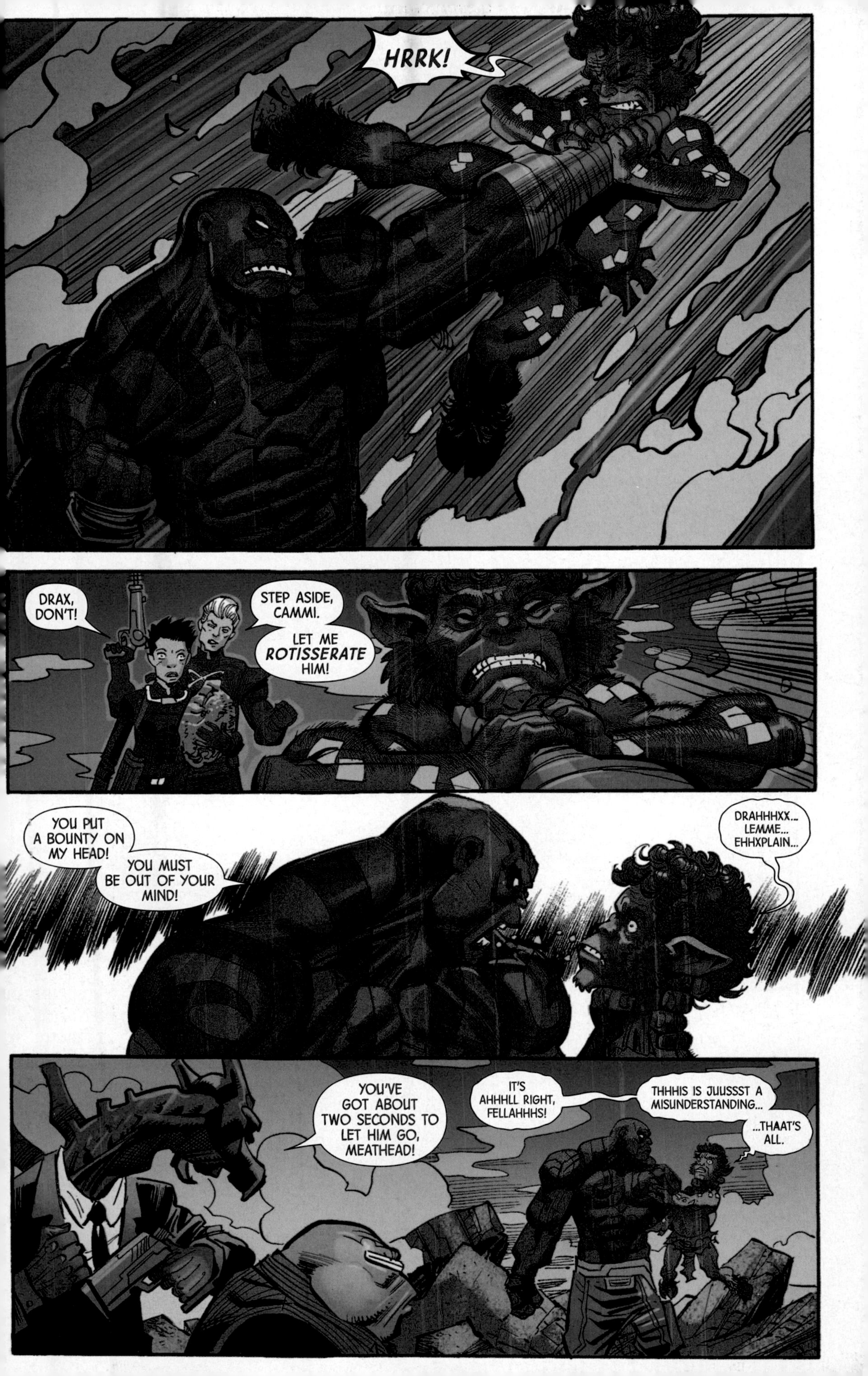
HRRK!
DRAX, DON'T!
STEP ASIDE, CAMMI.
LET ME ROTISSERATE HIM!
YOU PUT A BOUNTY ON MY HEAD!
YOU MUST BE OUT OF YOUR MIND!
DRAHHHXX... LEMME... EHHXPLAIN...
YOU'VE GOT ABOUT TWO SECONDS TO LET HIM GO, MEATHEAD!
IT'S AHHHLL RIGHT, FELLAHHHS!
THHHIS IS JUUSSST A MISUNDERSTANDING...
...THAAT'S ALL.

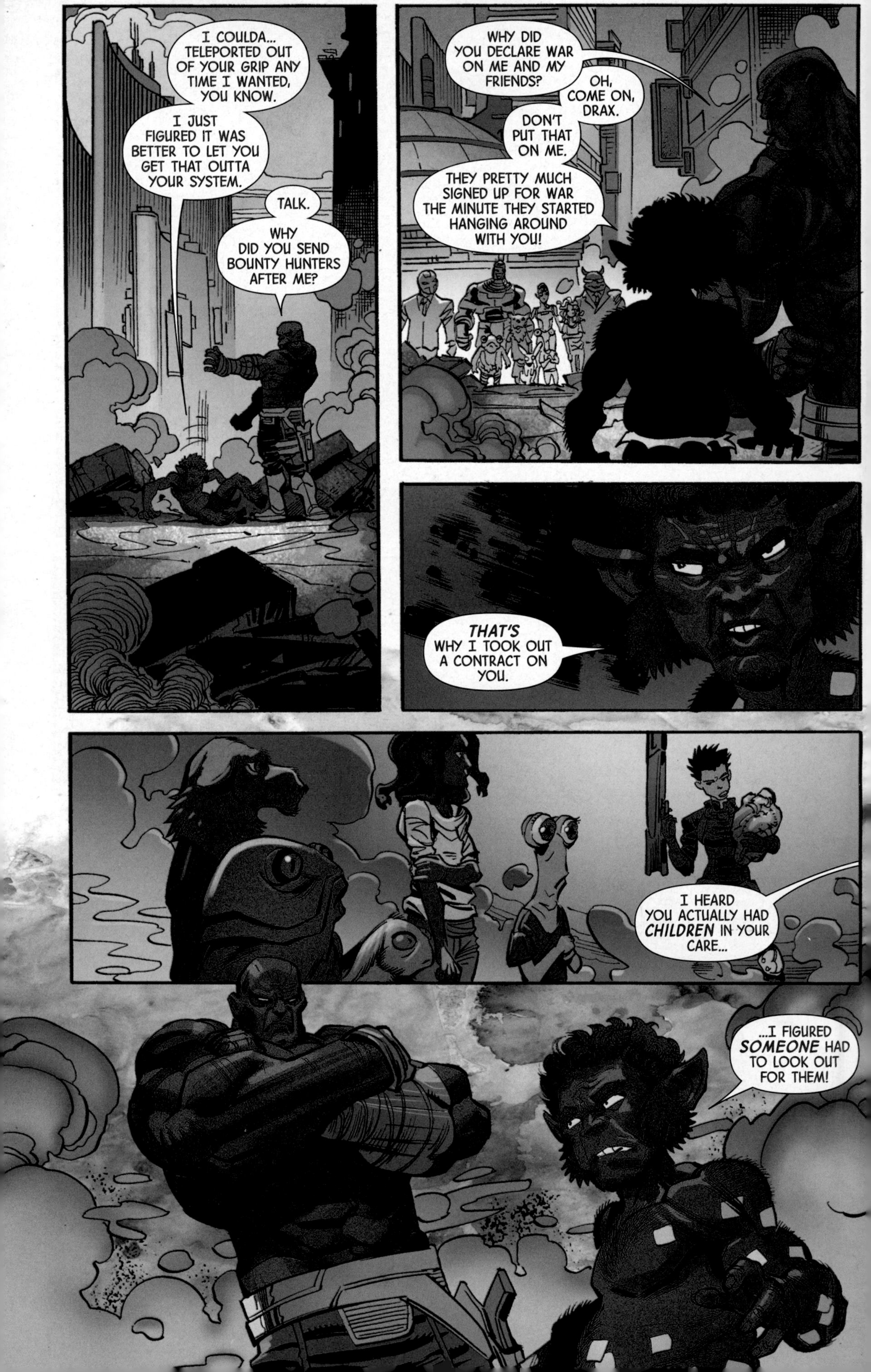
I COULDA... TELEPORTED OUT OF YOUR GRIP ANY TIME I WANTED, YOU KNOW.
I JUST FIGURED IT WAS BETTER TO LET YOU GET THAT OUTTA YOUR SYSTEM.
TALK.
WHY DID YOU SEND BOUNTY HUNTERS AFTER ME?
WHY DID YOU DECLARE WAR ON ME AND MY FRIENDS?
OH, COME ON, DRAX.
DON'T PUT THAT ON ME.
THEY PRETTY MUCH SIGNED UP FOR WAR THE MINUTE THEY STARTED HANGING AROUND WITH YOU!
THAT'S WHY I TOOK OUT A CONTRACT ON YOU.
I HEARD YOU ACTUALLY HAD **CHILDREN** IN YOUR CARE...
...I FIGURED ***SOMEONE*** HAD TO LOOK OUT FOR THEM!

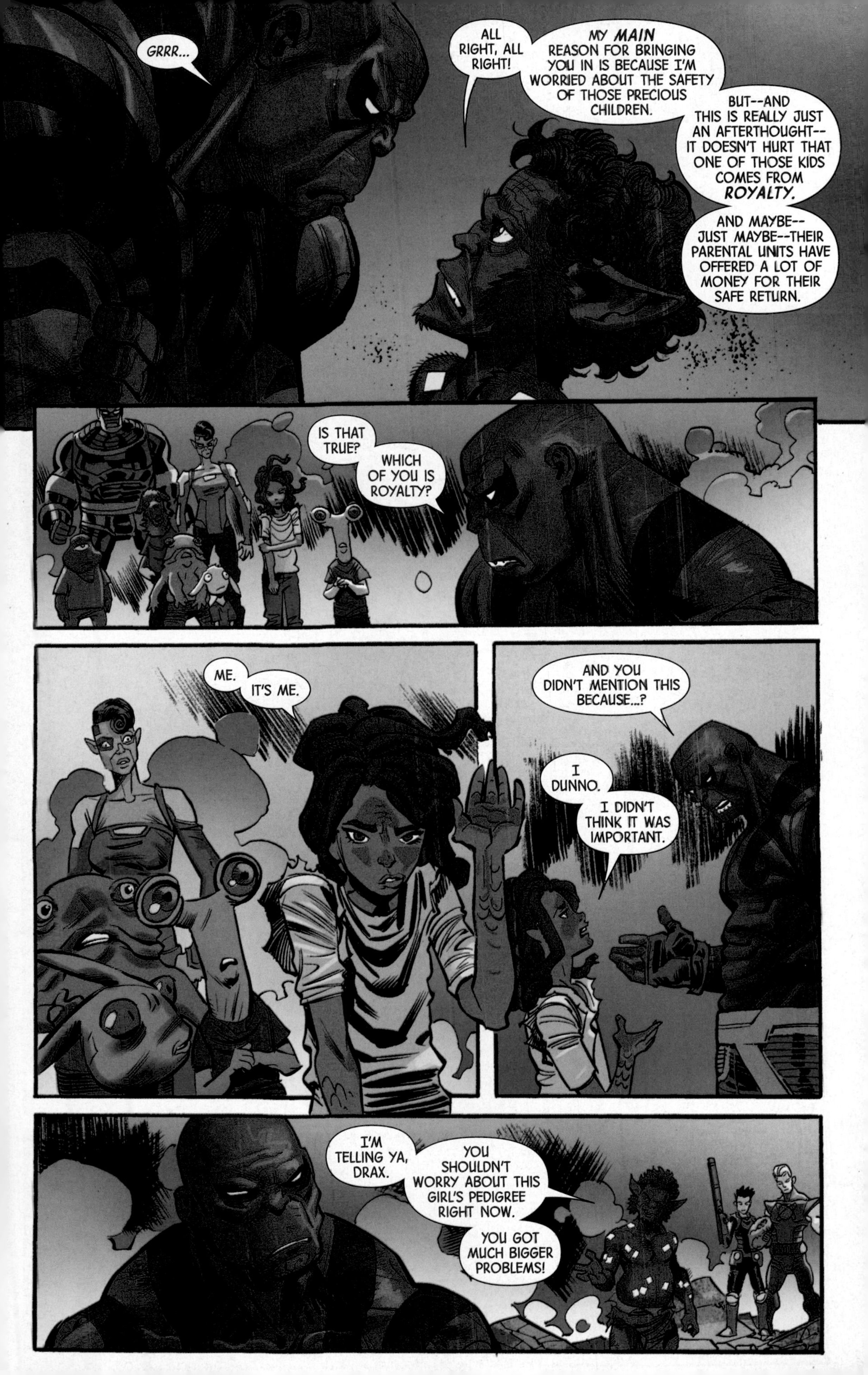
GRRR...
ALL RIGHT, ALL RIGHT!
MY MAIN REASON FOR BRINGING YOU IN IS BECAUSE I'M WORRIED ABOUT THE SAFETY OF THOSE PRECIOUS CHILDREN.
BUT--AND THIS IS REALLY JUST AN AFTERTHOUGHT--IT DOESN'T HURT THAT ONE OF THOSE KIDS COMES FROM ROYALTY.
AND MAYBE--JUST MAYBE--THEIR PARENTAL UNITS HAVE OFFERED A LOT OF MONEY FOR THEIR SAFE RETURN.
IS THAT TRUE?
WHICH OF YOU IS ROYALTY?
ME.
IT'S ME.
AND YOU DIDN'T MENTION THIS BECAUSE...?
I DUNNO.
I DIDN'T THINK IT WAS IMPORTANT.
I'M TELLING YA, DRAX.
YOU SHOULDN'T WORRY ABOUT THIS GIRL'S PEDIGREE RIGHT NOW.
YOU GOT MUCH BIGGER PROBLEMS!

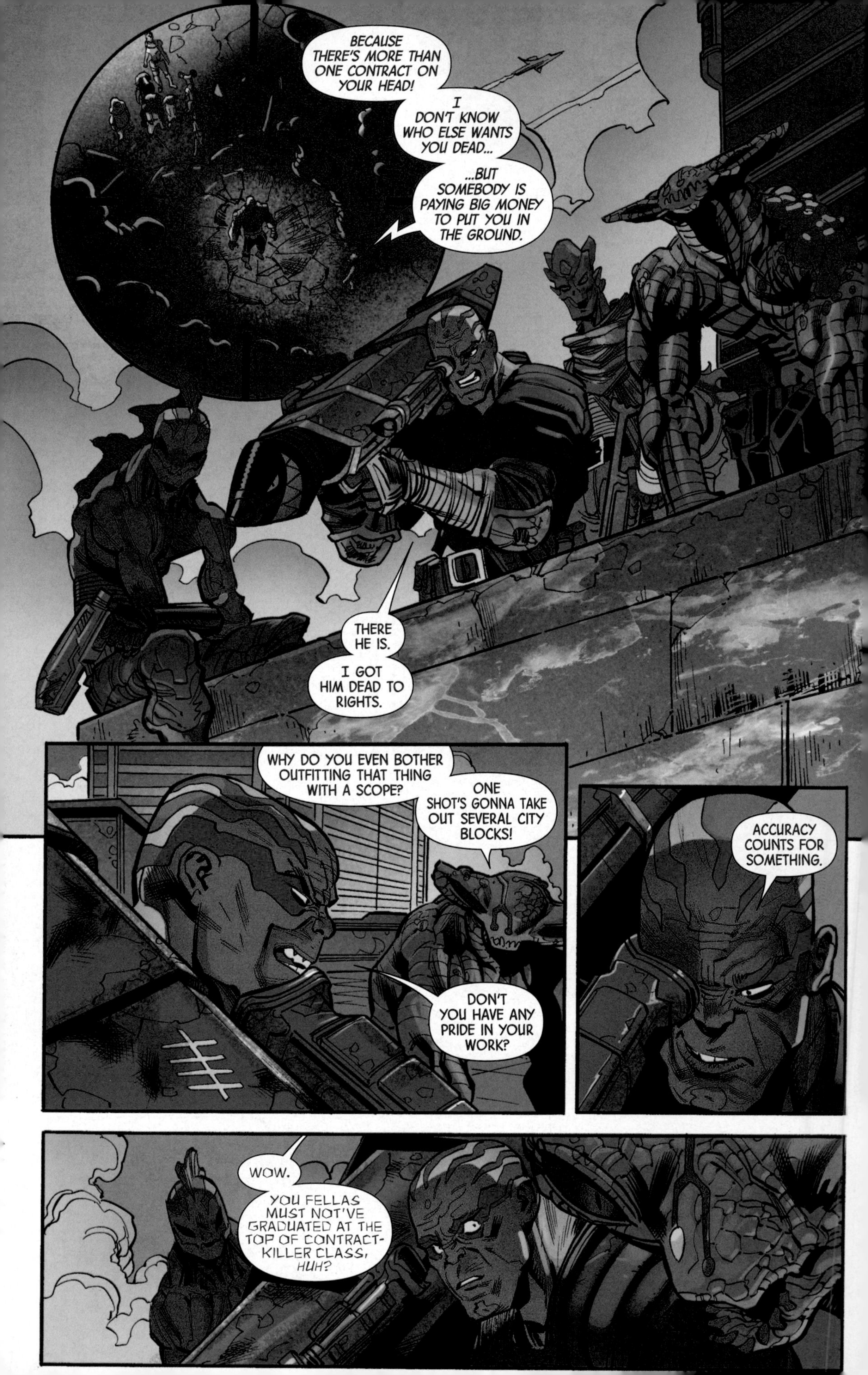
BECAUSE THERE'S MORE THAN ONE CONTRACT ON YOUR HEAD!
I DON'T KNOW WHO ELSE WANTS YOU DEAD...
...BUT SOMEBODY IS PAYING BIG MONEY TO PUT YOU IN THE GROUND.
THERE HE IS.
I GOT HIM DEAD TO RIGHTS.
WHY DO YOU EVEN BOTHER OUTFITTING THAT THING WITH A SCOPE?
ONE SHOT'S GONNA TAKE OUT SEVERAL CITY BLOCKS!
DON'T YOU HAVE ANY PRIDE IN YOUR WORK?
ACCURACY COUNTS FOR SOMETHING.
WOW.
YOU FELLAS MUST NOT'VE GRADUATED AT THE TOP OF CONTRACT-KILLER CLASS, HUH?

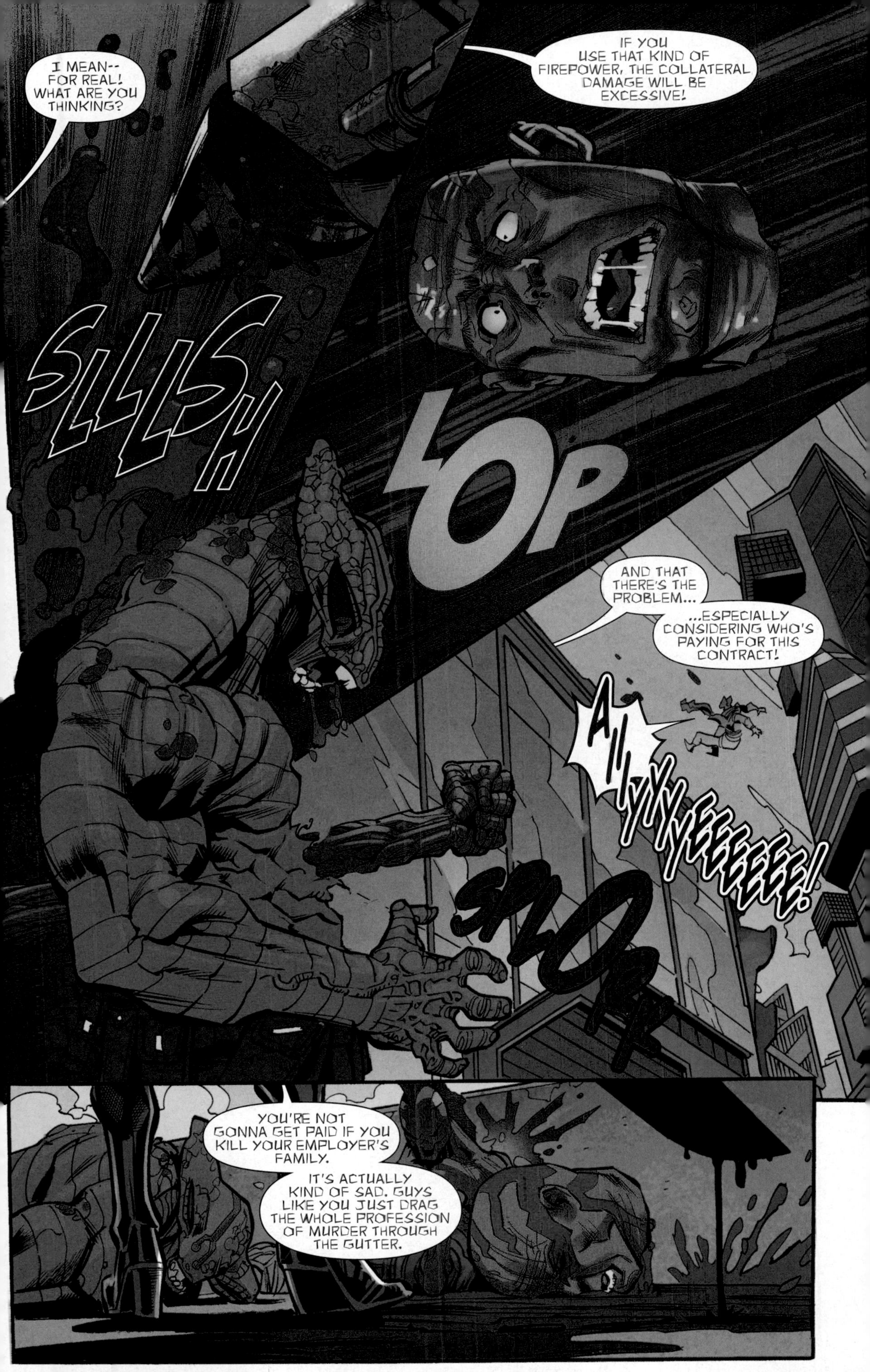
I MEAN-- FOR REAL! WHAT ARE YOU THINKING?
IF YOU USE THAT KIND OF FIREPOWER, THE COLLATERAL DAMAGE WILL BE EXCESSIVE!
SLLLSH
LOP
AND THAT THERE'S THE PROBLEM...
...ESPECIALLY CONSIDERING WHO'S PAYING FOR THIS CONTRACT!
AIIYYYEEEEEE!
SPLORP
YOU'RE NOT GONNA GET PAID IF YOU KILL YOUR EMPLOYER'S FAMILY.
IT'S ACTUALLY KIND OF SAD. GUYS LIKE YOU JUST DRAG THE WHOLE PROFESSION OF MURDER THROUGH THE GUTTER.

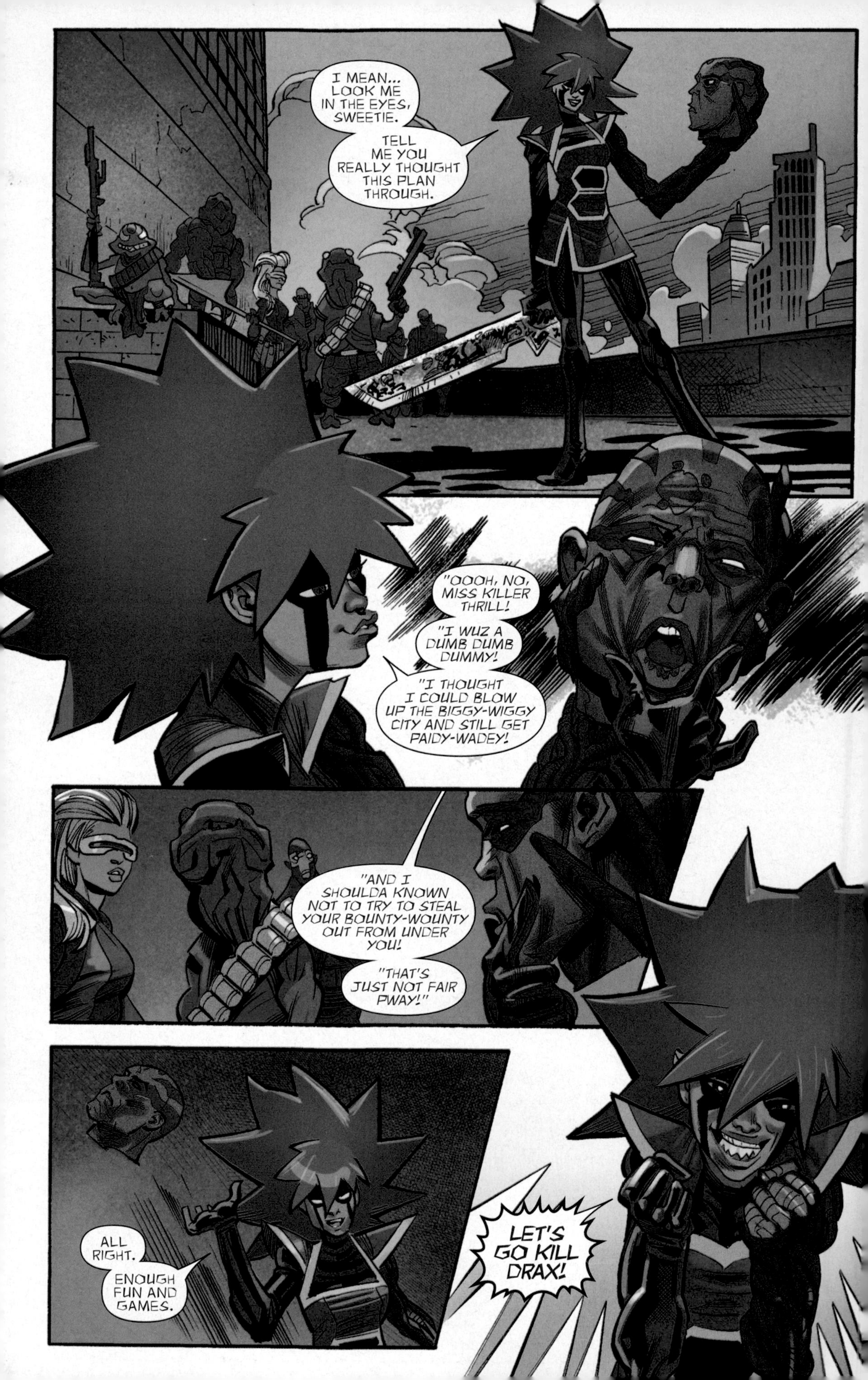
I MEAN... LOOK ME IN THE EYES, SWEETIE.
TELL ME YOU REALLY THOUGHT THIS PLAN THROUGH.
"OOOH, NO, MISS KILLER THRILL!
"I WUZ A DUMB DUMB DUMMY!
"I THOUGHT I COULD BLOW UP THE BIGGY-WIGGY CITY AND STILL GET PAIDY-WADEY!
"AND I SHOULDA KNOWN NOT TO TRY TO STEAL YOUR BOUNTY-WOUNTY OUT FROM UNDER YOU!
"THAT'S JUST NOT FAIR PWAY!"
ALL RIGHT.
ENOUGH FUN AND GAMES.
LET'S GO KILL DRAX!

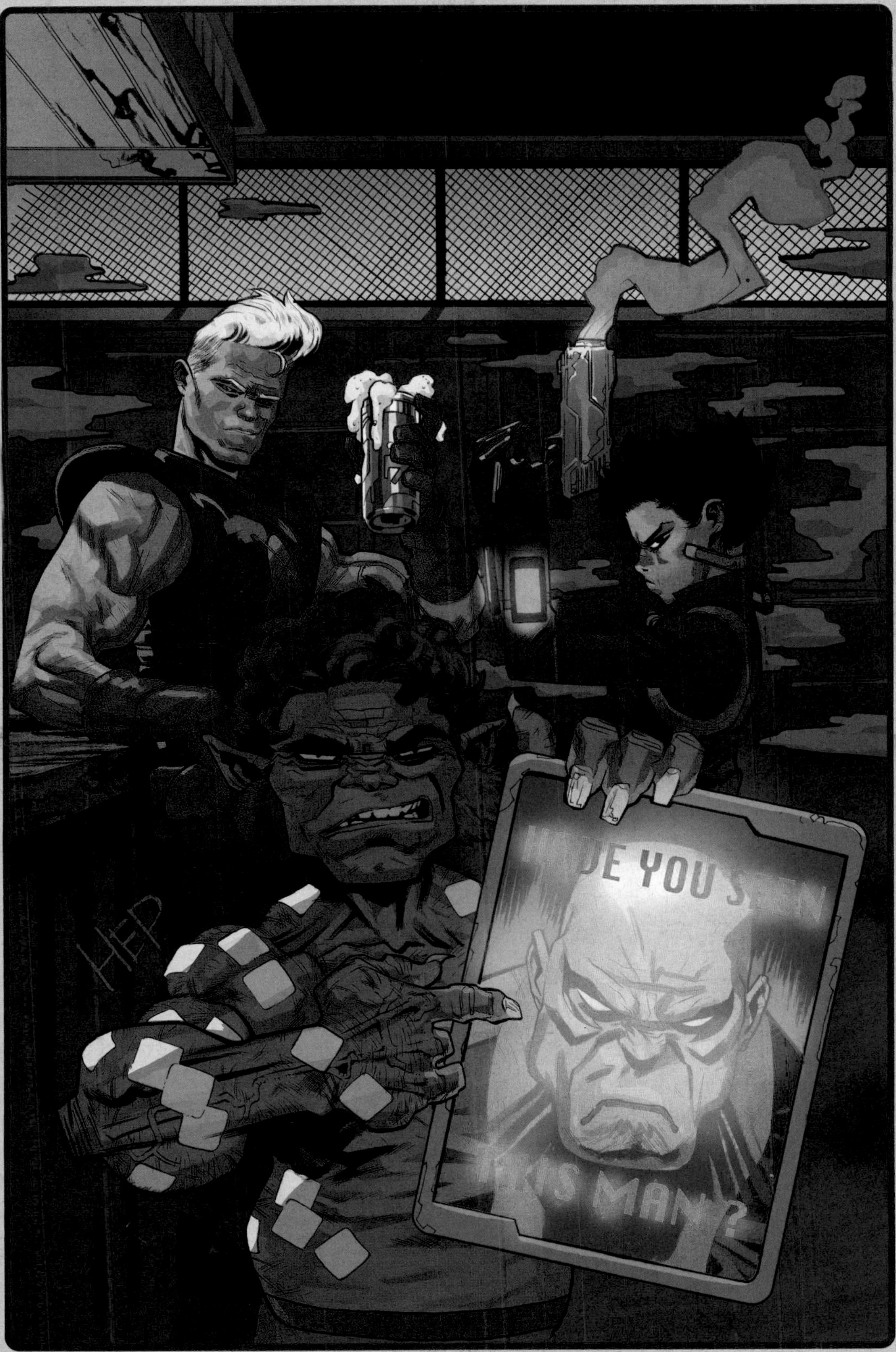
HEP
DE YOU S
IS MAN?

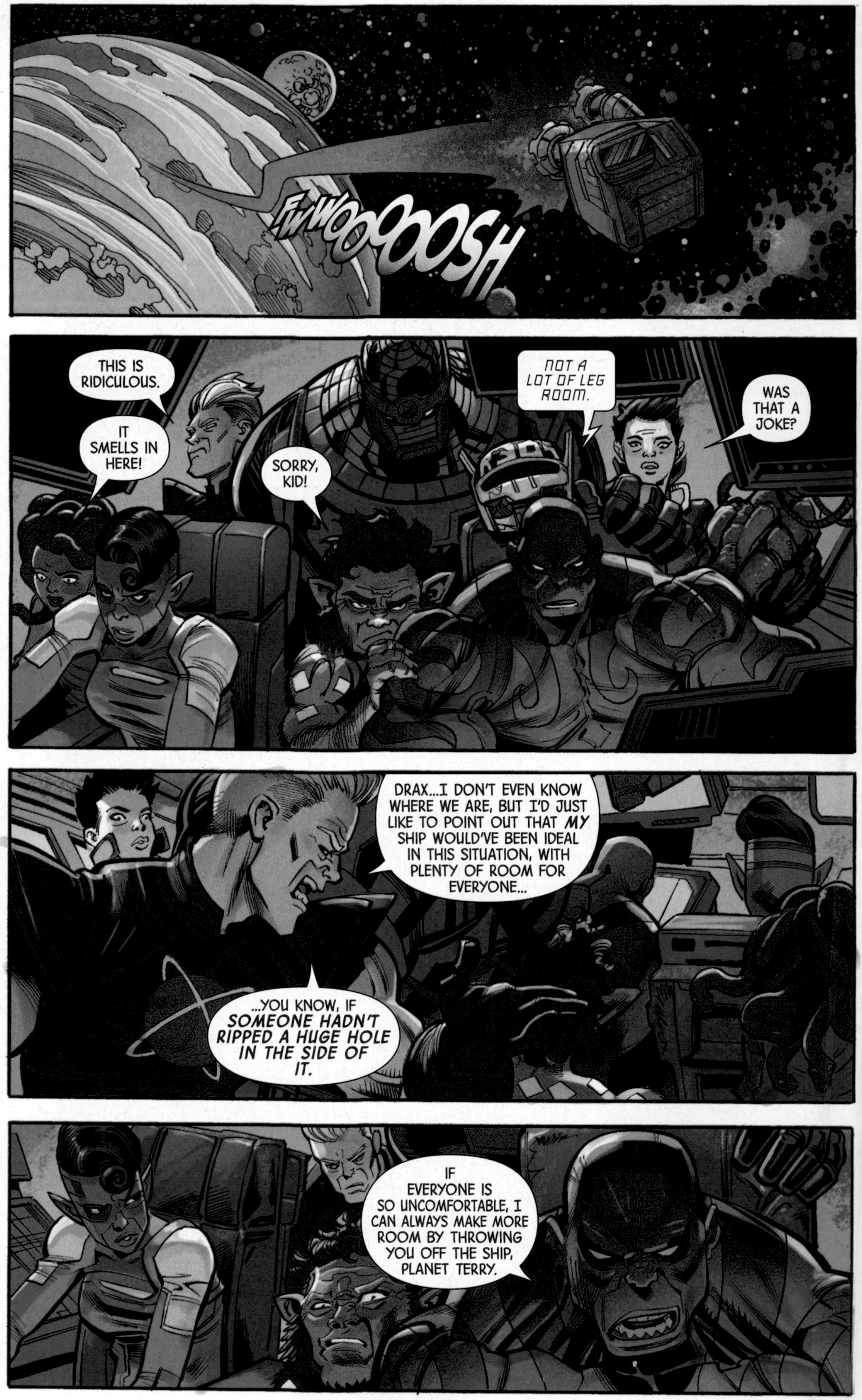
FWWOOOOOOSH
THIS IS RIDICULOUS.
IT SMELLS IN HERE!
SORRY, KID!
NOT A LOT OF LEG ROOM.
WAS THAT A JOKE?
DRAX...I DON'T EVEN KNOW WHERE WE ARE, BUT I'D JUST LIKE TO POINT OUT THAT MY SHIP WOULD'VE BEEN IDEAL IN THIS SITUATION, WITH PLENTY OF ROOM FOR EVERYONE...
...YOU KNOW, IF SOMEONE HADN'T RIPPED A HUGE HOLE IN THE SIDE OF IT.
IF EVERYONE IS SO UNCOMFORTABLE, I CAN ALWAYS MAKE MORE ROOM BY THROWING YOU OFF THE SHIP, PLANET TERRY.

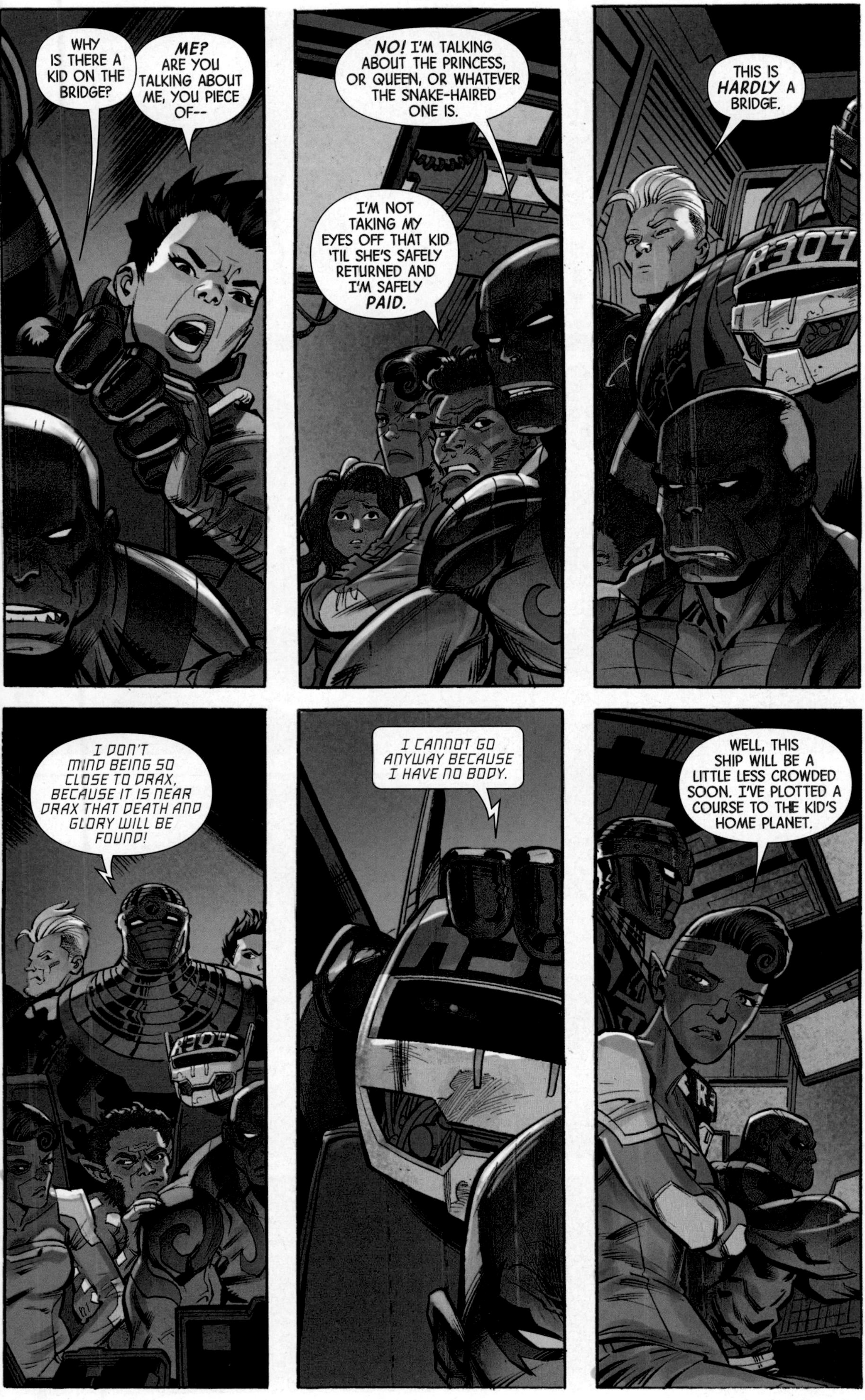
WHY IS THERE A KID ON THE BRIDGE?
ME? ARE YOU TALKING ABOUT ME, YOU PIECE OF--
NO! I'M TALKING ABOUT THE PRINCESS, OR QUEEN, OR WHATEVER THE SNAKE-HAIRED ONE IS.
I'M NOT TAKING MY EYES OFF THAT KID 'TIL SHE'S SAFELY RETURNED AND I'M SAFELY PAID.
THIS IS HARDLY A BRIDGE.
R304
I DON'T MIND BEING SO CLOSE TO DRAX, BECAUSE IT IS NEAR DRAX THAT DEATH AND GLORY WILL BE FOUND!
I CANNOT GO ANYWAY BECAUSE I HAVE NO BODY.
WELL, THIS SHIP WILL BE A LITTLE LESS CROWDED SOON. I'VE PLOTTED A COURSE TO THE KID'S HOME PLANET.

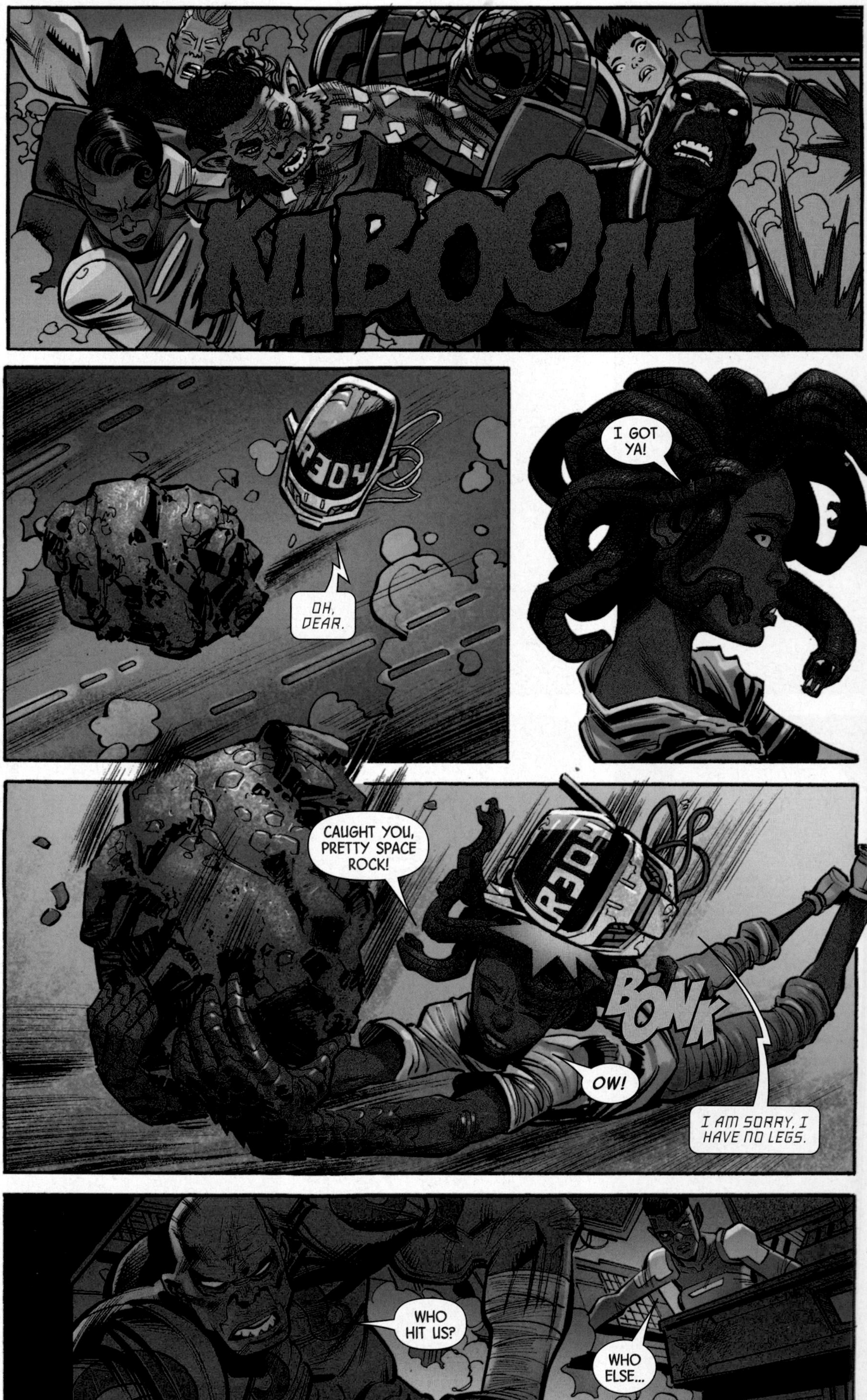
KABOOM
OH, DEAR.
I GOT YA!
CAUGHT YOU, PRETTY SPACE ROCK!
BONK
OW!
I AM SORRY, I HAVE NO LEGS.
WHO HIT US?
WHO ELSE...

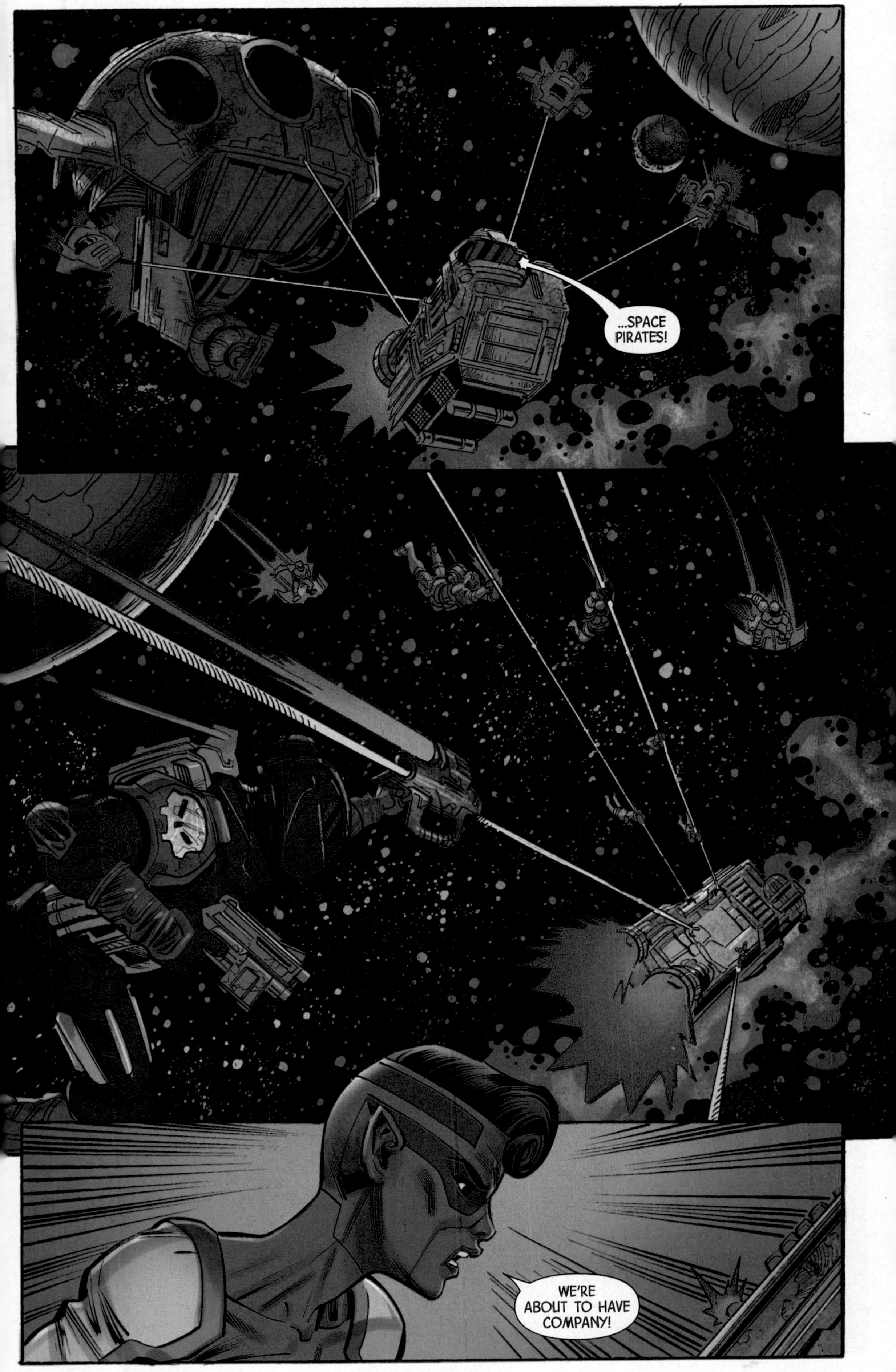
...SPACE PIRATES!
WE'RE ABOUT TO HAVE COMPANY!

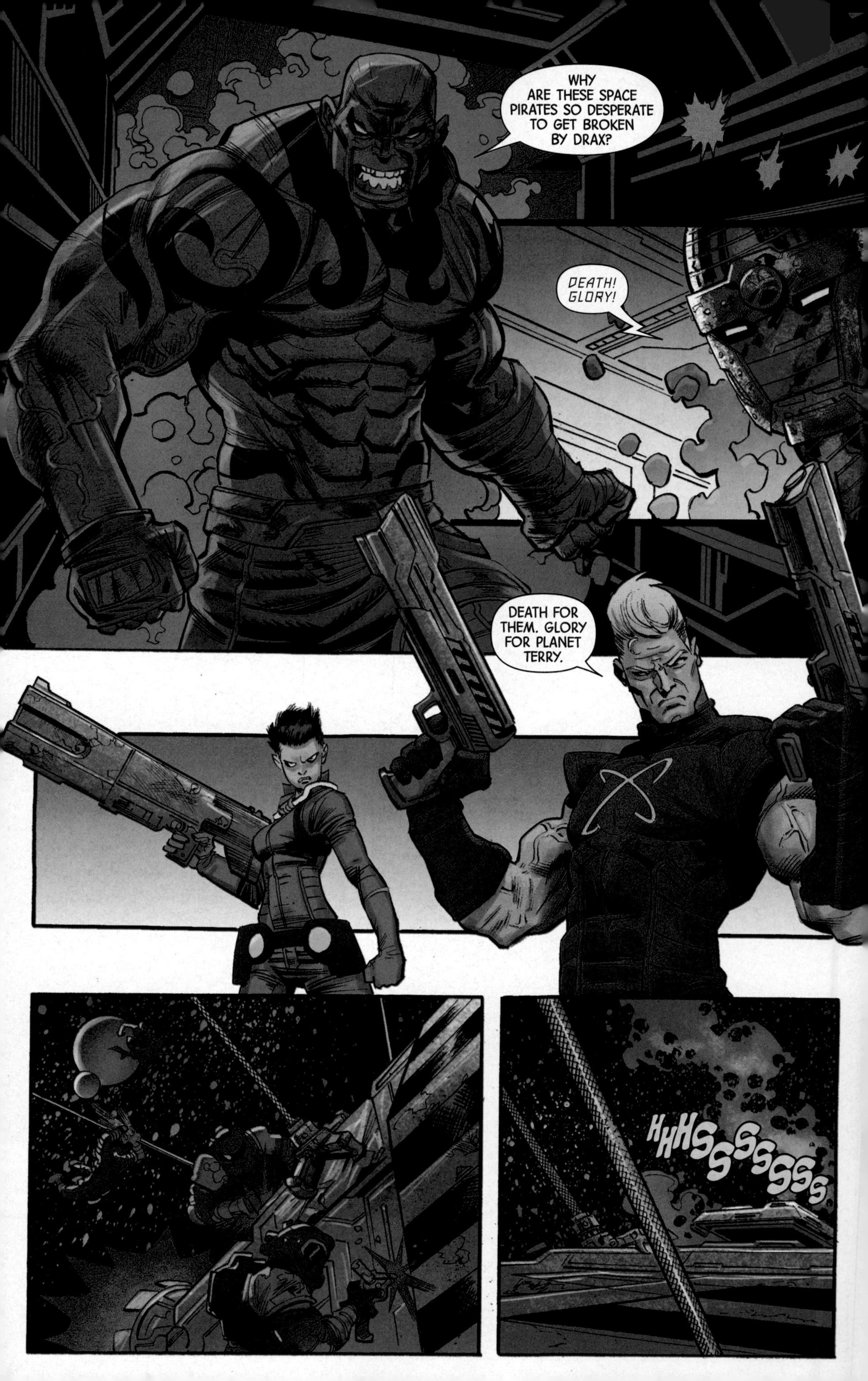
WHY ARE THESE SPACE PIRATES SO DESPERATE TO GET BROKEN BY DRAX?
DEATH! GLORY!
DEATH FOR THEM. GLORY FOR PLANET TERRY.
HHHSSSSSSS

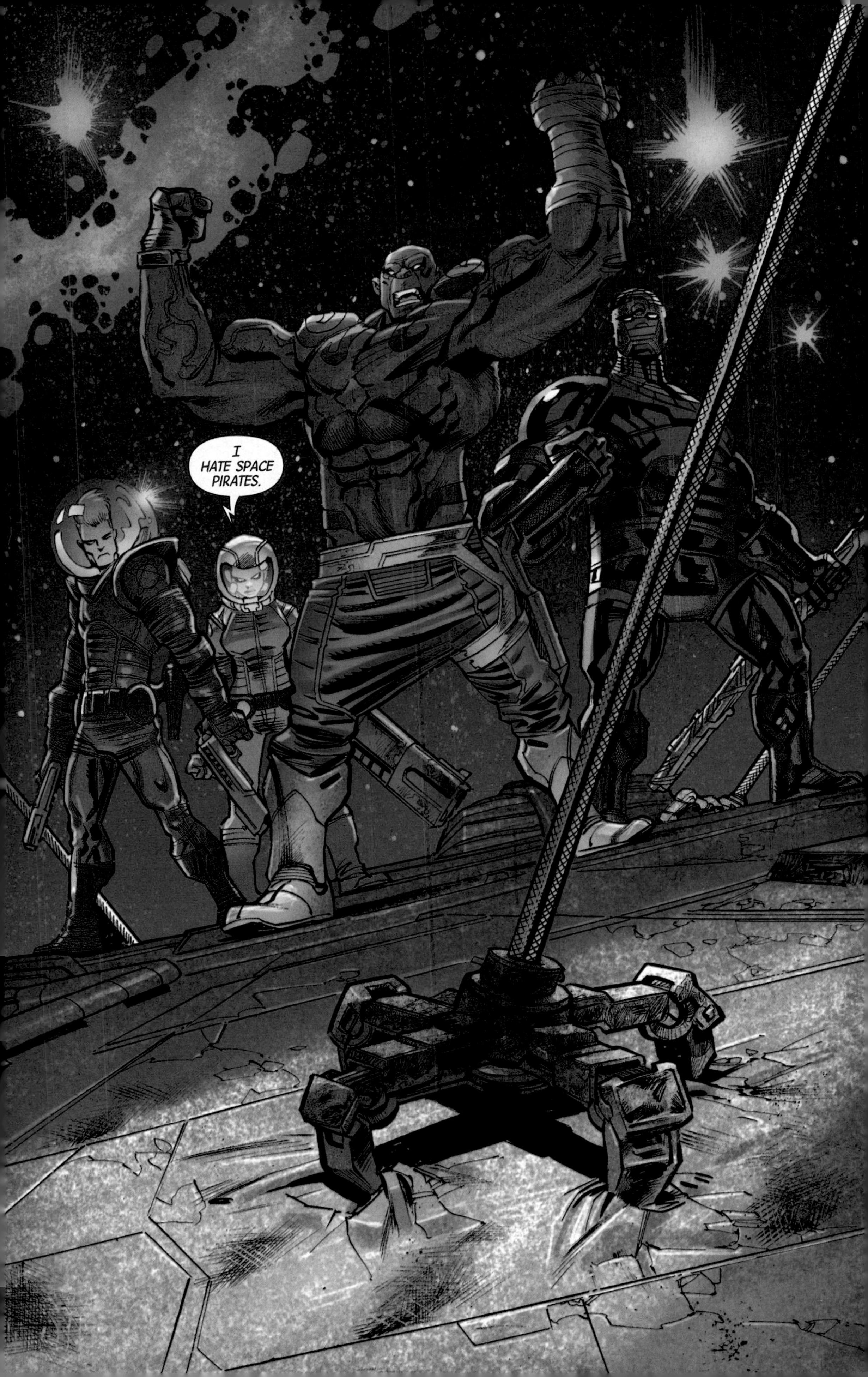
I HATE SPACE PIRATES.

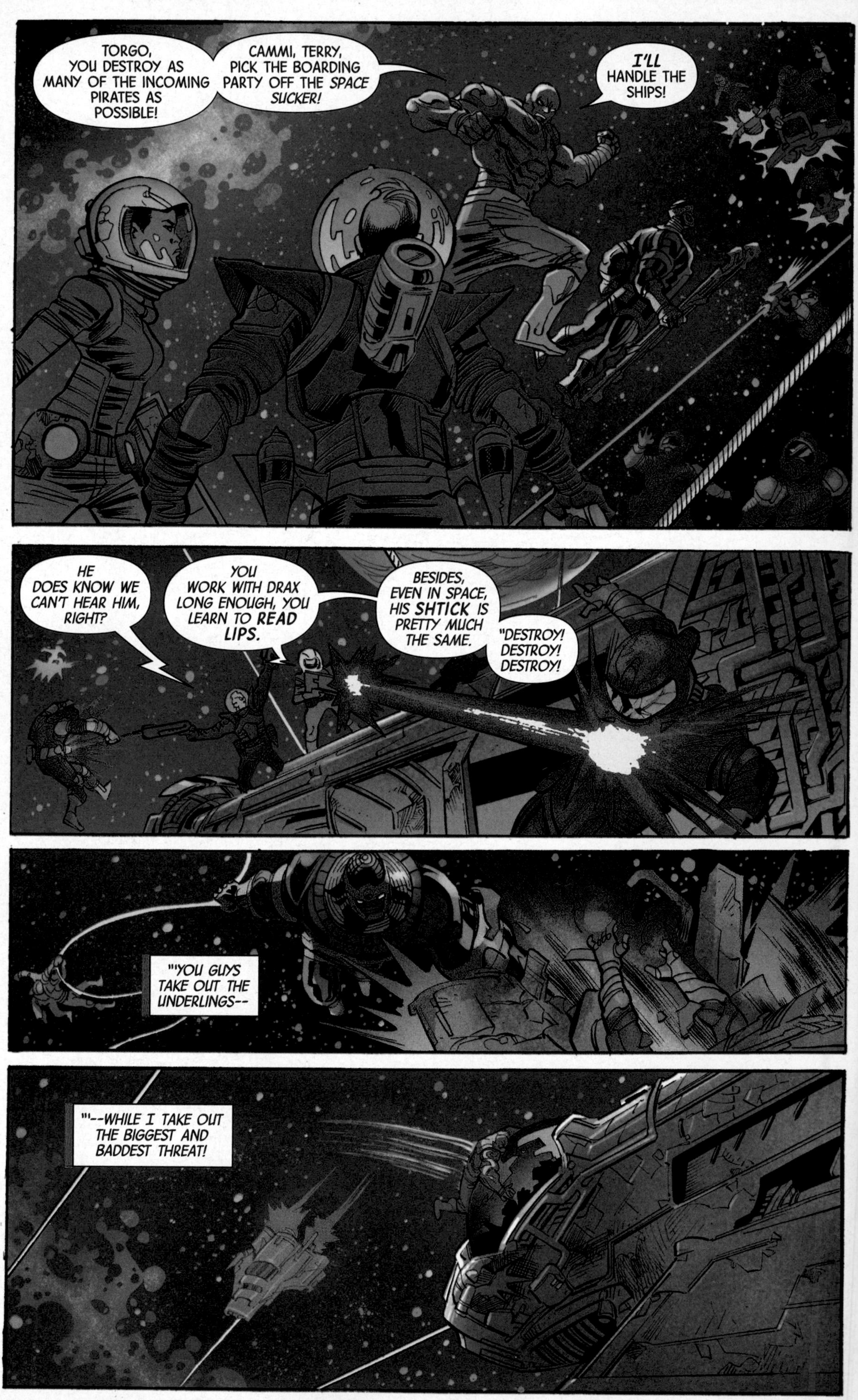
TORGO, YOU DESTROY AS MANY OF THE INCOMING PIRATES AS POSSIBLE!
CAMMI, TERRY, PICK THE BOARDING PARTY OFF THE SPACE SUCKER!
I'LL HANDLE THE SHIPS!
HE DOES KNOW WE CAN'T HEAR HIM, RIGHT?
YOU WORK WITH DRAX LONG ENOUGH, YOU LEARN TO READ LIPS.
BESIDES, EVEN IN SPACE, HIS SHTICK IS PRETTY MUCH THE SAME.
"DESTROY! DESTROY! DESTROY!
"'YOU GUYS TAKE OUT THE UNDERLINGS--
"'--WHILE I TAKE OUT THE BIGGEST AND BADDEST THREAT!

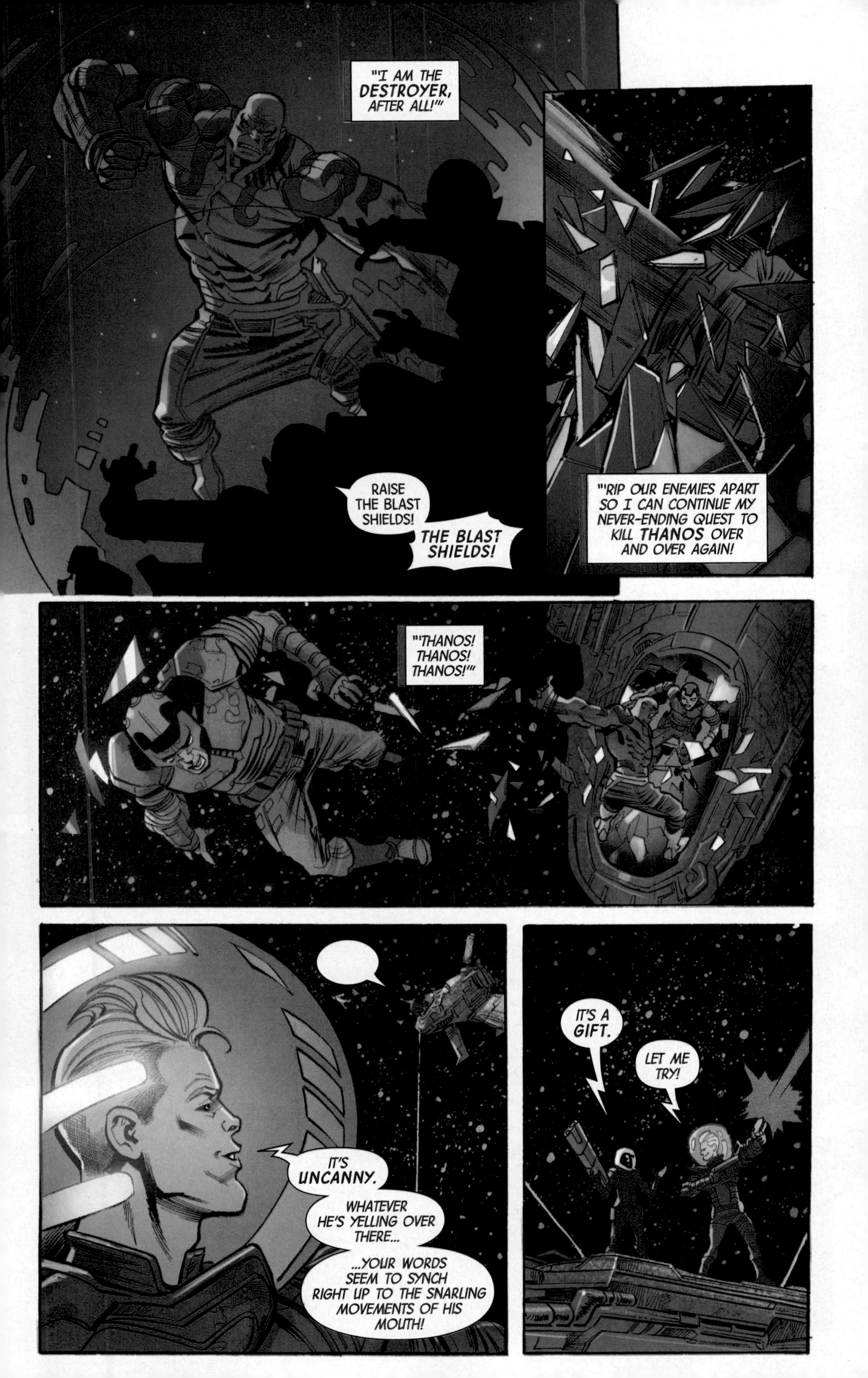
"I AM THE DESTROYER, AFTER ALL!"
RAISE THE BLAST SHIELDS!
THE BLAST SHIELDS!
"RIP OUR ENEMIES APART SO I CAN CONTINUE MY NEVER-ENDING QUEST TO KILL THANOS OVER AND OVER AGAIN!
"THANOS! THANOS! THANOS!"
IT'S UNCANNY.
WHATEVER HE'S YELLING OVER THERE...
...YOUR WORDS SEEM TO SYNCH RIGHT UP TO THE SNARLING MOVEMENTS OF HIS MOUTH!
IT'S A GIFT.
LET ME TRY!

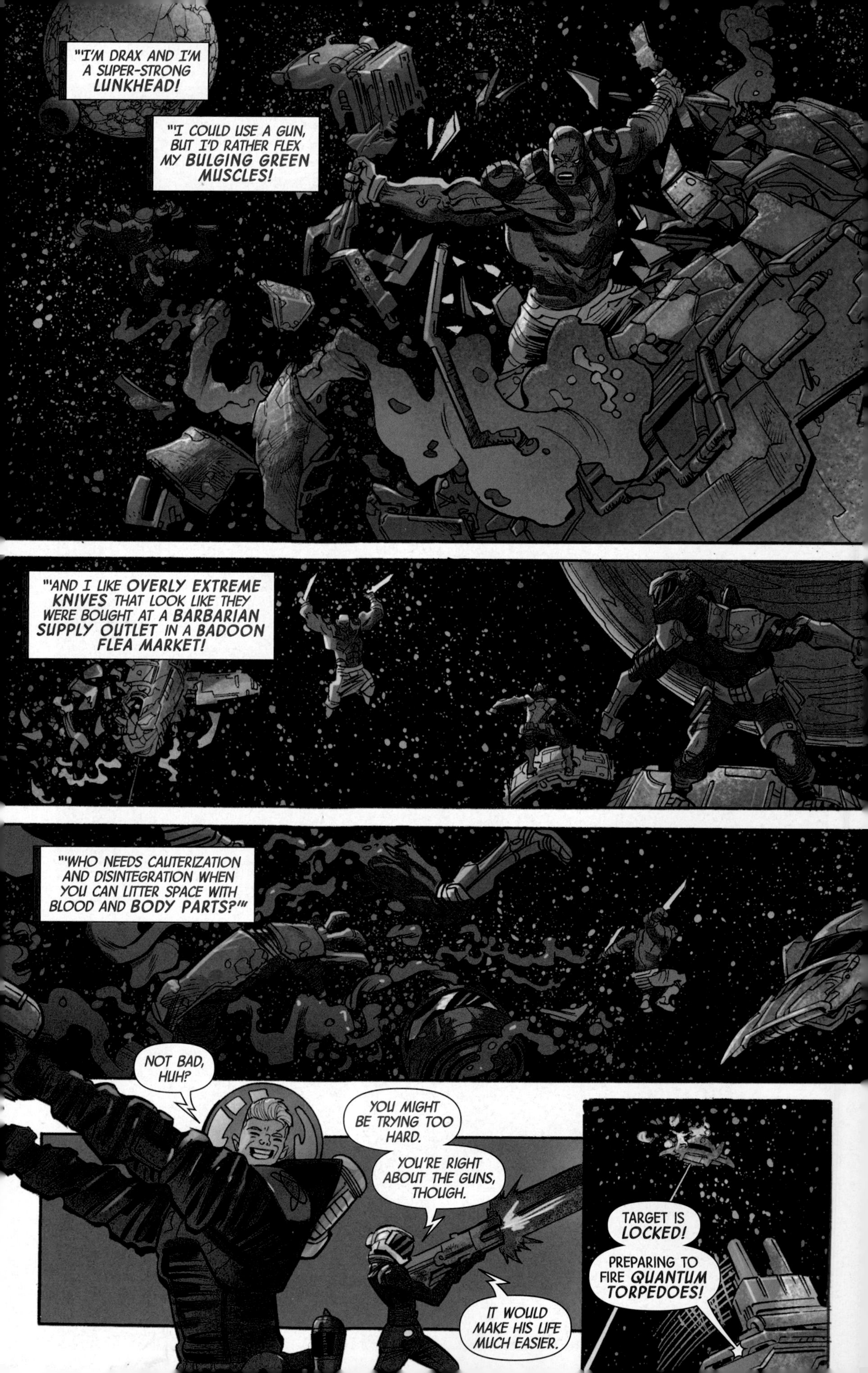
"I'M DRAX AND I'M A SUPER-STRONG LUNKHEAD!
"I COULD USE A GUN, BUT I'D RATHER FLEX MY BULGING GREEN MUSCLES!
"AND I LIKE OVERLY EXTREME KNIVES THAT LOOK LIKE THEY WERE BOUGHT AT A BARBARIAN SUPPLY OUTLET IN A BADOON FLEA MARKET!
"'WHO NEEDS CAUTERIZATION AND DISINTEGRATION WHEN YOU CAN LITTER SPACE WITH BLOOD AND BODY PARTS?'"
NOT BAD, HUH?
YOU MIGHT BE TRYING TOO HARD.
YOU'RE RIGHT ABOUT THE GUNS, THOUGH.
IT WOULD MAKE HIS LIFE MUCH EASIER.
TARGET IS LOCKED!
PREPARING TO FIRE QUANTUM TORPEDOES!

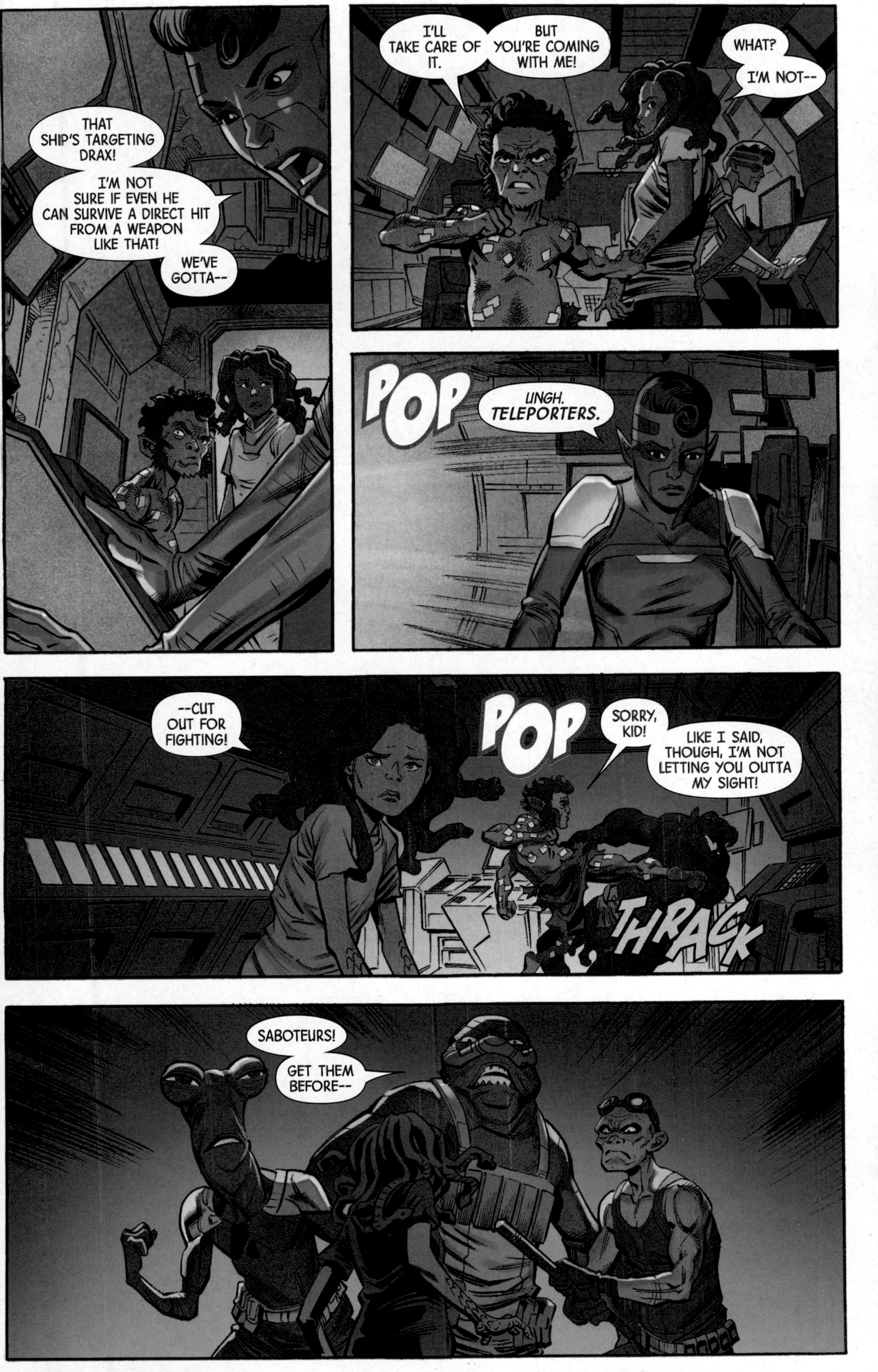

THAT SHIP'S TARGETING DRAX!
I'M NOT SURE IF EVEN HE CAN SURVIVE A DIRECT HIT FROM A WEAPON LIKE THAT!
WE'VE GOTTA--
I'LL TAKE CARE OF IT.
BUT YOU'RE COMING WITH ME!
WHAT?
I'M NOT--
POP
UNGH. TELEPORTERS.
--CUT OUT FOR FIGHTING!
POP
SORRY, KID!
LIKE I SAID, THOUGH, I'M NOT LETTING YOU OUTTA MY SIGHT!
THRACK
SABOTEURS!
GET THEM BEFORE--

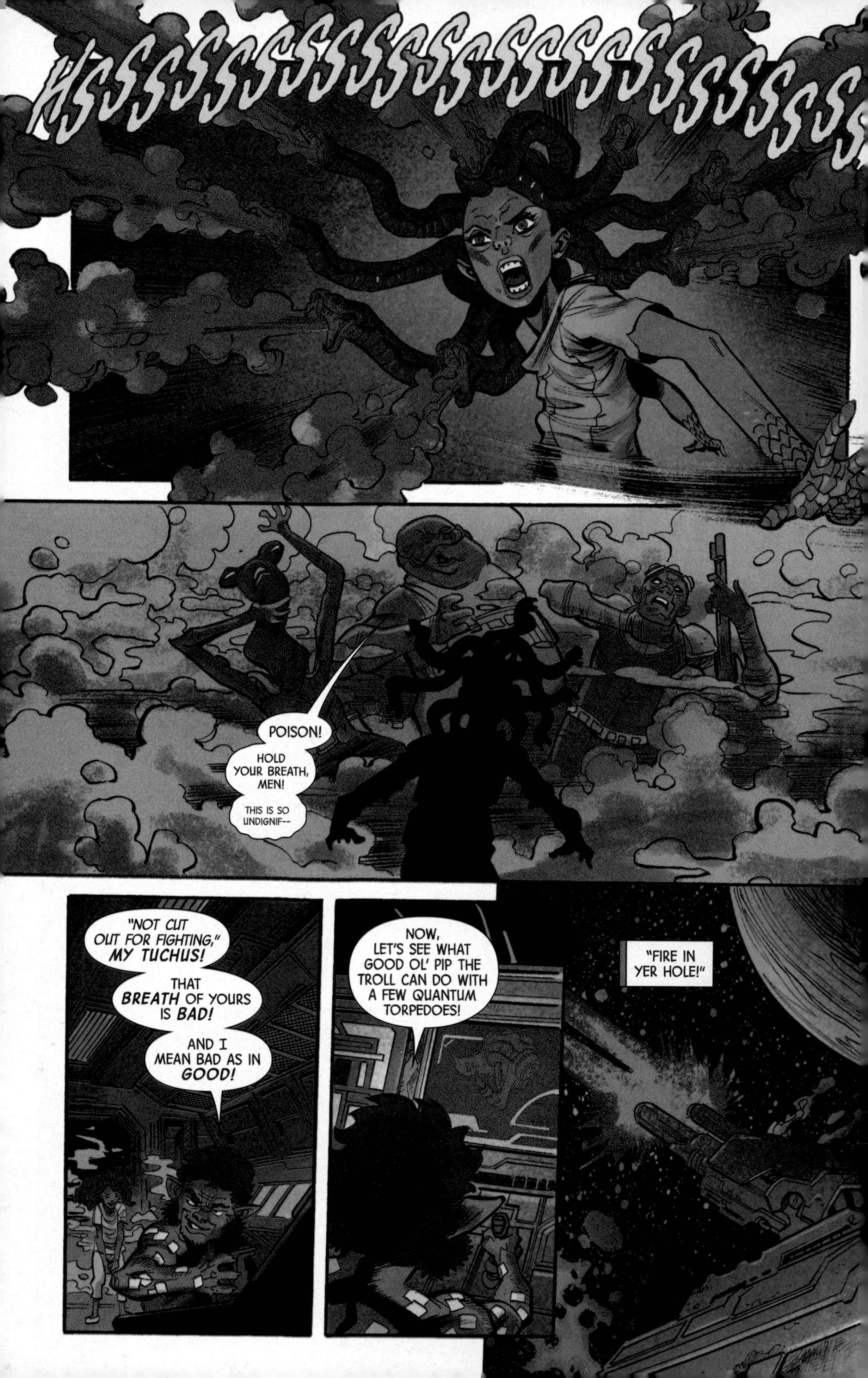
HSSSSSSSSSSSSSSSSSSSSSSSSS
POISON!
HOLD YOUR BREATH, MEN!
THIS IS SO UNDIGNIF--
"NOT CUT OUT FOR FIGHTING," MY TUCHUS!
THAT BREATH OF YOURS IS BAD!
AND I MEAN BAD AS IN GOOD!
NOW, LET'S SEE WHAT GOOD OL' PIP THE TROLL CAN DO WITH A FEW QUANTUM TORPEDOES!
"FIRE IN YER HOLE!"

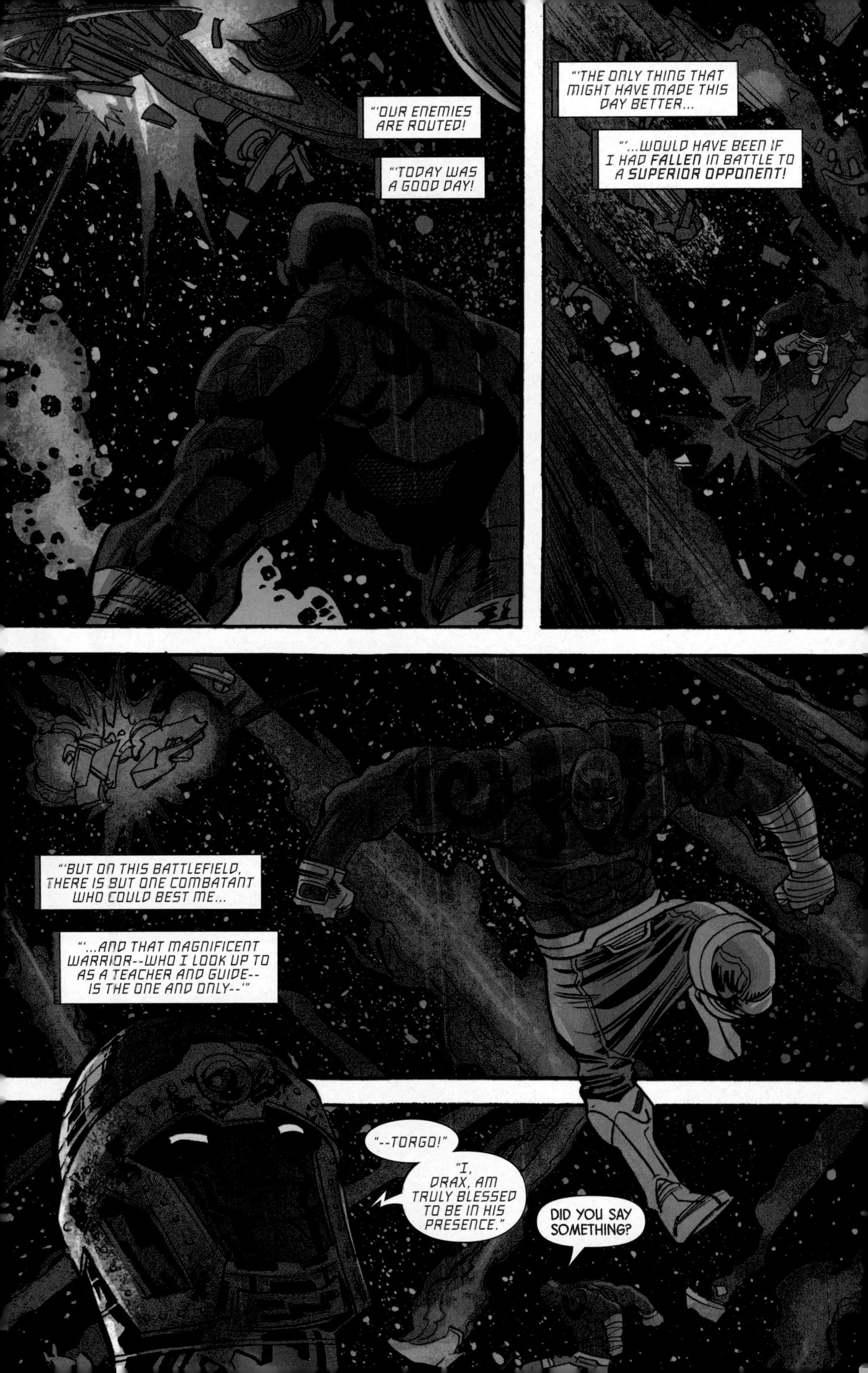
"'OUR ENEMIES ARE ROUTED!
"'TODAY WAS A GOOD DAY!
"'THE ONLY THING THAT MIGHT HAVE MADE THIS DAY BETTER...
"'...WOULD HAVE BEEN IF I HAD FALLEN IN BATTLE TO A SUPERIOR OPPONENT!
"'BUT ON THIS BATTLEFIELD, THERE IS BUT ONE COMBATANT WHO COULD BEST ME...
"'...AND THAT MAGNIFICENT WARRIOR--WHO I LOOK UP TO AS A TEACHER AND GUIDE--IS THE ONE AND ONLY--'"
"--TORGO!"
"I, DRAX, AM TRULY BLESSED TO BE IN HIS PRESENCE."
DID YOU SAY SOMETHING?

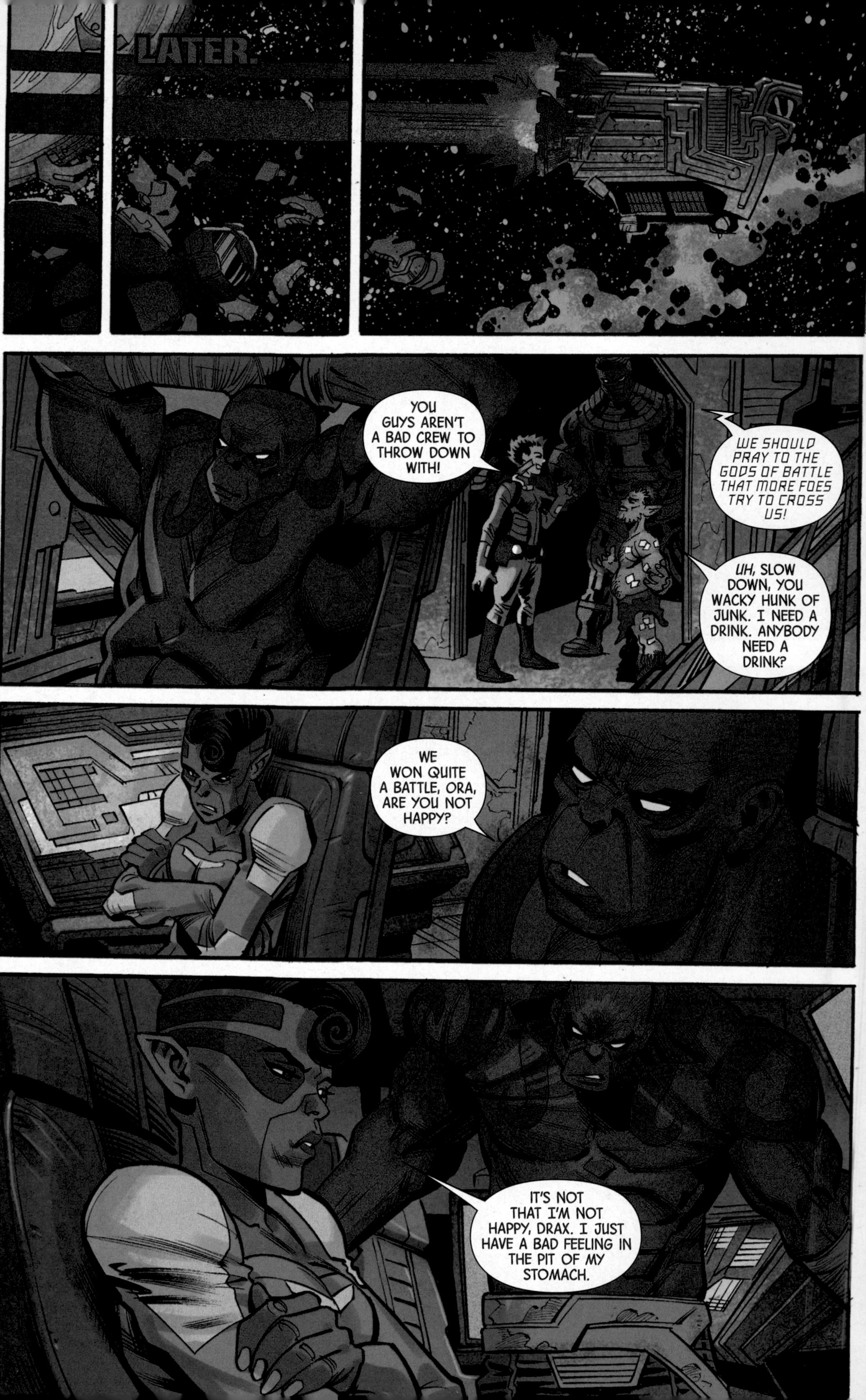
LATER.
YOU GUYS AREN'T A BAD CREW TO THROW DOWN WITH!
WE SHOULD PRAY TO THE GODS OF BATTLE THAT MORE FOES TRY TO CROSS US!
UH, SLOW DOWN, YOU WACKY HUNK OF JUNK. I NEED A DRINK. ANYBODY NEED A DRINK?
WE WON QUITE A BATTLE, ORA, ARE YOU NOT HAPPY?
IT'S NOT THAT I'M NOT HAPPY, DRAX. I JUST HAVE A BAD FEELING IN THE PIT OF MY STOMACH.

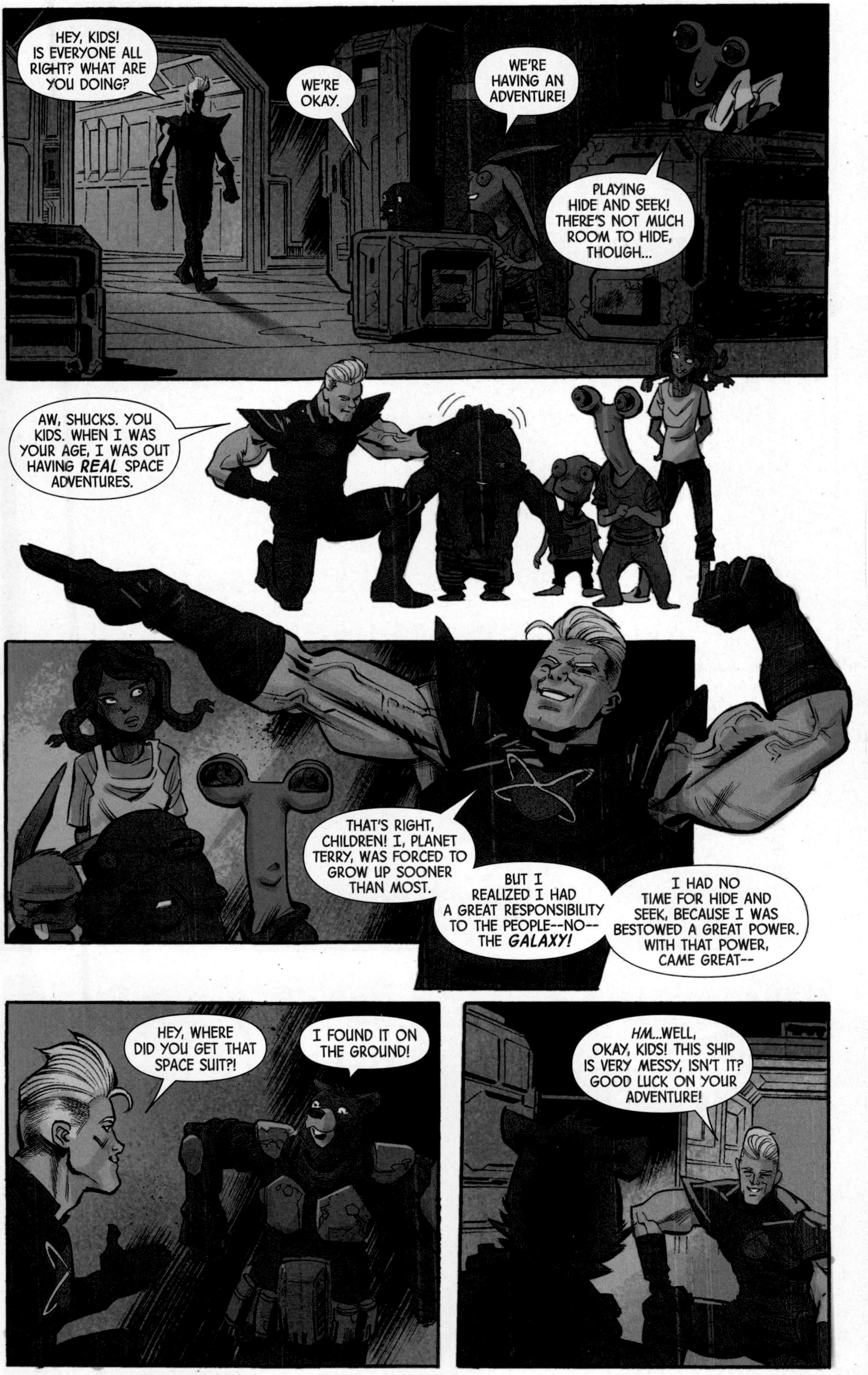
HEY, KIDS! IS EVERYONE ALL RIGHT? WHAT ARE YOU DOING?
WE'RE OKAY.
WE'RE HAVING AN ADVENTURE!
PLAYING HIDE AND SEEK! THERE'S NOT MUCH ROOM TO HIDE, THOUGH...
AW, SHUCKS. YOU KIDS. WHEN I WAS YOUR AGE, I WAS OUT HAVING REAL SPACE ADVENTURES.
THAT'S RIGHT, CHILDREN! I, PLANET TERRY, WAS FORCED TO GROW UP SOONER THAN MOST.
BUT I REALIZED I HAD A GREAT RESPONSIBILITY TO THE PEOPLE--NO--THE GALAXY!
I HAD NO TIME FOR HIDE AND SEEK, BECAUSE I WAS BESTOWED A GREAT POWER. WITH THAT POWER, CAME GREAT--
HEY, WHERE DID YOU GET THAT SPACE SUIT?!
I FOUND IT ON THE GROUND!
HM...WELL, OKAY, KIDS! THIS SHIP IS VERY MESSY, ISN'T IT? GOOD LUCK ON YOUR ADVENTURE!

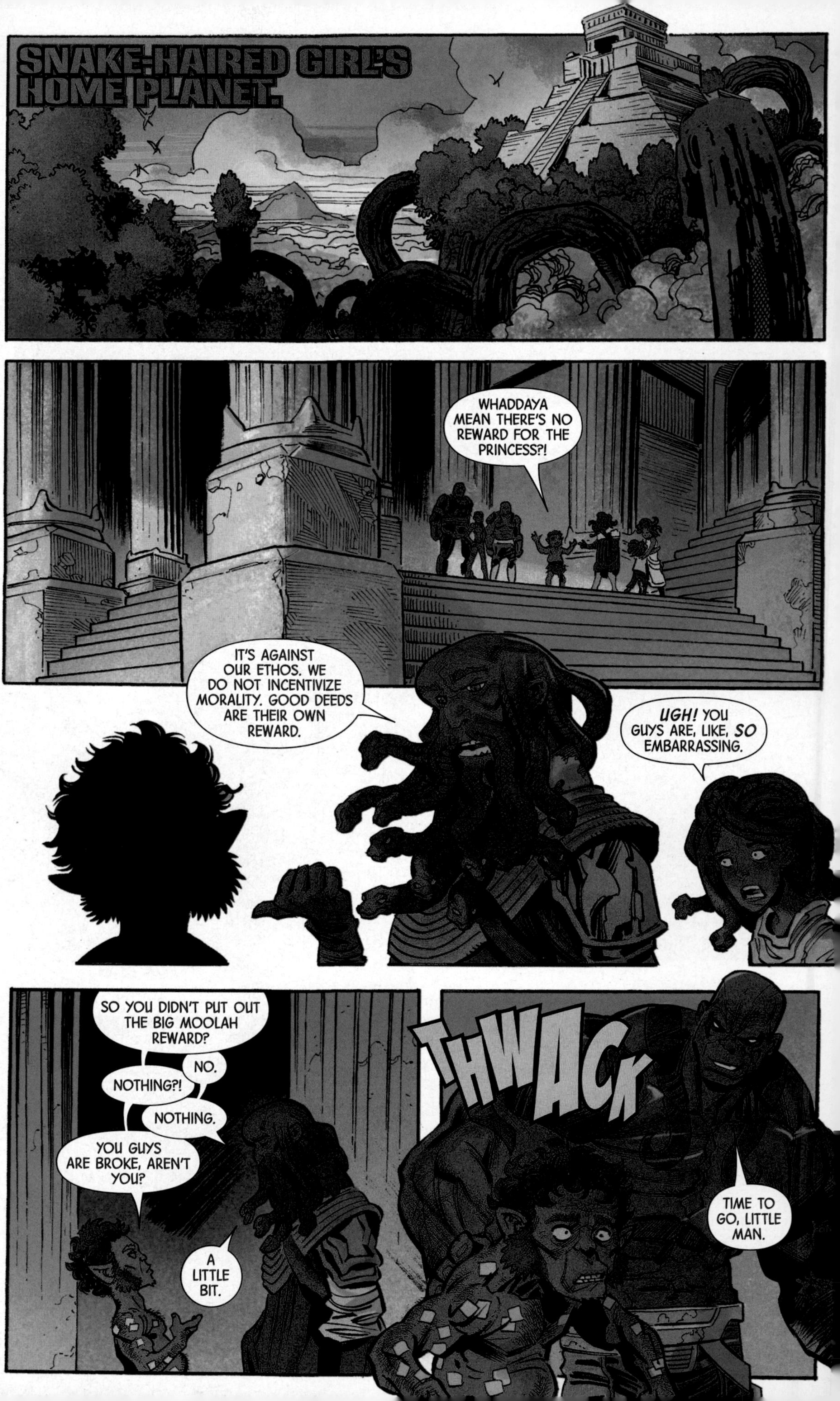
SNAKE-HAIRED GIRL'S HOME PLANET.
WHADDAYA MEAN THERE'S NO REWARD FOR THE PRINCESS?!
IT'S AGAINST OUR ETHOS. WE DO NOT INCENTIVIZE MORALITY. GOOD DEEDS ARE THEIR OWN REWARD.
UGH! YOU GUYS ARE, LIKE, SO EMBARRASSING.
SO YOU DIDN'T PUT OUT THE BIG MOOLAH REWARD?
NO.
NOTHING?!
NOTHING.
YOU GUYS ARE BROKE, AREN'T YOU?
A LITTLE BIT.
THWACK
TIME TO GO, LITTLE MAN.

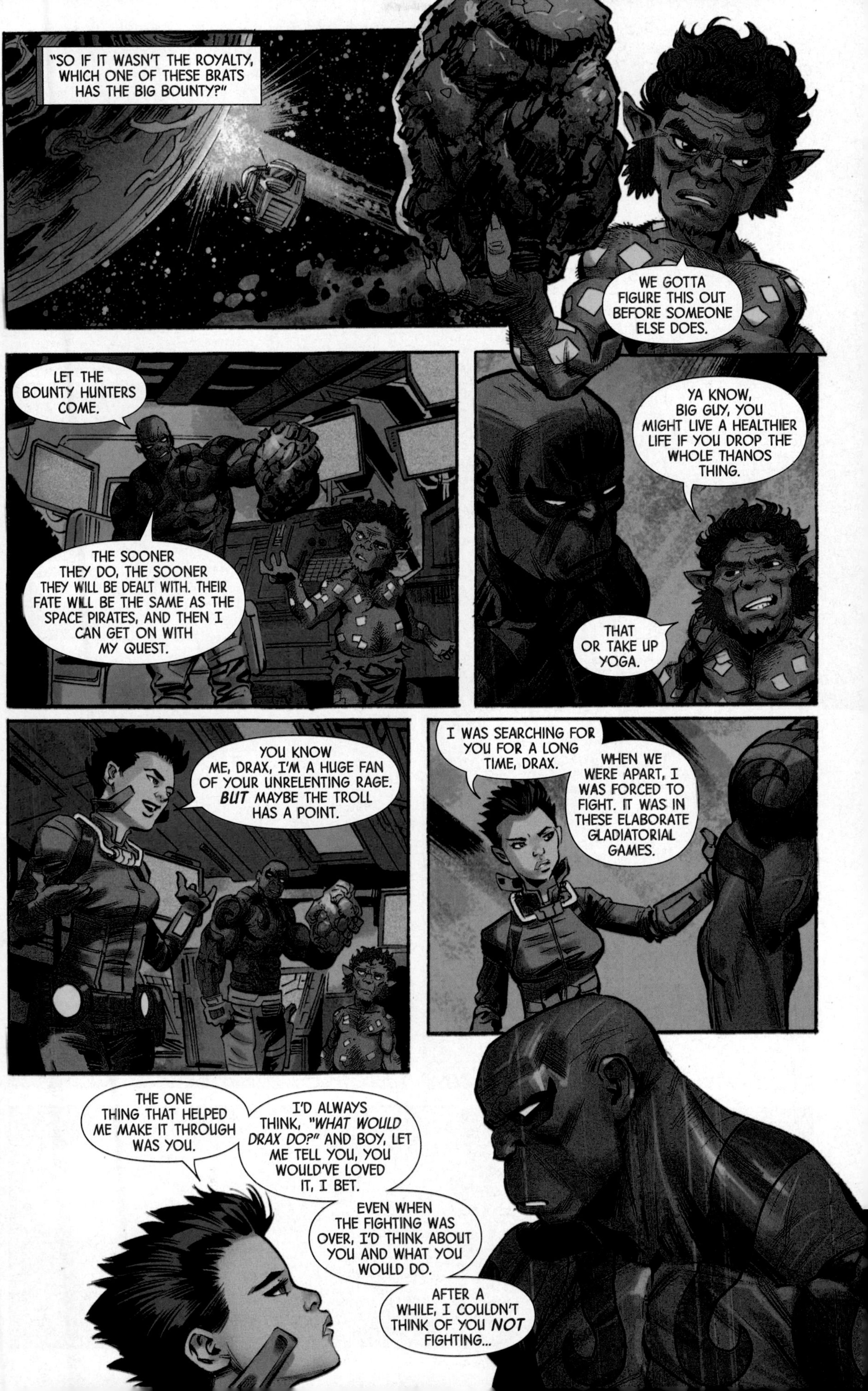
"SO IF IT WASN'T THE ROYALTY, WHICH ONE OF THESE BRATS HAS THE BIG BOUNTY?"
WE GOTTA FIGURE THIS OUT BEFORE SOMEONE ELSE DOES.
LET THE BOUNTY HUNTERS COME.
THE SOONER THEY DO, THE SOONER THEY WILL BE DEALT WITH. THEIR FATE WILL BE THE SAME AS THE SPACE PIRATES, AND THEN I CAN GET ON WITH MY QUEST.
YA KNOW, BIG GUY, YOU MIGHT LIVE A HEALTHIER LIFE IF YOU DROP THE WHOLE THANOS THING.
THAT OR TAKE UP YOGA.
YOU KNOW ME, DRAX, I'M A HUGE FAN OF YOUR UNRELENTING RAGE. ***BUT*** MAYBE THE TROLL HAS A POINT.
I WAS SEARCHING FOR YOU FOR A LONG TIME, DRAX.
WHEN WE WERE APART, I WAS FORCED TO FIGHT. IT WAS IN THESE ELABORATE GLADIATORIAL GAMES.
THE ONE THING THAT HELPED ME MAKE IT THROUGH WAS YOU.
I'D ALWAYS THINK, *"WHAT WOULD DRAX DO?"* AND BOY, LET ME TELL YOU, YOU WOULD'VE LOVED IT, I BET.
EVEN WHEN THE FIGHTING WAS OVER, I'D THINK ABOUT YOU AND WHAT YOU WOULD DO.
AFTER A WHILE, I COULDN'T THINK OF YOU ***NOT*** FIGHTING...

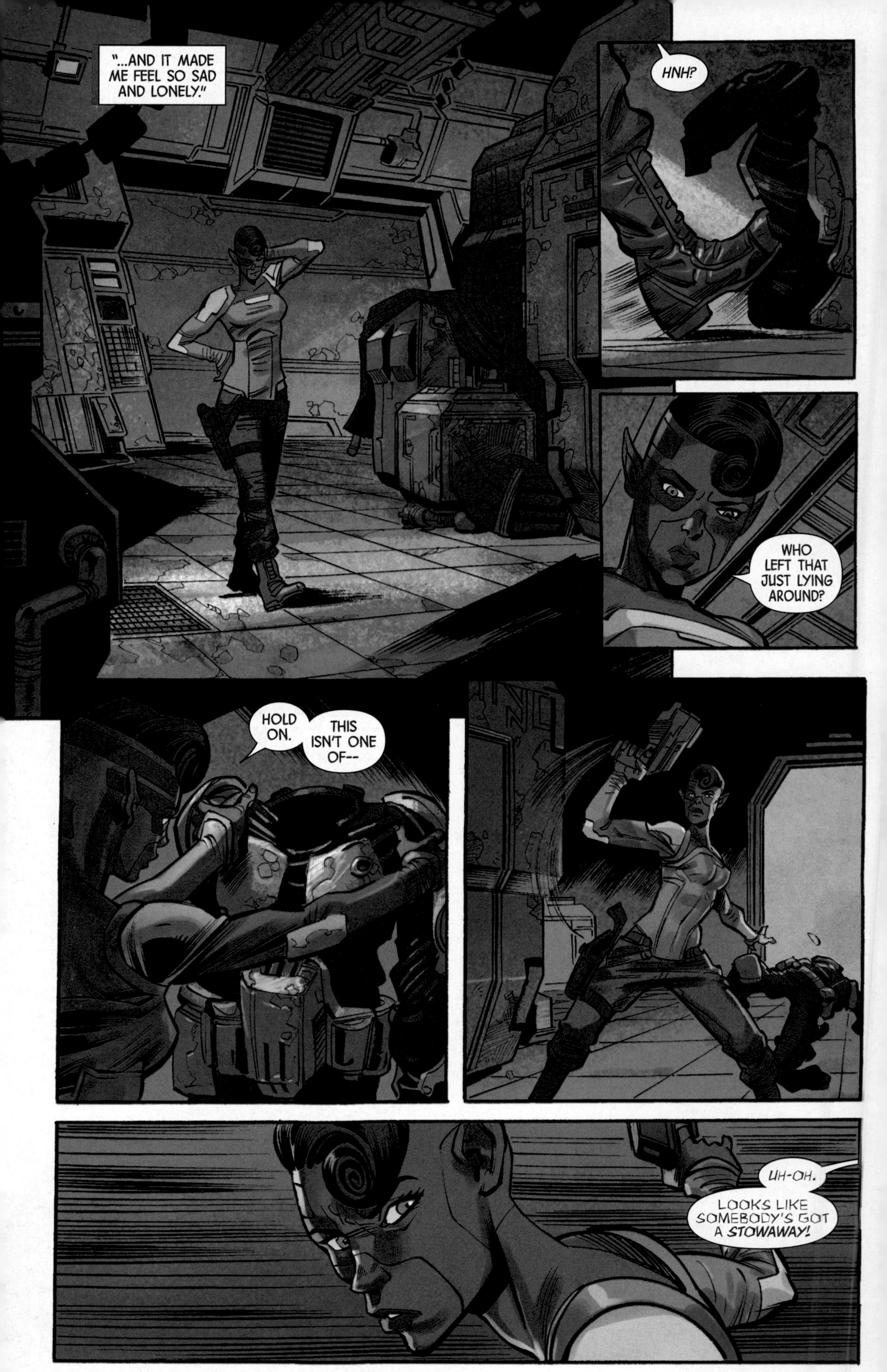
"...AND IT MADE ME FEEL SO SAD AND LONELY."
HNH?
WHO LEFT THAT JUST LYING AROUND?
HOLD ON.
THIS ISN'T ONE OF--
UH-OH.
LOOKS LIKE SOMEBODY'S GOT A *STOWAWAY!*

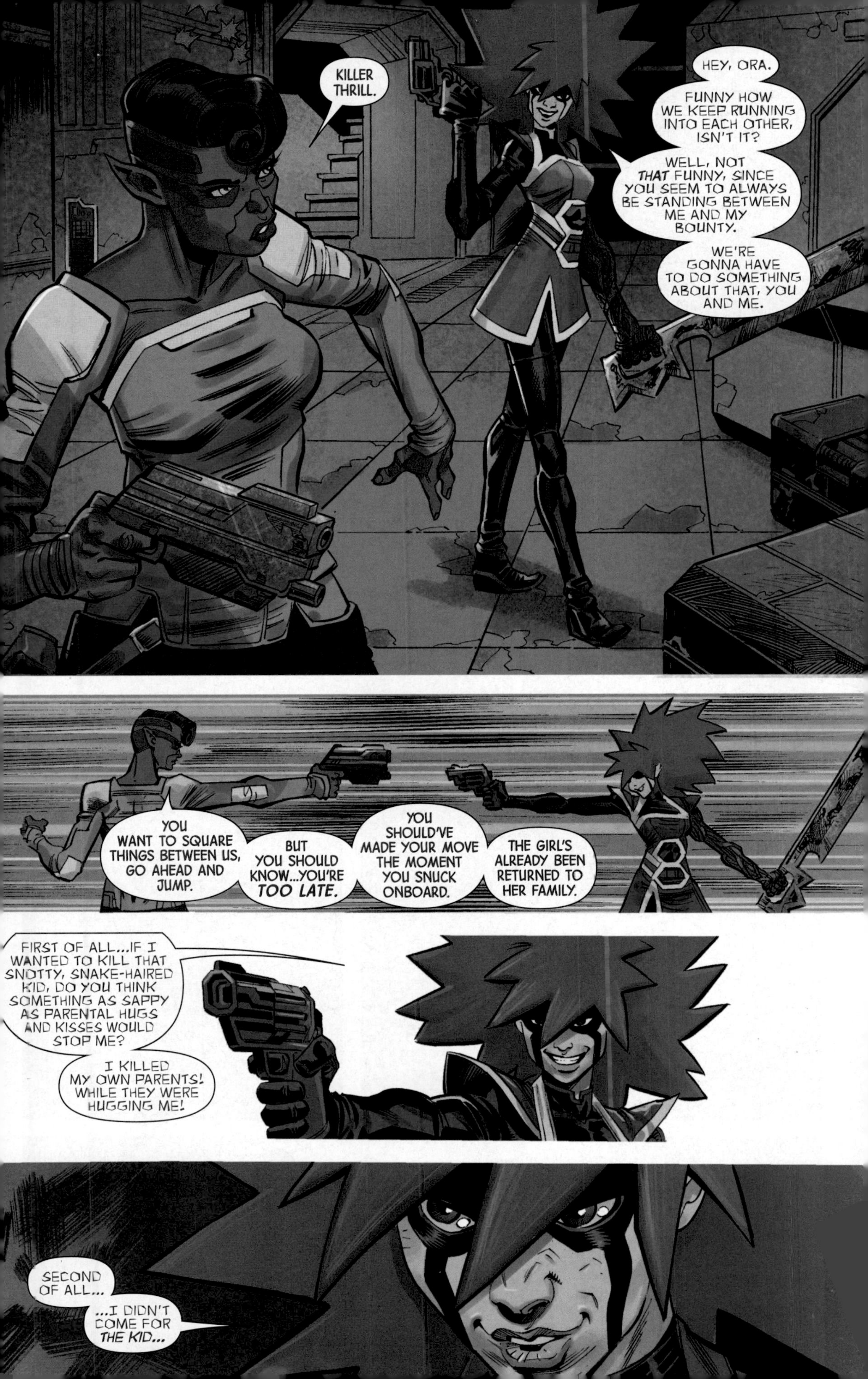
KILLER THRILL.
HEY, ORA.
FUNNY HOW WE KEEP RUNNING INTO EACH OTHER, ISN'T IT?
WELL, NOT THAT FUNNY, SINCE YOU SEEM TO ALWAYS BE STANDING BETWEEN ME AND MY BOUNTY.
WE'RE GONNA HAVE TO DO SOMETHING ABOUT THAT, YOU AND ME.
YOU WANT TO SQUARE THINGS BETWEEN US, GO AHEAD AND JUMP.
BUT YOU SHOULD KNOW...YOU'RE TOO LATE.
YOU SHOULD'VE MADE YOUR MOVE THE MOMENT YOU SNUCK ONBOARD.
THE GIRL'S ALREADY BEEN RETURNED TO HER FAMILY.
FIRST OF ALL...IF I WANTED TO KILL THAT SNOTTY, SNAKE-HAIRED KID, DO YOU THINK SOMETHING AS SAPPY AS PARENTAL HUGS AND KISSES WOULD STOP ME?
I KILLED MY OWN PARENTS! WHILE THEY WERE HUGGING ME!
SECOND OF ALL...
...I DIDN'T COME FOR THE KID...

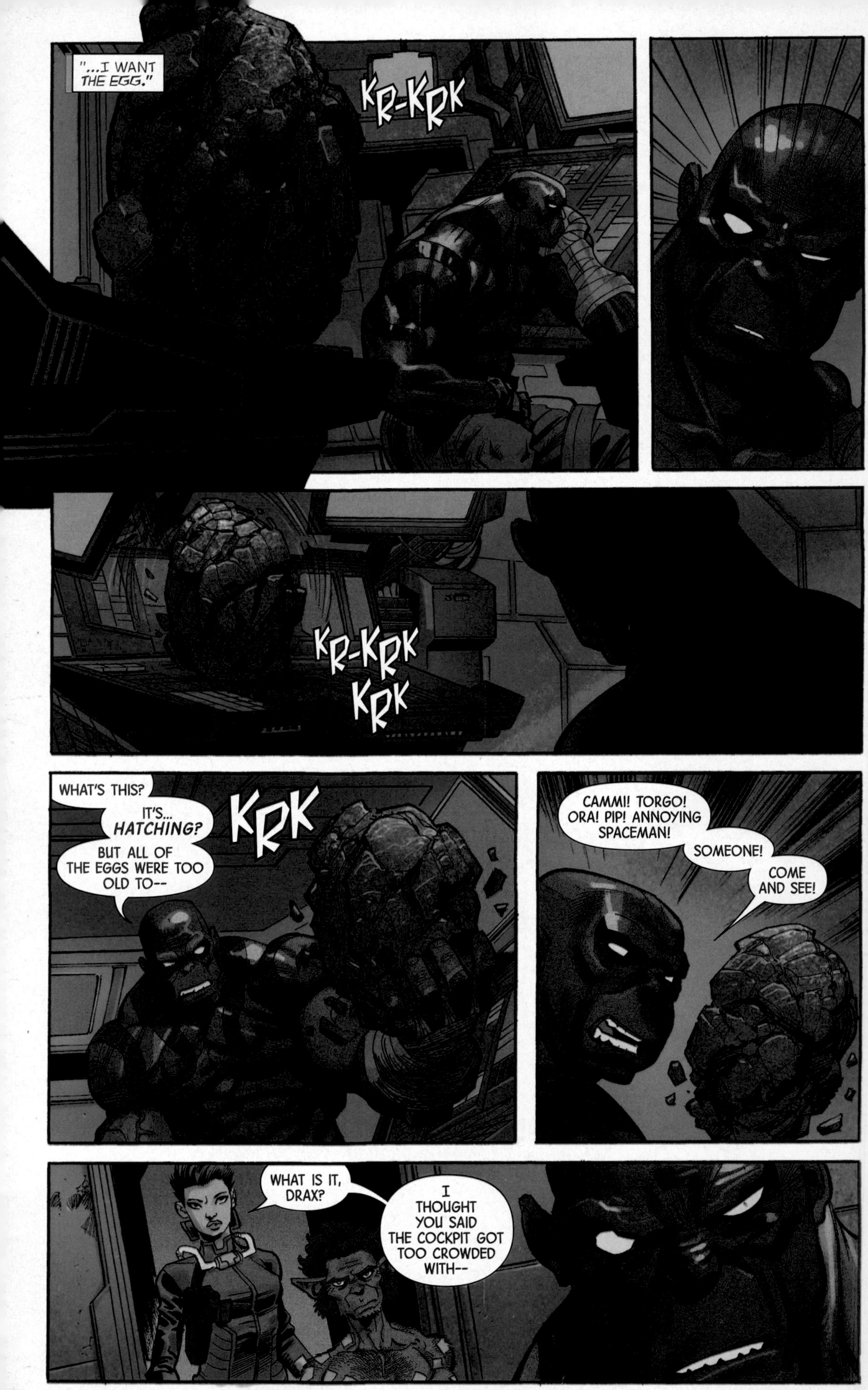
"...I WANT THE EGG."
KR-KRK
KR-KRK
KRK
WHAT'S THIS?
IT'S... HATCHING?
BUT ALL OF THE EGGS WERE TOO OLD TO--
KRK
CAMMI! TORGO! ORA! PIP! ANNOYING SPACEMAN!
SOMEONE!
COME AND SEE!
WHAT IS IT, DRAX?
I THOUGHT YOU SAID THE COCKPIT GOT TOO CROWDED WITH--

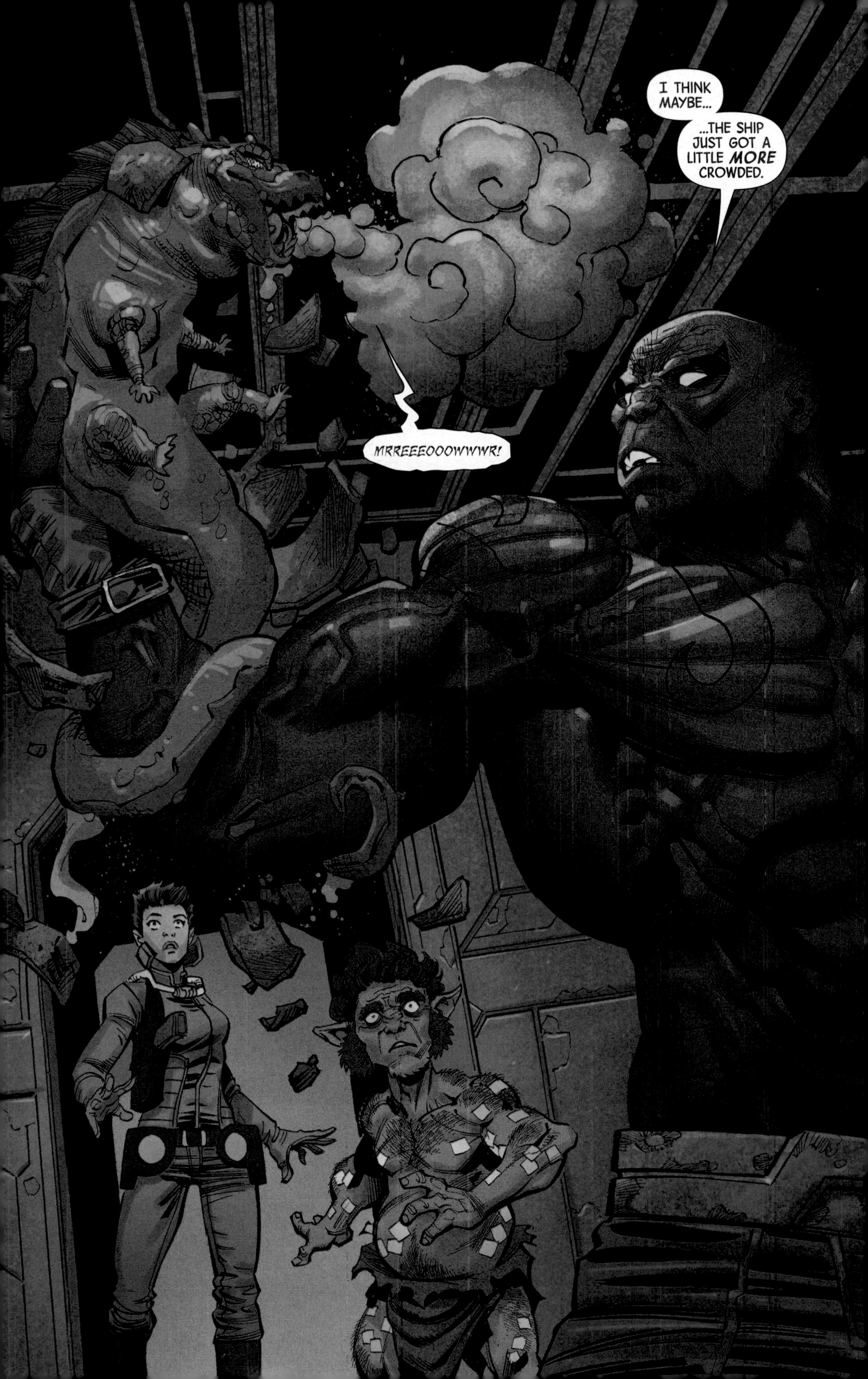
I THINK MAYBE...
...THE SHIP JUST GOT A LITTLE MORE CROWDED.
MRREEEOOOWWWR!

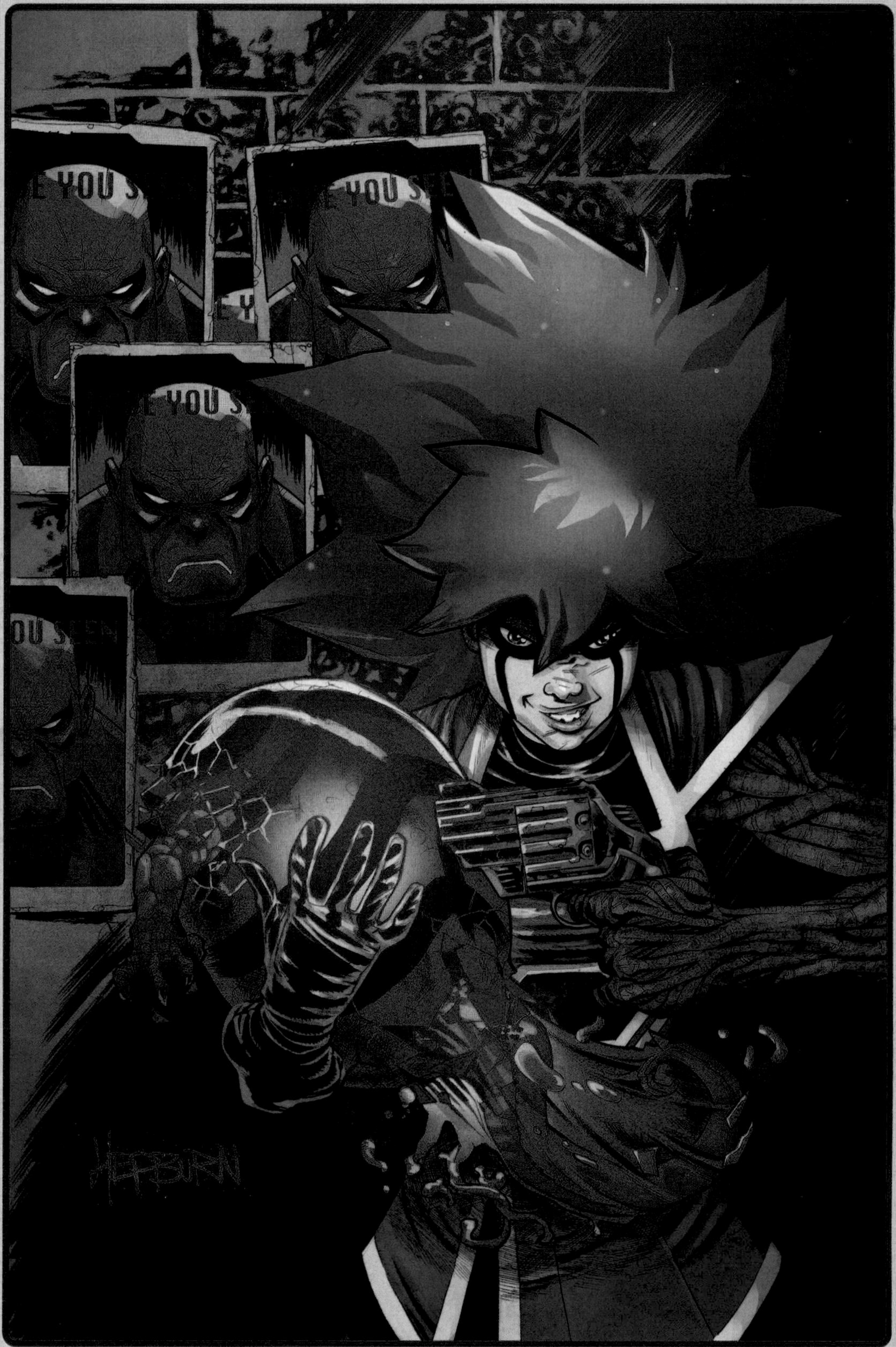
HEPBURN

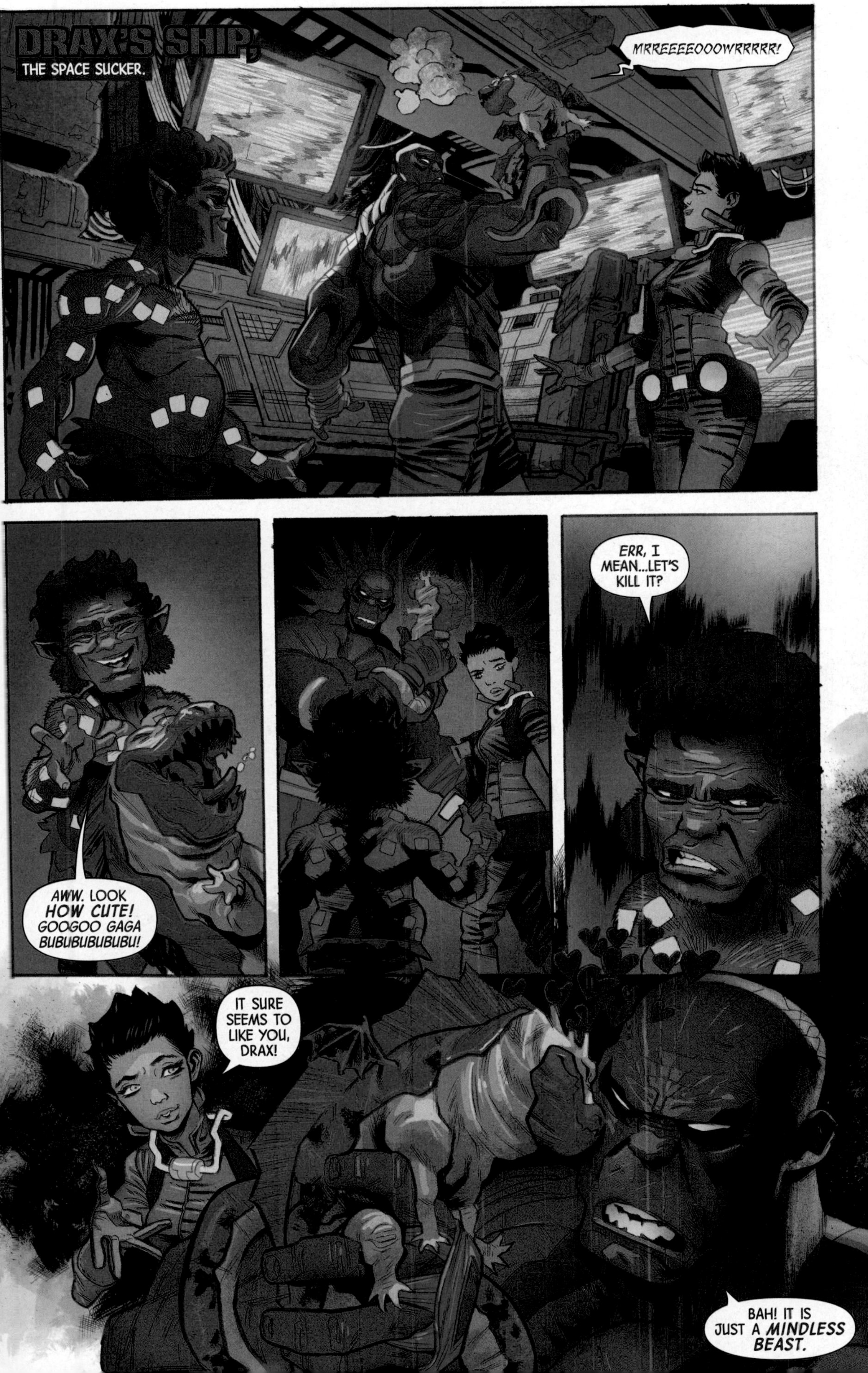
DRAX'S SHIP,
THE SPACE SUCKER.
MRREEEEEOOOWRRRRR!
AWW. LOOK HOW CUTE! GOOGOO GAGA BUBUBUBUBUBU!
ERR, I MEAN...LET'S KILL IT?
IT SURE SEEMS TO LIKE YOU, DRAX!
BAH! IT IS JUST A MINDLESS BEAST.

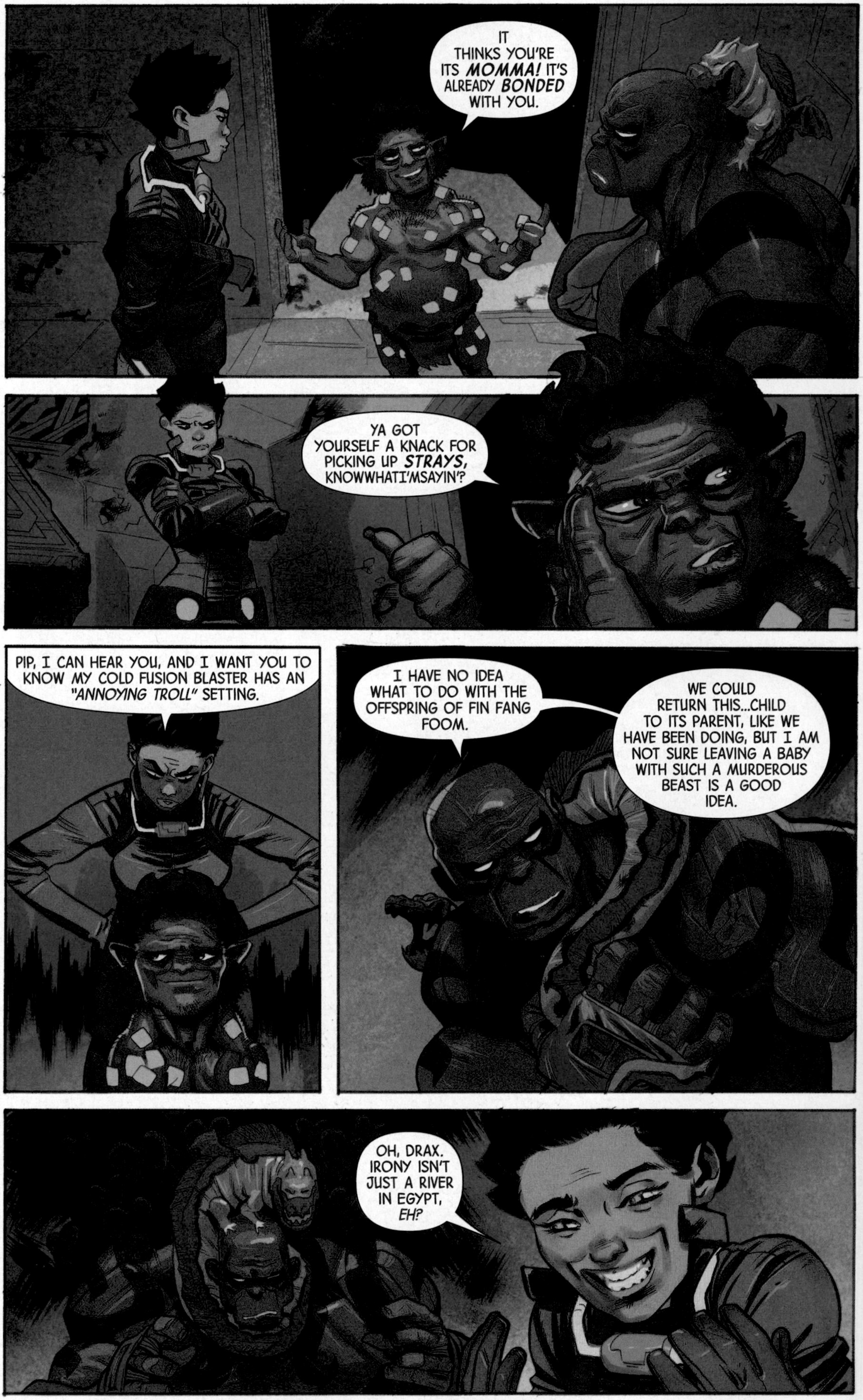
IT THINKS YOU'RE ITS MOMMA! IT'S ALREADY BONDED WITH YOU.
YA GOT YOURSELF A KNACK FOR PICKING UP STRAYS, KNOWWHATI'MSAYIN'?
PIP, I CAN HEAR YOU, AND I WANT YOU TO KNOW MY COLD FUSION BLASTER HAS AN "ANNOYING TROLL" SETTING.
I HAVE NO IDEA WHAT TO DO WITH THE OFFSPRING OF FIN FANG FOOM.
WE COULD RETURN THIS...CHILD TO ITS PARENT, LIKE WE HAVE BEEN DOING, BUT I AM NOT SURE LEAVING A BABY WITH SUCH A MURDEROUS BEAST IS A GOOD IDEA.
OH, DRAX. IRONY ISN'T JUST A RIVER IN EGYPT, EH?

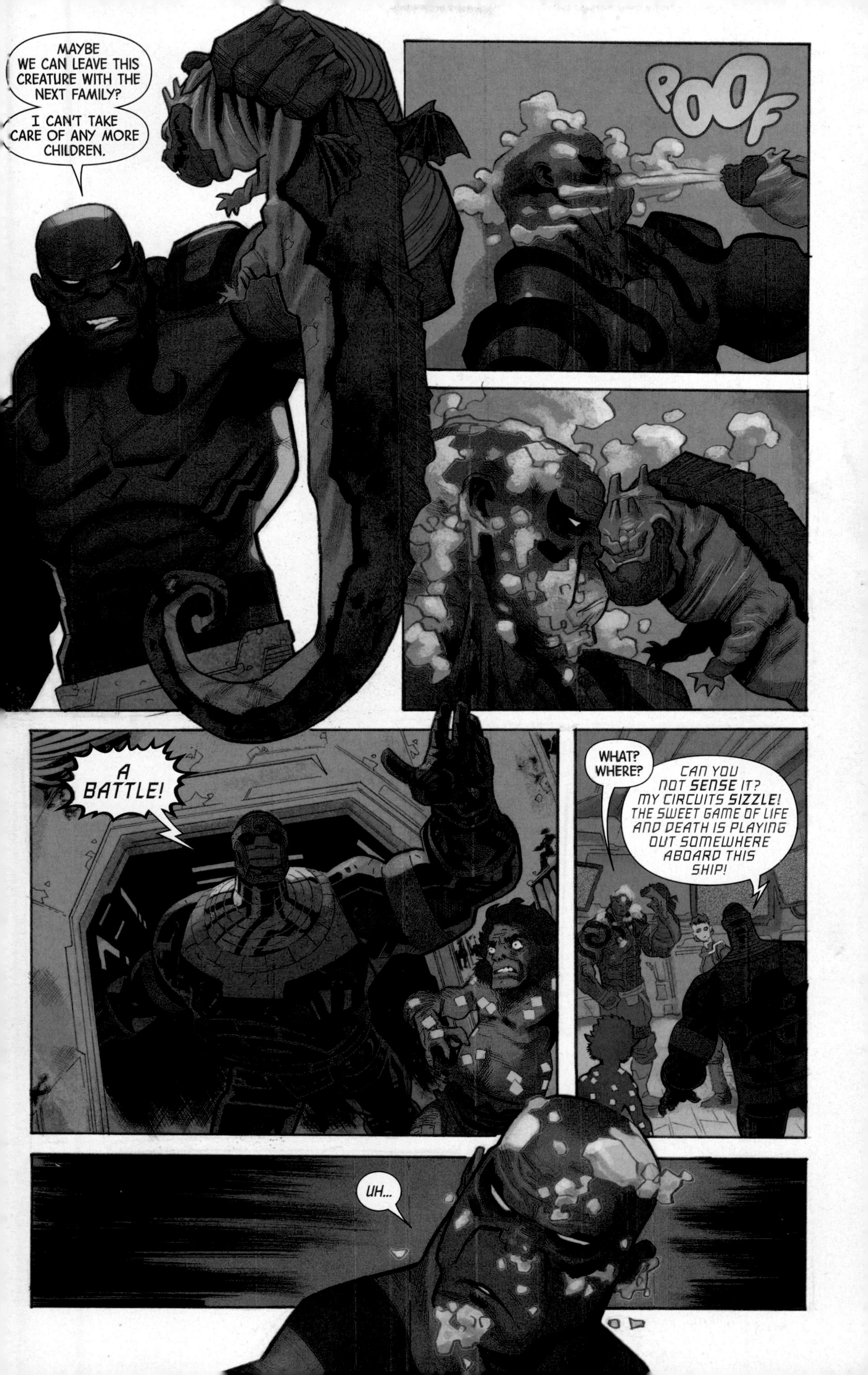
MAYBE WE CAN LEAVE THIS CREATURE WITH THE NEXT FAMILY?
I CAN'T TAKE CARE OF ANY MORE CHILDREN.
POOF
A BATTLE!
WHAT? WHERE?
CAN YOU NOT SENSE IT? MY CIRCUITS SIZZLE! THE SWEET GAME OF LIFE AND DEATH IS PLAYING OUT SOMEWHERE ABOARD THIS SHIP!
UH...

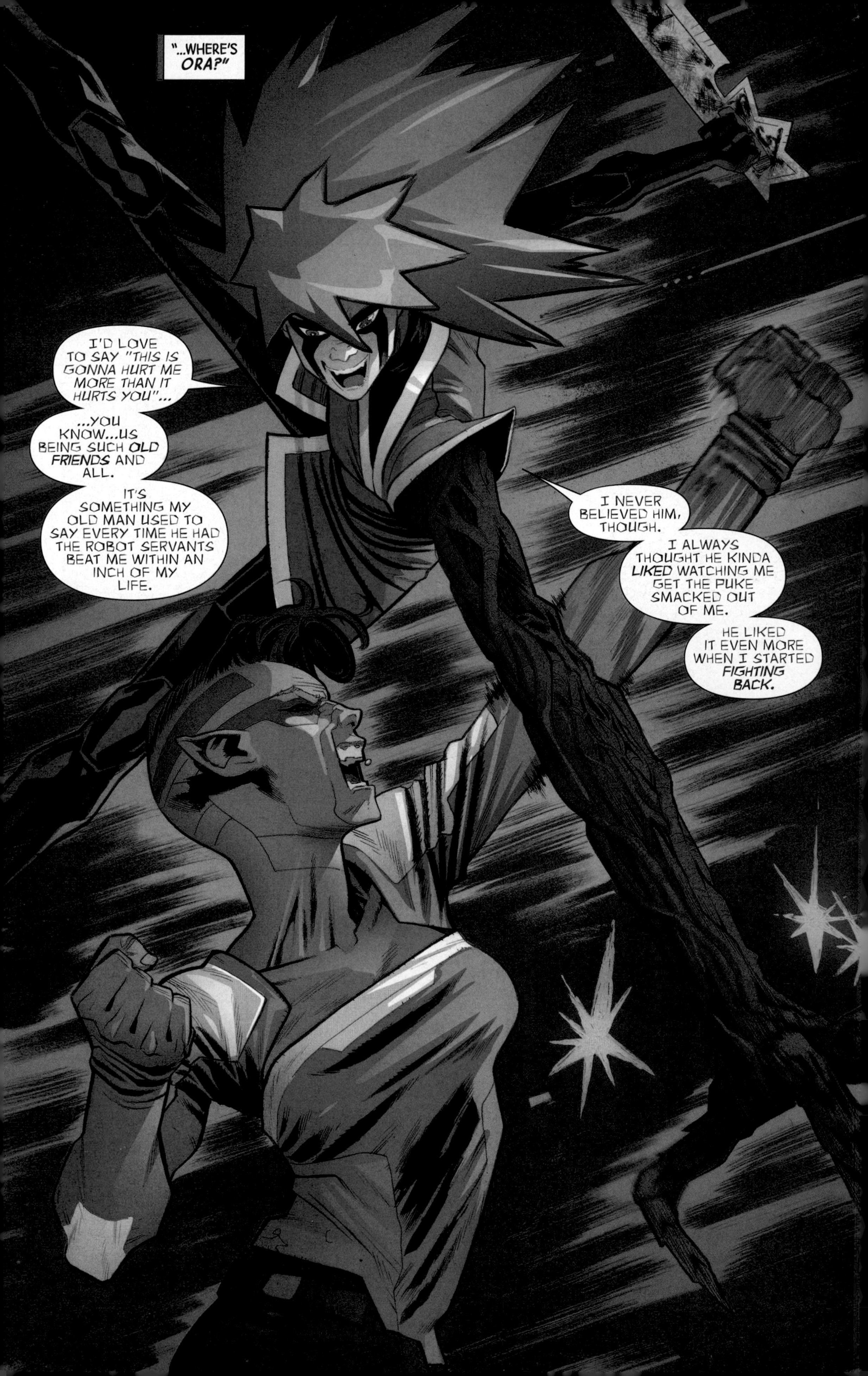
"...WHERE'S ORA?"
I'D LOVE TO SAY "THIS IS GONNA HURT ME MORE THAN IT HURTS YOU"...
...YOU KNOW...US BEING SUCH OLD FRIENDS AND ALL.
IT'S SOMETHING MY OLD MAN USED TO SAY EVERY TIME HE HAD THE ROBOT SERVANTS BEAT ME WITHIN AN INCH OF MY LIFE.
I NEVER BELIEVED HIM, THOUGH.
I ALWAYS THOUGHT HE KINDA LIKED WATCHING ME GET THE PUKE SMACKED OUT OF ME.
HE LIKED IT EVEN MORE WHEN I STARTED FIGHTING BACK.

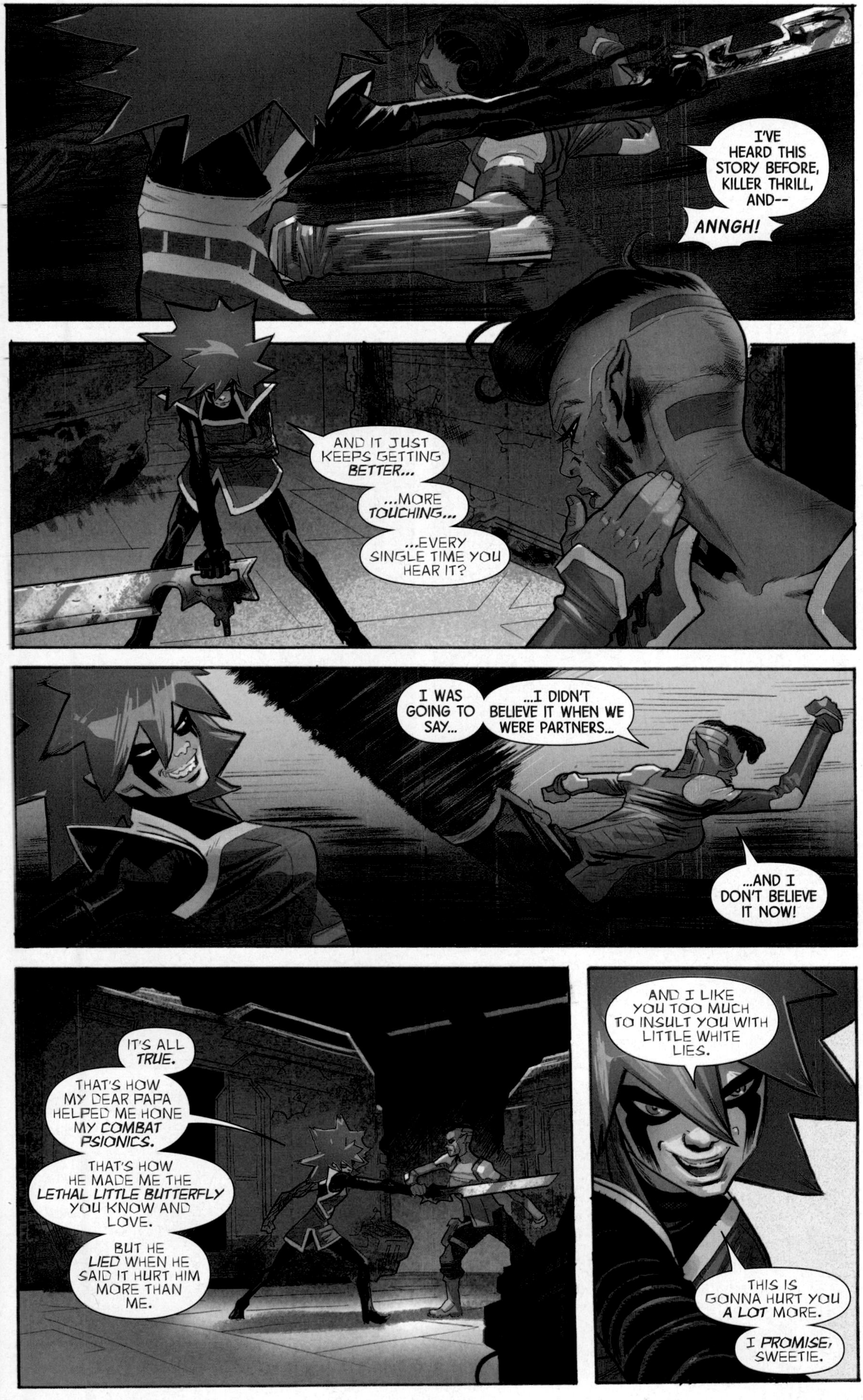
I'VE HEARD THIS STORY BEFORE, KILLER THRILL, AND--
ANNGH!
AND IT JUST KEEPS GETTING BETTER...
...MORE TOUCHING...
...EVERY SINGLE TIME YOU HEAR IT?
I WAS GOING TO SAY...
...I DIDN'T BELIEVE IT WHEN WE WERE PARTNERS...
...AND I DON'T BELIEVE IT NOW!
IT'S ALL TRUE.
THAT'S HOW MY DEAR PAPA HELPED ME HONE MY COMBAT PSIONICS.
THAT'S HOW HE MADE ME THE LETHAL LITTLE BUTTERFLY YOU KNOW AND LOVE.
BUT HE LIED WHEN HE SAID IT HURT HIM MORE THAN ME.
AND I LIKE YOU TOO MUCH TO INSULT YOU WITH LITTLE WHITE LIES.
THIS IS GONNA HURT YOU A LOT MORE.
I PROMISE, SWEETIE.

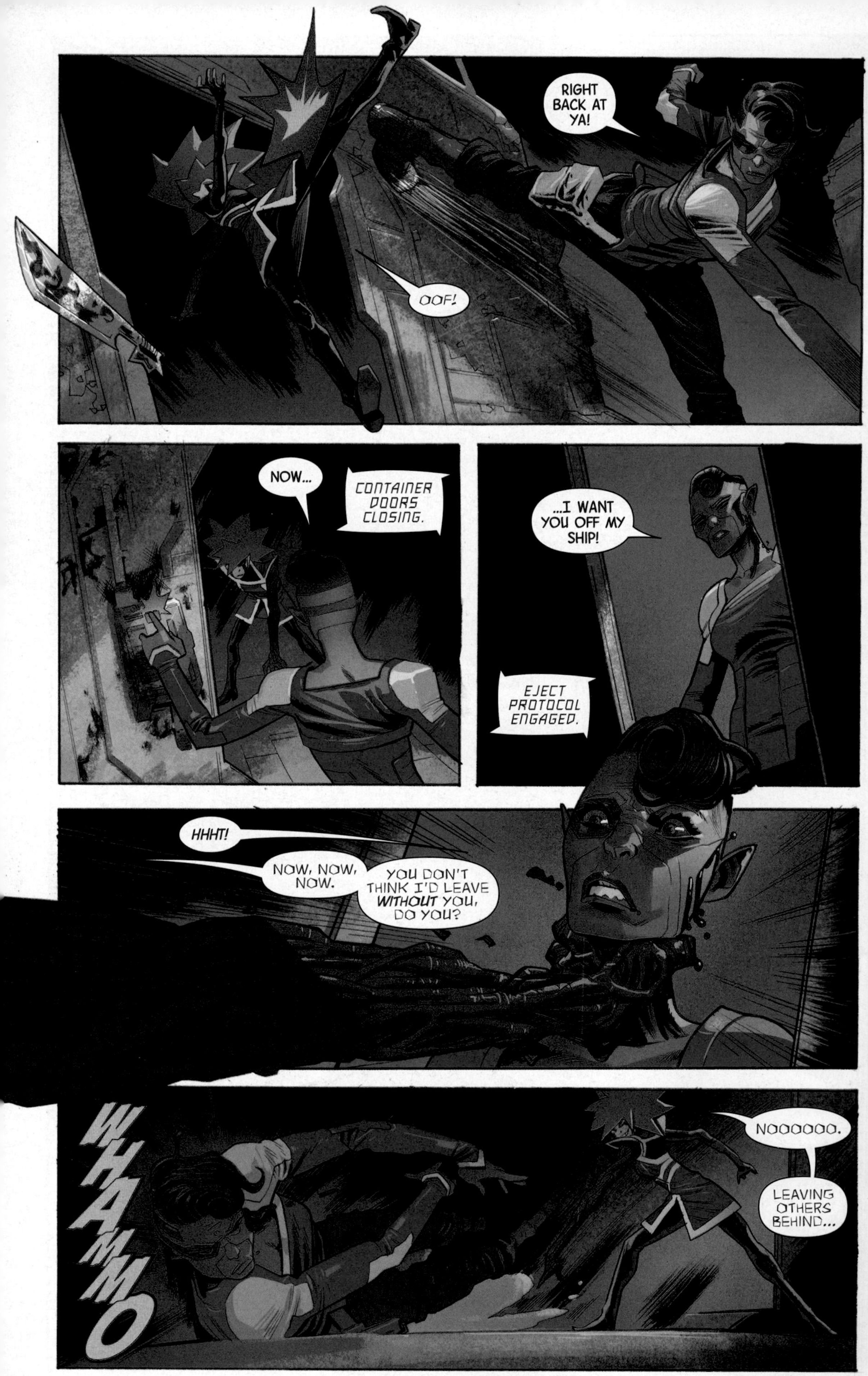
RIGHT BACK AT YA!
OOF!
NOW...
CONTAINER DOORS CLOSING.
...I WANT YOU OFF MY SHIP!
EJECT PROTOCOL ENGAGED.
HHHT!
NOW, NOW, NOW.
YOU DON'T THINK I'D LEAVE WITHOUT YOU, DO YOU?
WHAMMO
NOOOOOO.
LEAVING OTHERS BEHIND...

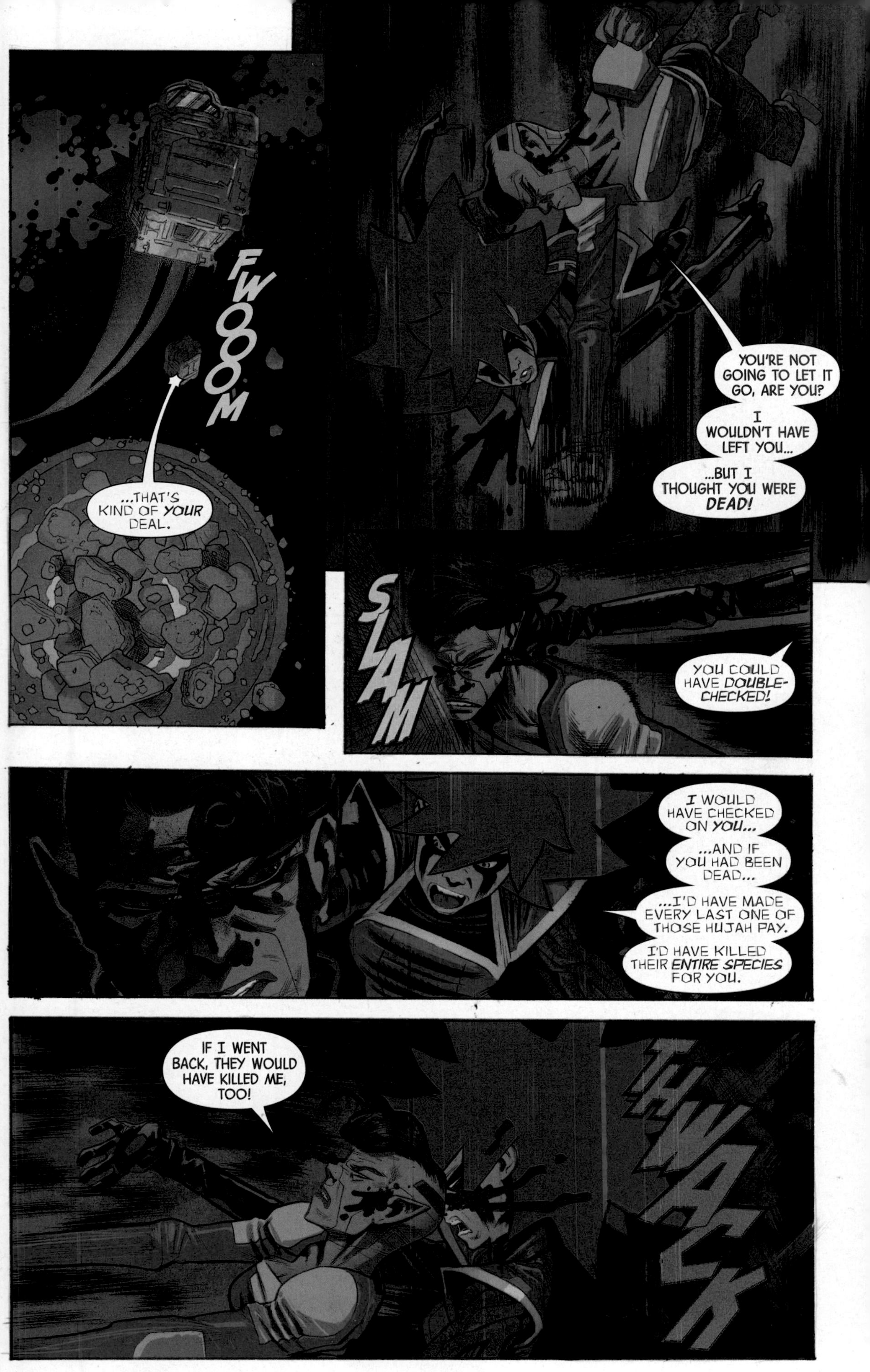

FWOOOOM
...THAT'S KIND OF YOUR DEAL.
YOU'RE NOT GOING TO LET IT GO, ARE YOU?
I WOULDN'T HAVE LEFT YOU...
...BUT I THOUGHT YOU WERE DEAD!
SLAM
YOU COULD HAVE DOUBLE-CHECKED!
I WOULD HAVE CHECKED ON YOU...
...AND IF YOU HAD BEEN DEAD...
...I'D HAVE MADE EVERY LAST ONE OF THOSE HUJAH PAY.
I'D HAVE KILLED THEIR ENTIRE SPECIES FOR YOU.
IF I WENT BACK, THEY WOULD HAVE KILLED ME, TOO!
THWACK

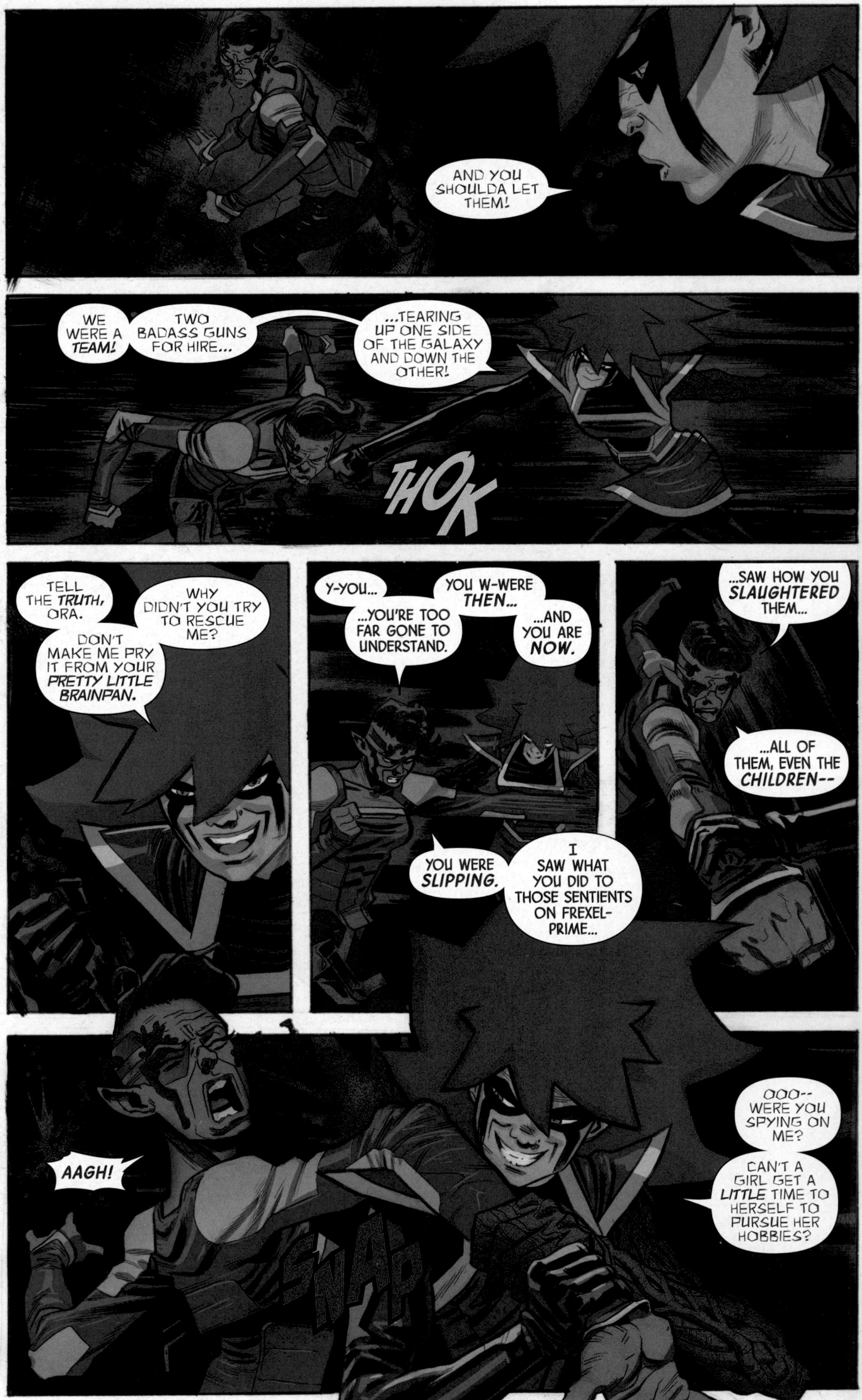
AND YOU SHOULDA LET THEM!
WE WERE A TEAM!
TWO BADASS GUNS FOR HIRE...
...TEARING UP ONE SIDE OF THE GALAXY AND DOWN THE OTHER!
THOK
TELL THE TRUTH, ORA.
WHY DIDN'T YOU TRY TO RESCUE ME?
DON'T MAKE ME PRY IT FROM YOUR PRETTY LITTLE BRAINPAN.
Y-YOU...
...YOU'RE TOO FAR GONE TO UNDERSTAND.
YOU W-WERE THEN...
...AND YOU ARE NOW.
YOU WERE SLIPPING.
I SAW WHAT YOU DID TO THOSE SENTIENTS ON FREXEL-PRIME...
...SAW HOW YOU SLAUGHTERED THEM...
...ALL OF THEM, EVEN THE CHILDREN--
AAGH!
SNAP
OOO--WERE YOU SPYING ON ME?
CAN'T A GIRL GET A LITTLE TIME TO HERSELF TO PURSUE HER HOBBIES?

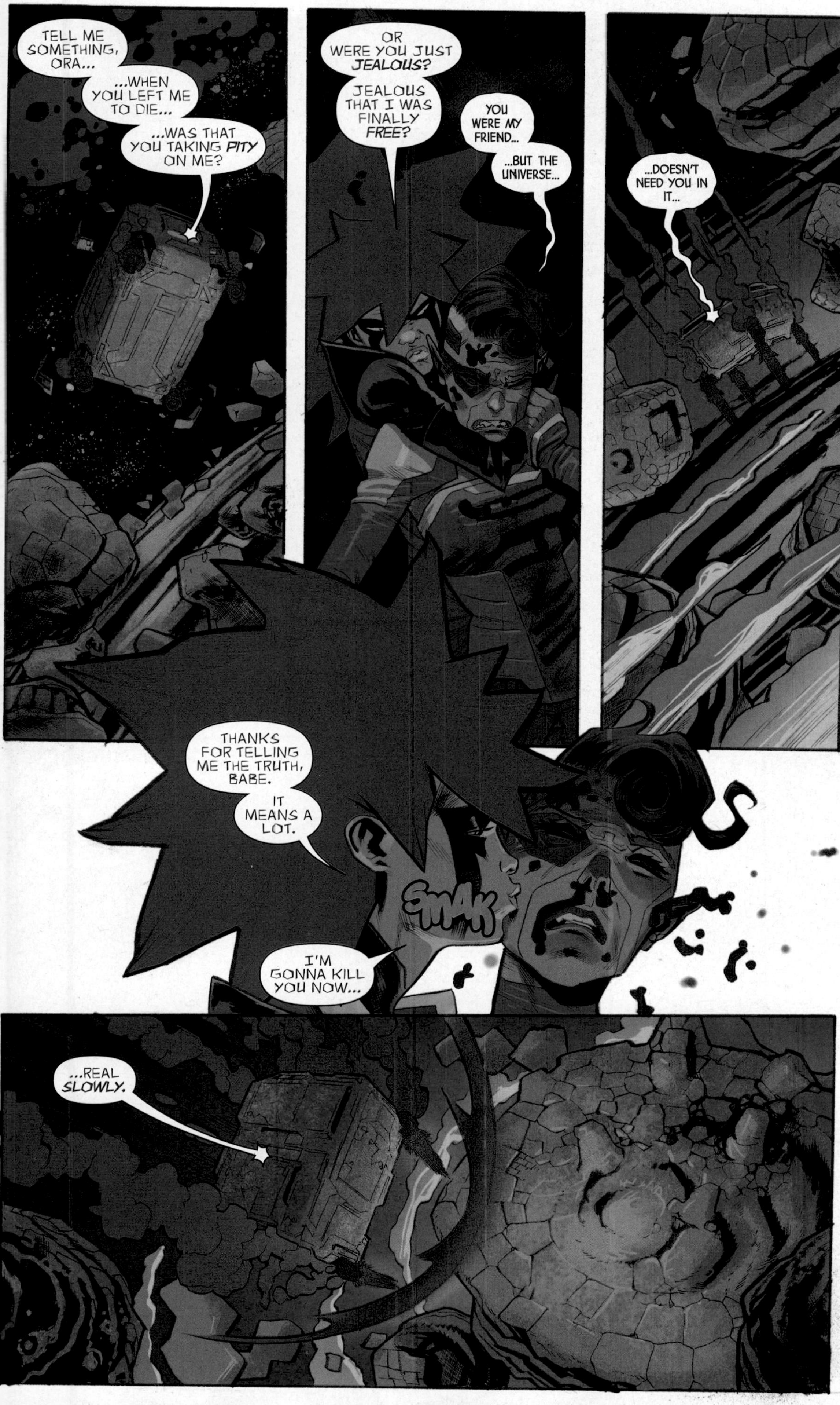
TELL ME SOMETHING, ORA...
...WHEN YOU LEFT ME TO DIE...
...WAS THAT YOU TAKING PITY ON ME?
OR WERE YOU JUST JEALOUS?
JEALOUS THAT I WAS FINALLY FREE?
YOU WERE MY FRIEND...
...BUT THE UNIVERSE...
...DOESN'T NEED YOU IN IT...
THANKS FOR TELLING ME THE TRUTH, BABE.
IT MEANS A LOT.
SMAK
I'M GONNA KILL YOU NOW...
...REAL SLOWLY.

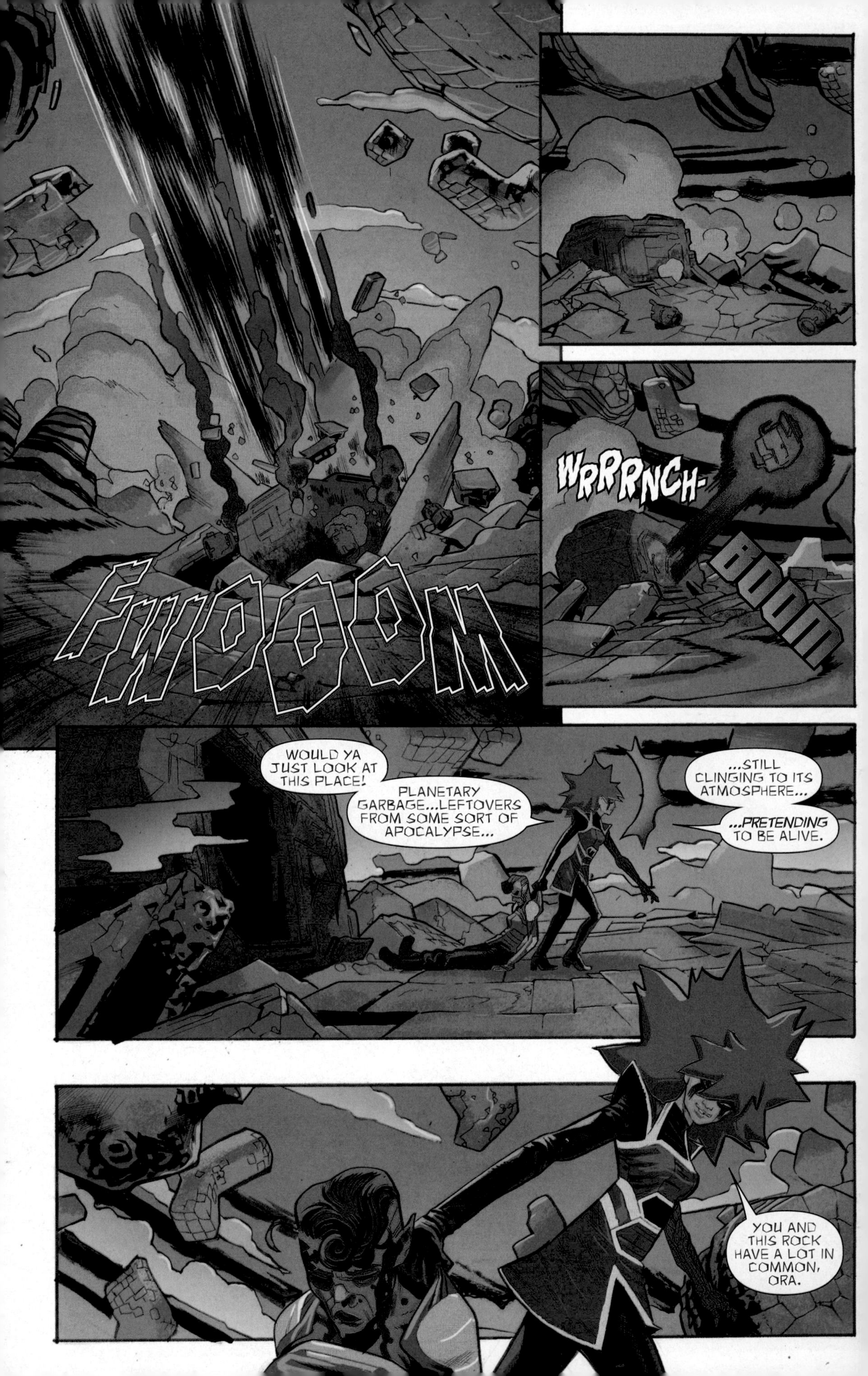
FWOOOM
WRRRNCH-
BOOM
WOULD YA JUST LOOK AT THIS PLACE!
PLANETARY GARBAGE...LEFTOVERS FROM SOME SORT OF APOCALYPSE...
...STILL CLINGING TO ITS ATMOSPHERE...
...PRETENDING TO BE ALIVE.
YOU AND THIS ROCK HAVE A LOT IN COMMON, ORA.

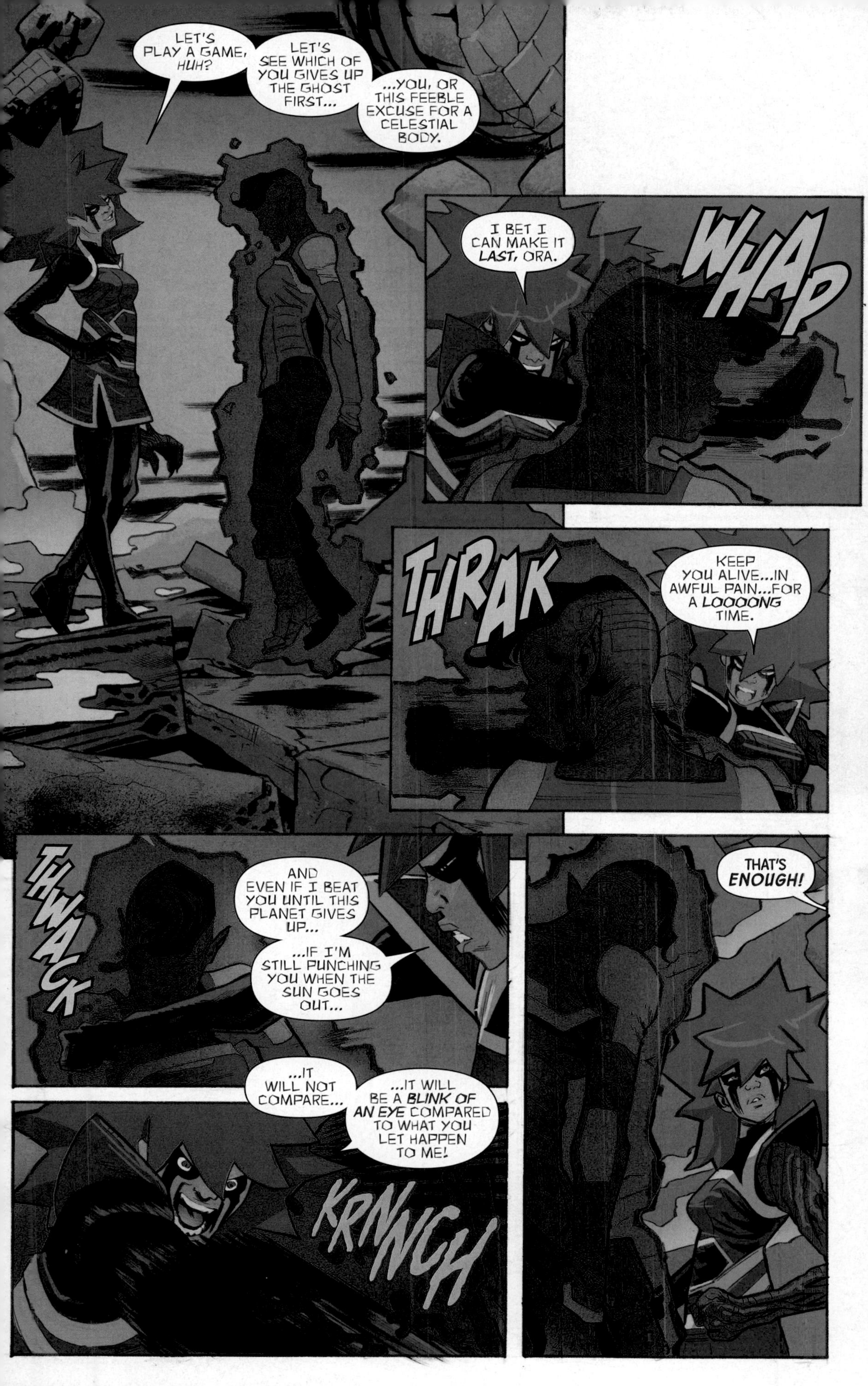

LET'S PLAY A GAME, HUH?
LET'S SEE WHICH OF YOU GIVES UP THE GHOST FIRST...
...YOU, OR THIS FEEBLE EXCUSE FOR A CELESTIAL BODY.
I BET I CAN MAKE IT LAST, ORA.
WHAP
THRAK
KEEP YOU ALIVE...IN AWFUL PAIN...FOR A LOOOONG TIME.
THWACK
AND EVEN IF I BEAT YOU UNTIL THIS PLANET GIVES UP...
...IF I'M STILL PUNCHING YOU WHEN THE SUN GOES OUT...
...IT WILL NOT COMPARE...
...IT WILL BE A BLINK OF AN EYE COMPARED TO WHAT YOU LET HAPPEN TO ME!
KRNNCH
THAT'S ENOUGH!

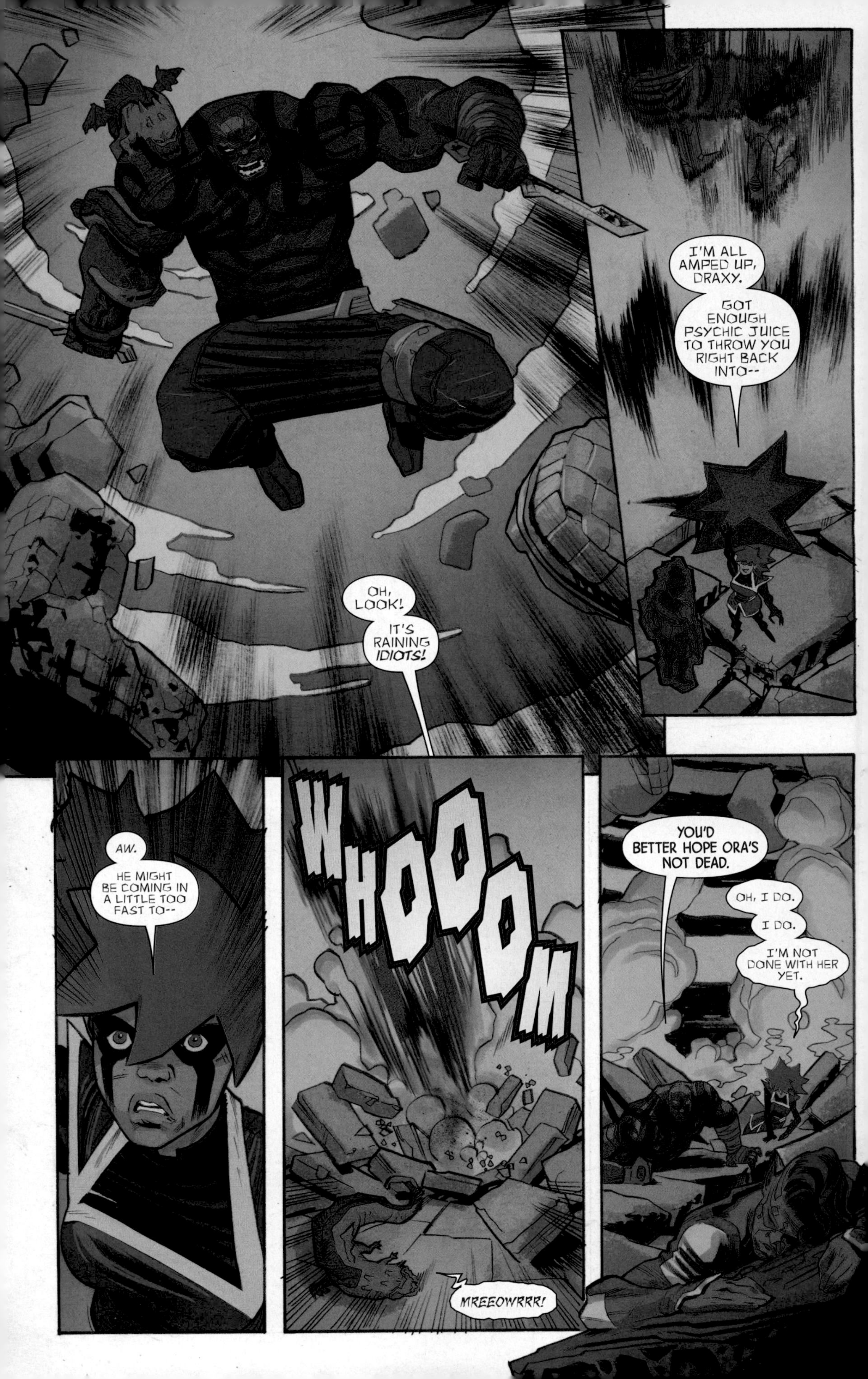
I'M ALL AMPED UP, DRAXY.
GOT ENOUGH PSYCHIC JUICE TO THROW YOU RIGHT BACK INTO--
OH, LOOK!
IT'S RAINING *IDIOTS!*
AW.
HE MIGHT BE COMING IN A LITTLE TOO FAST TO--
WHOOOOM
MREEOWRRR!
YOU'D BETTER HOPE ORA'S NOT DEAD.
OH, I DO.
I DO.
I'M NOT DONE WITH HER YET.

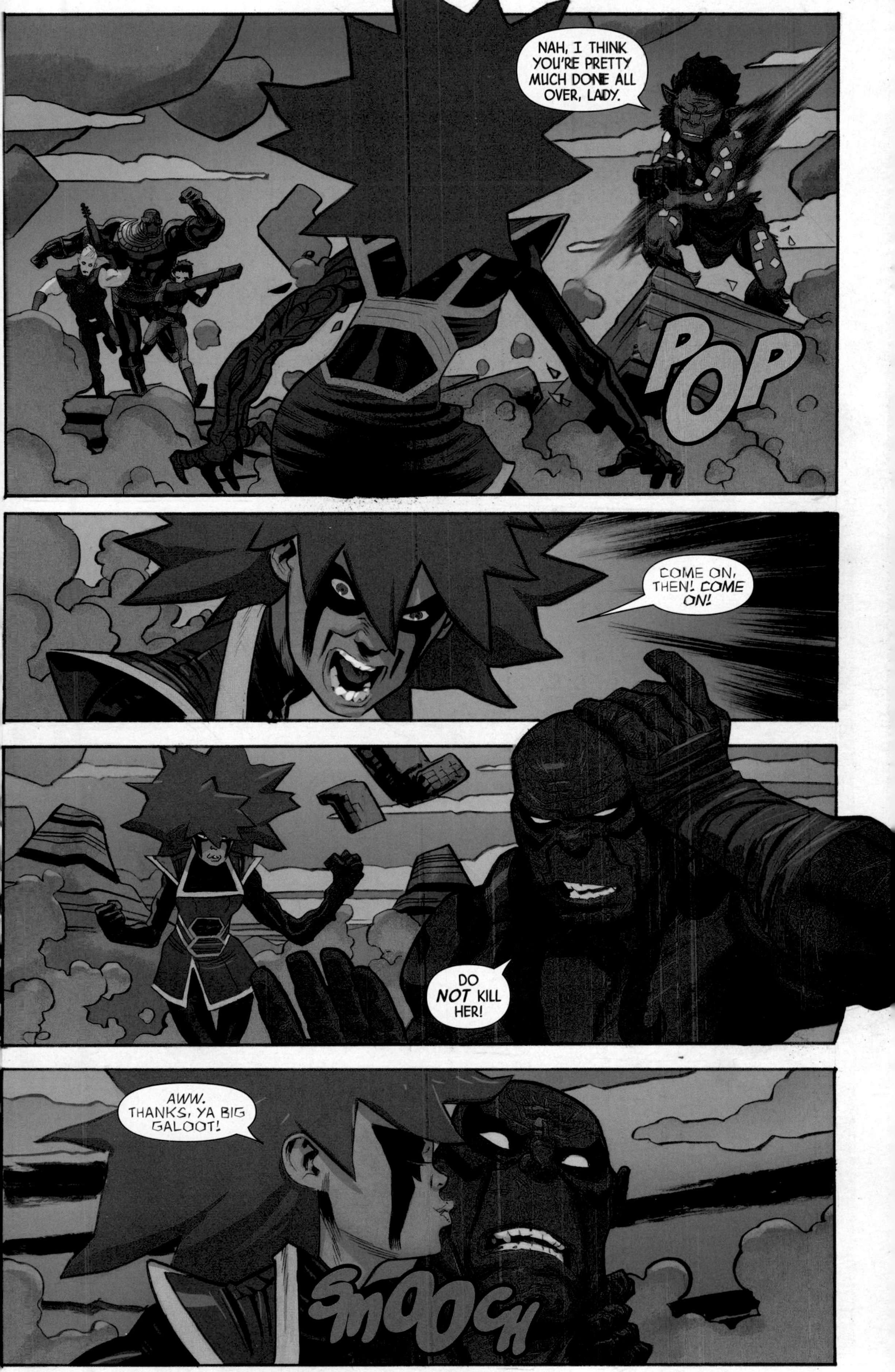
NAH, I THINK YOU'RE PRETTY MUCH DONE ALL OVER, LADY.
POP
COME ON, THEN! COME ON!
DO NOT KILL HER!
AWW. THANKS, YA BIG GALOOT!
SMOOCH

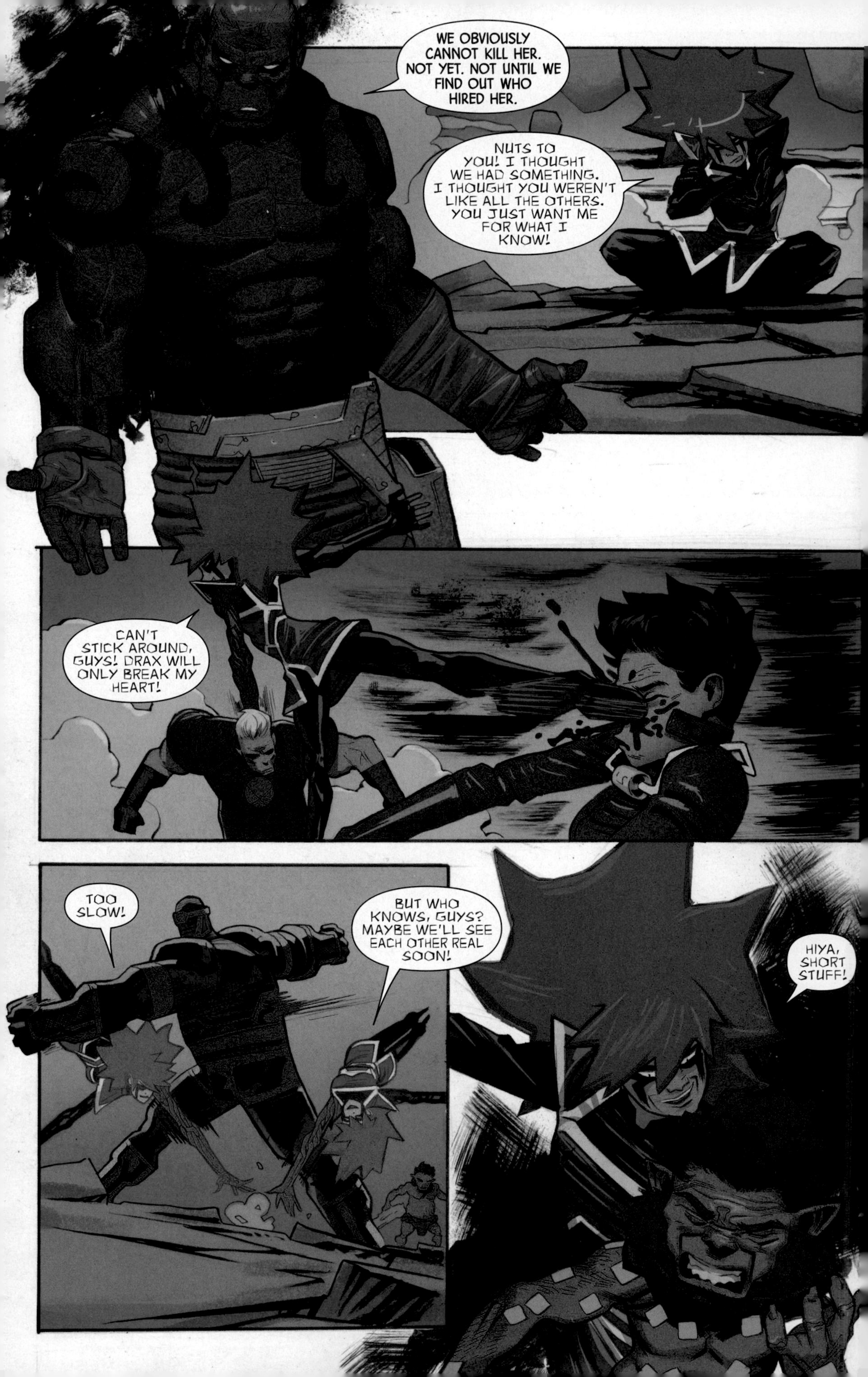
WE OBVIOUSLY CANNOT KILL HER. NOT YET. NOT UNTIL WE FIND OUT WHO HIRED HER.
NUTS TO YOU! I THOUGHT WE HAD SOMETHING. I THOUGHT YOU WEREN'T LIKE ALL THE OTHERS. YOU JUST WANT ME FOR WHAT I KNOW!
CAN'T STICK AROUND, GUYS! DRAX WILL ONLY BREAK MY HEART!
TOO SLOW!
BUT WHO KNOWS, GUYS? MAYBE WE'LL SEE EACH OTHER REAL SOON!
HIYA, SHORT STUFF!

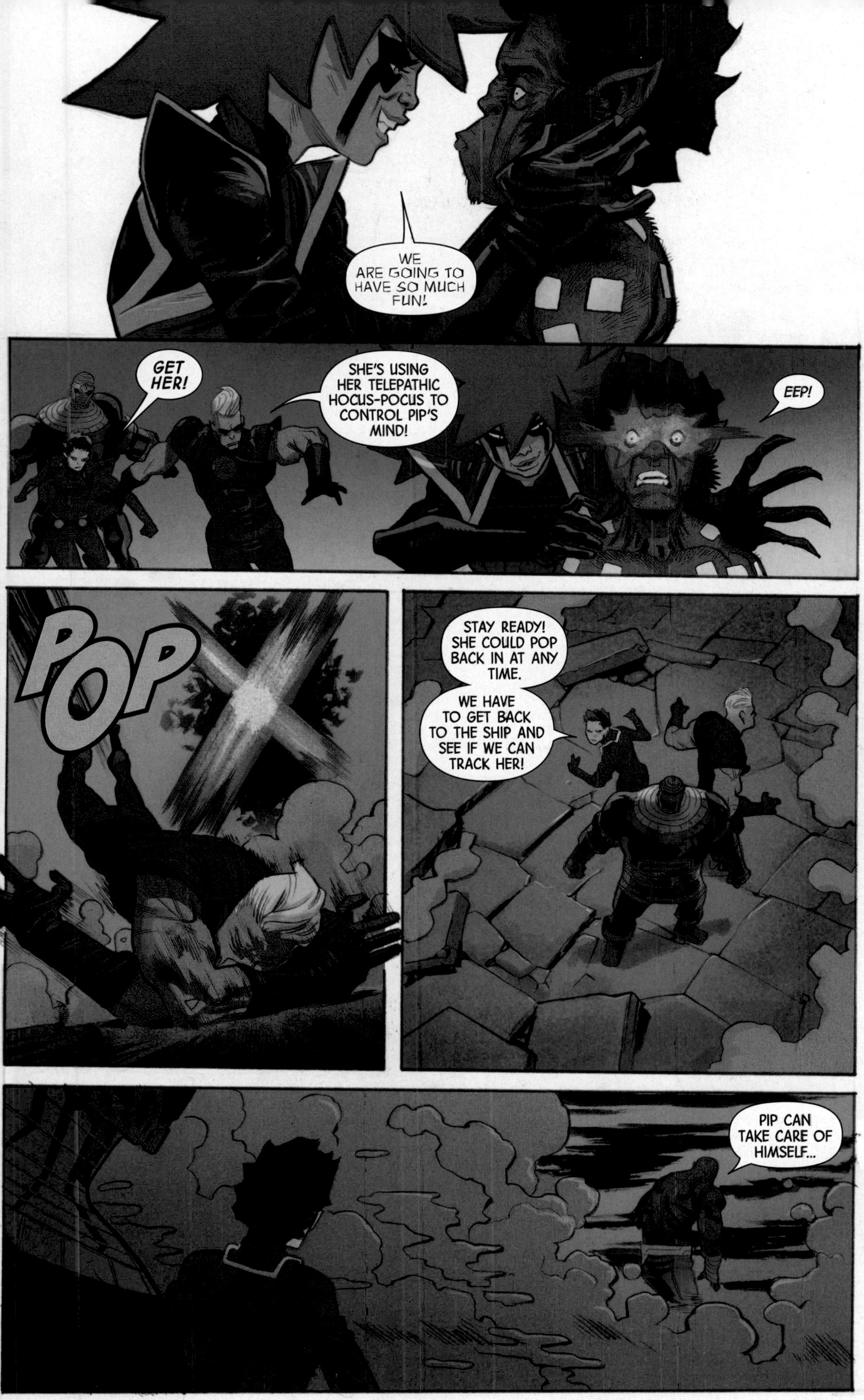
WE ARE GOING TO HAVE SO MUCH FUN!
GET HER!
SHE'S USING HER TELEPATHIC HOCUS-POCUS TO CONTROL PIP'S MIND!
EEP!
POP
STAY READY! SHE COULD POP BACK IN AT ANY TIME.
WE HAVE TO GET BACK TO THE SHIP AND SEE IF WE CAN TRACK HER!
PIP CAN TAKE CARE OF HIMSELF...

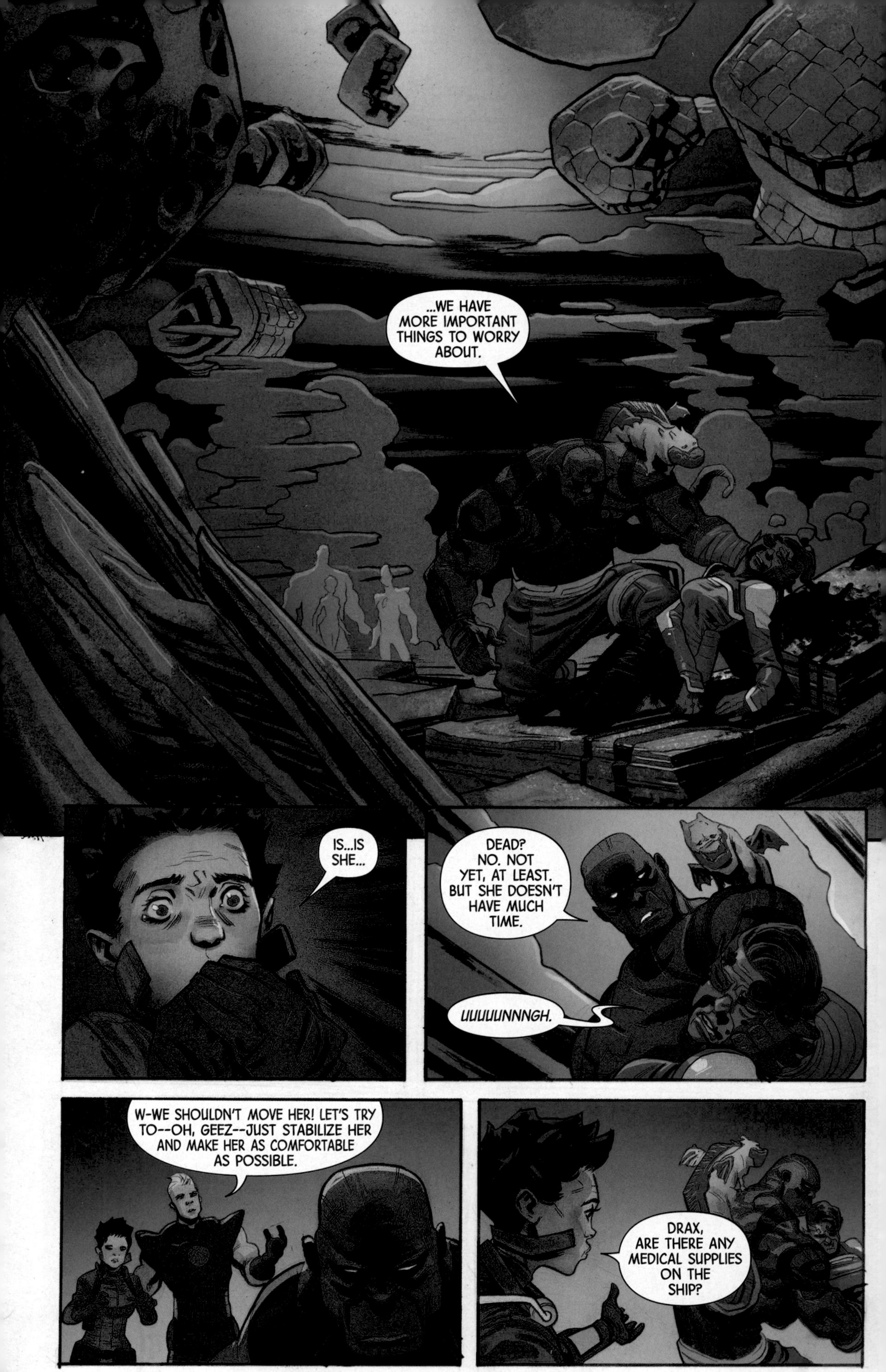
...WE HAVE MORE IMPORTANT THINGS TO WORRY ABOUT.
IS...IS SHE...
DEAD? NO. NOT YET, AT LEAST. BUT SHE DOESN'T HAVE MUCH TIME.
UUUUUNNNGH.
W-WE SHOULDN'T MOVE HER! LET'S TRY TO--OH, GEEZ--JUST STABILIZE HER AND MAKE HER AS COMFORTABLE AS POSSIBLE.
DRAX, ARE THERE ANY MEDICAL SUPPLIES ON THE SHIP?

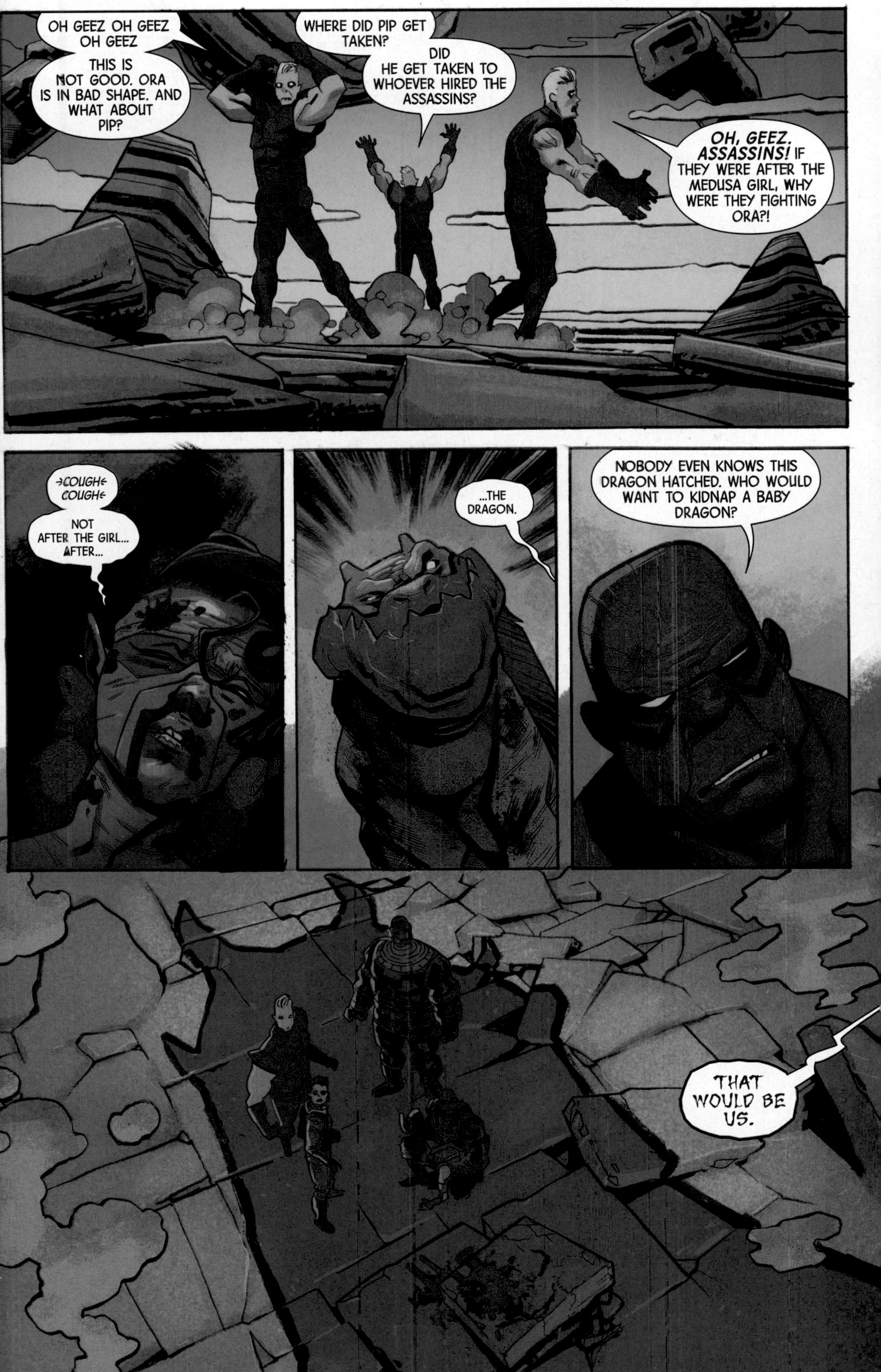
OH GEEZ OH GEEZ OH GEEZ
THIS IS NOT GOOD. ORA IS IN BAD SHAPE. AND WHAT ABOUT PIP?
WHERE DID PIP GET TAKEN?
DID HE GET TAKEN TO WHOEVER HIRED THE ASSASSINS?
OH, GEEZ. ASSASSINS! IF THEY WERE AFTER THE MEDUSA GIRL, WHY WERE THEY FIGHTING ORA?!
COUGH COUGH
NOT AFTER THE GIRL... AFTER...
...THE DRAGON.
NOBODY EVEN KNOWS THIS DRAGON HATCHED. WHO WOULD WANT TO KIDNAP A BABY DRAGON?
THAT WOULD BE US.

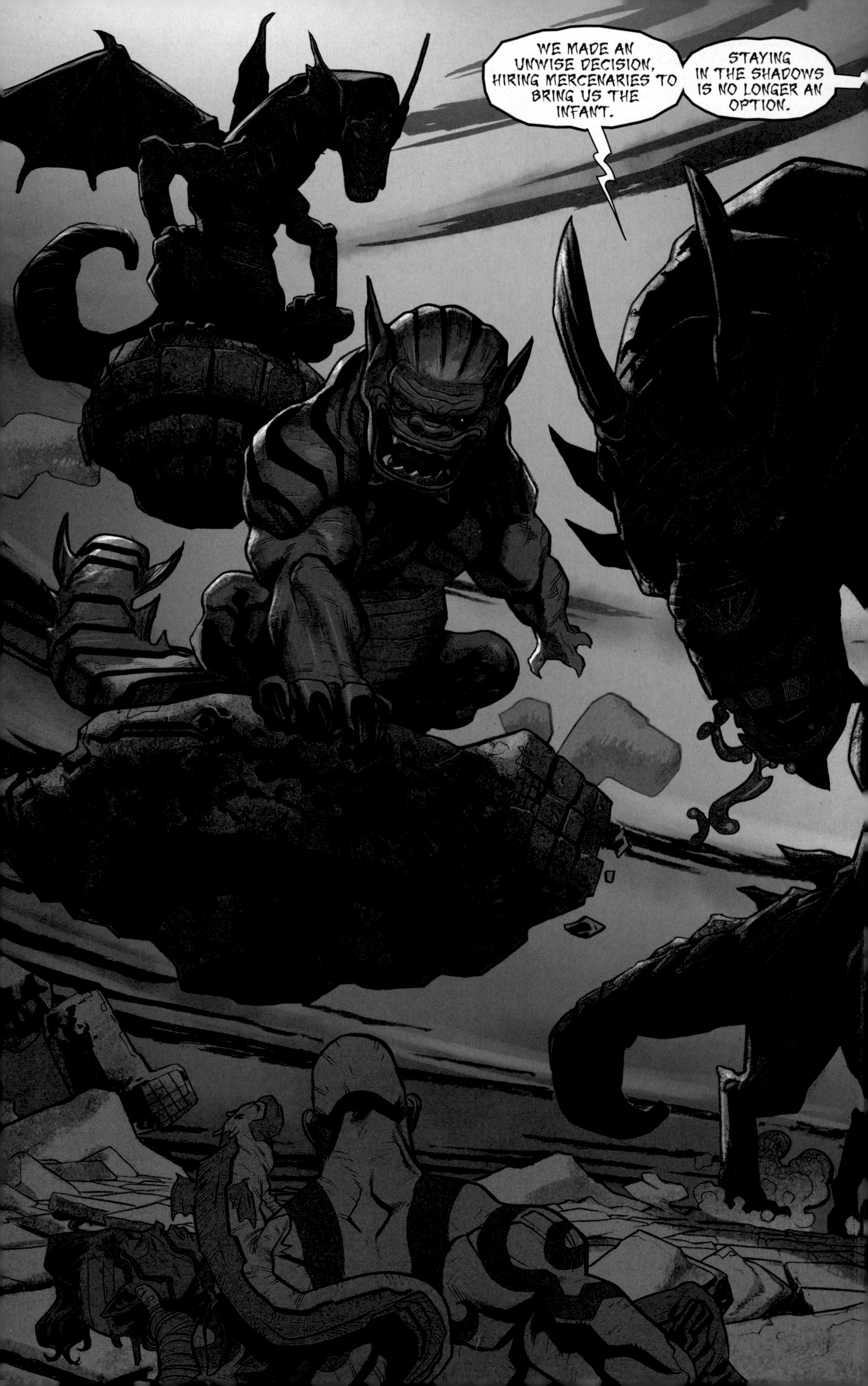
WE MADE AN UNWISE DECISION, HIRING MERCENARIES TO BRING US THE INFANT.
STAYING IN THE SHADOWS IS NO LONGER AN OPTION.

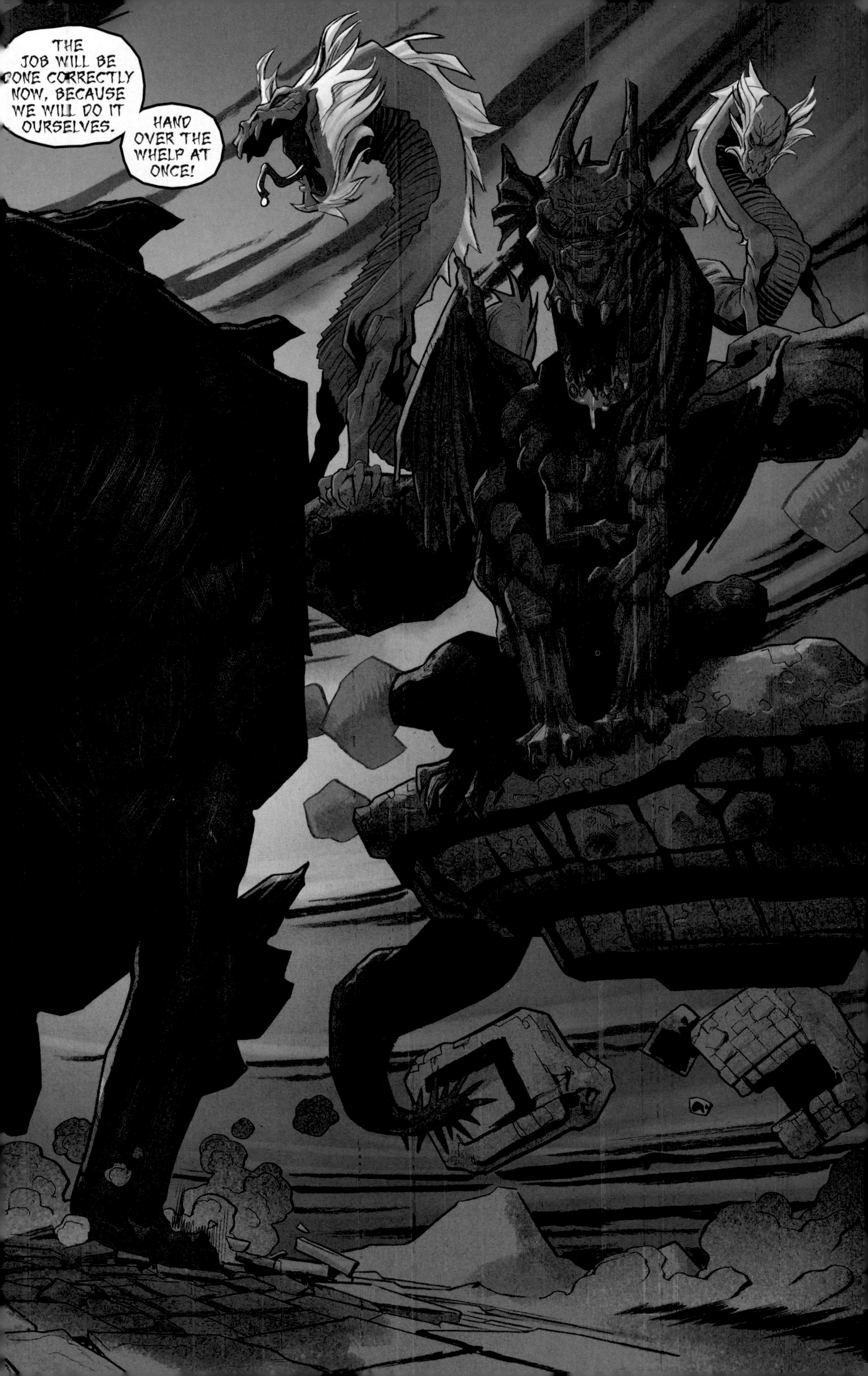
THE JOB WILL BE DONE CORRECTLY NOW, BECAUSE WE WILL DO IT OURSELVES.
HAND OVER THE WHELP AT ONCE!

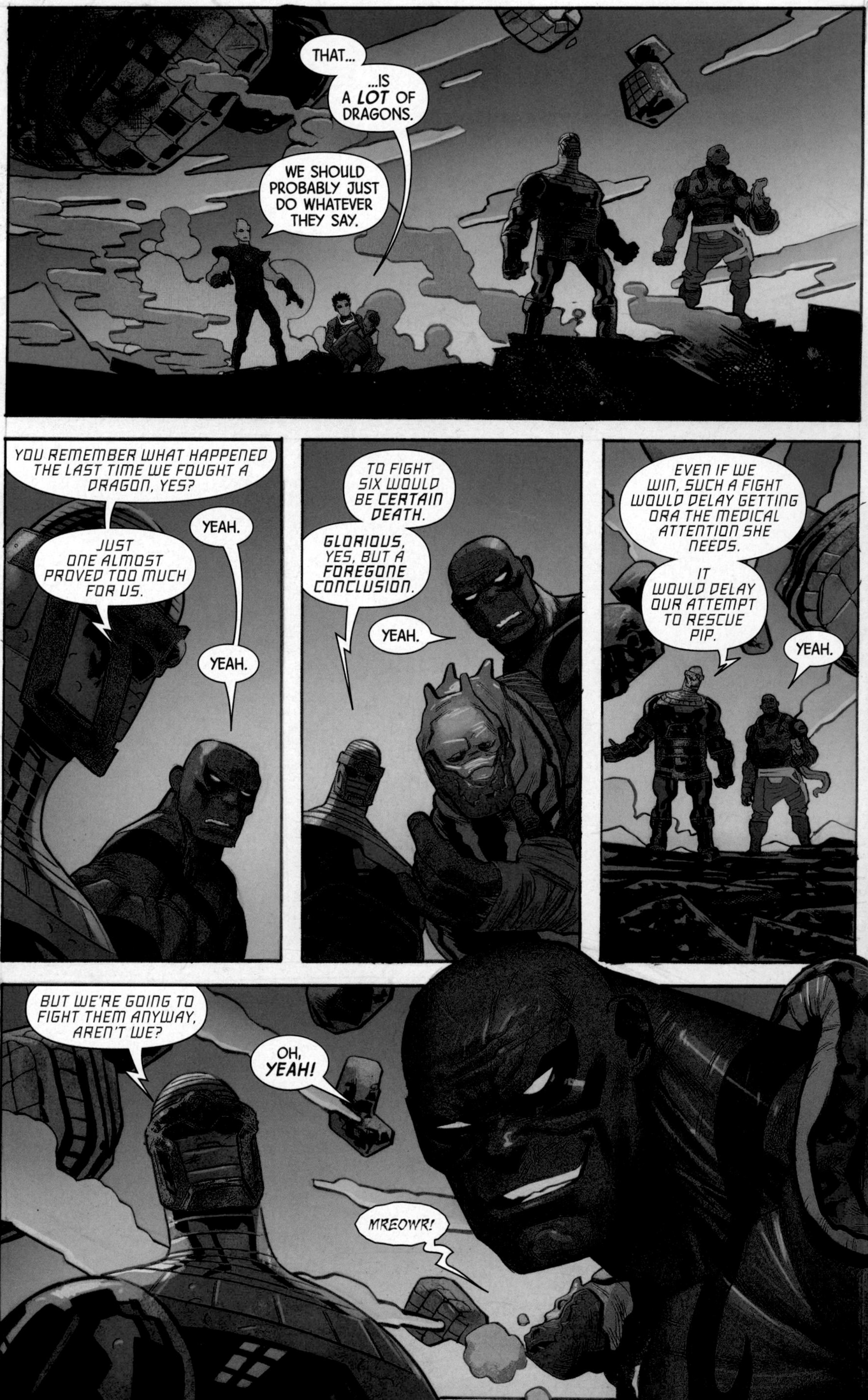
THAT...
...IS A LOT OF DRAGONS.
WE SHOULD PROBABLY JUST DO WHATEVER THEY SAY.
YOU REMEMBER WHAT HAPPENED THE LAST TIME WE FOUGHT A DRAGON, YES?
YEAH.
JUST ONE ALMOST PROVED TOO MUCH FOR US.
YEAH.
TO FIGHT SIX WOULD BE CERTAIN DEATH.
GLORIOUS, YES, BUT A FOREGONE CONCLUSION.
YEAH.
EVEN IF WE WIN, SUCH A FIGHT WOULD DELAY GETTING ORA THE MEDICAL ATTENTION SHE NEEDS.
IT WOULD DELAY OUR ATTEMPT TO RESCUE PIP.
YEAH.
BUT WE'RE GOING TO FIGHT THEM ANYWAY, AREN'T WE?
OH, YEAH!
MREOWR!

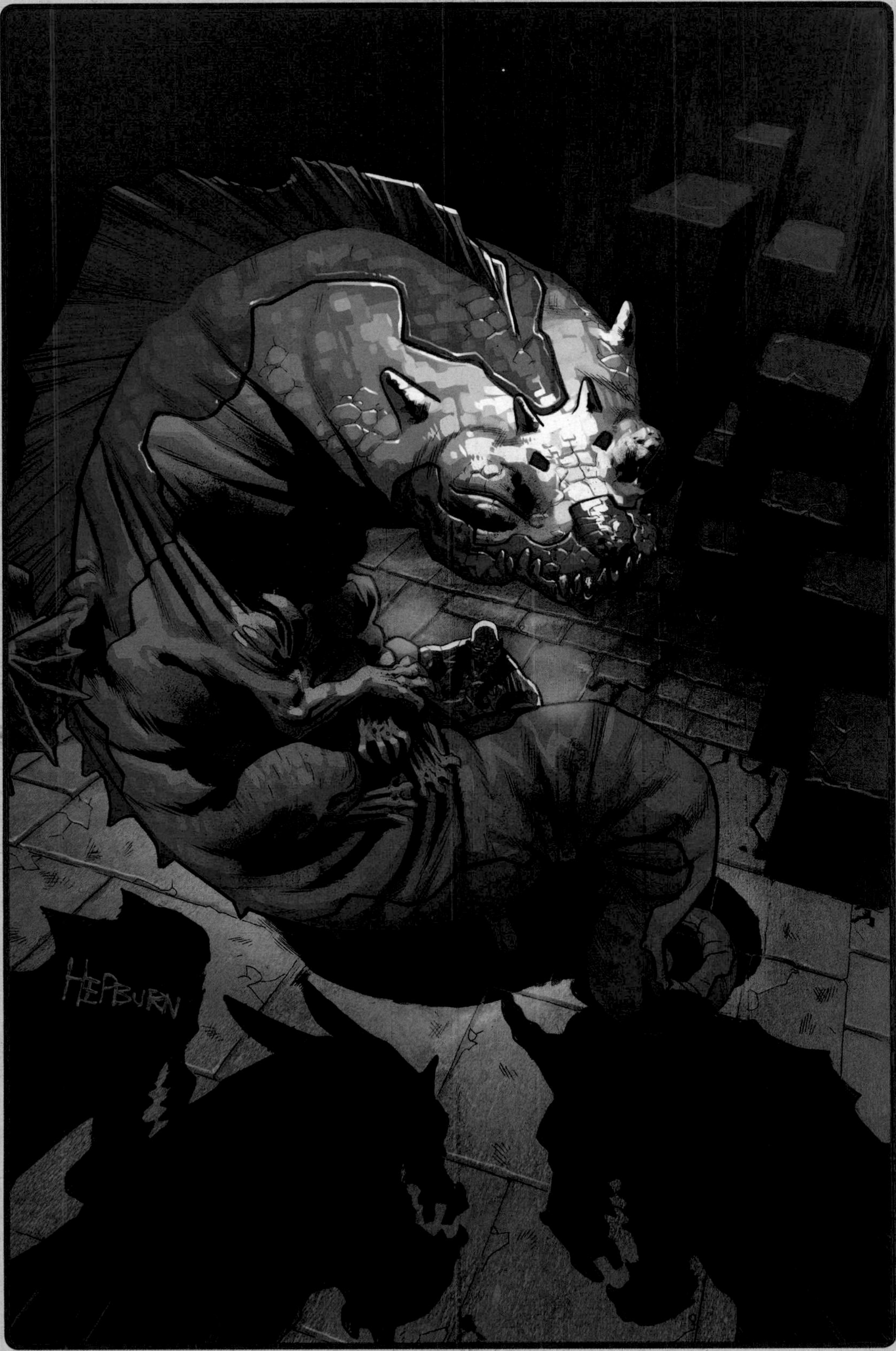
HEPBURN

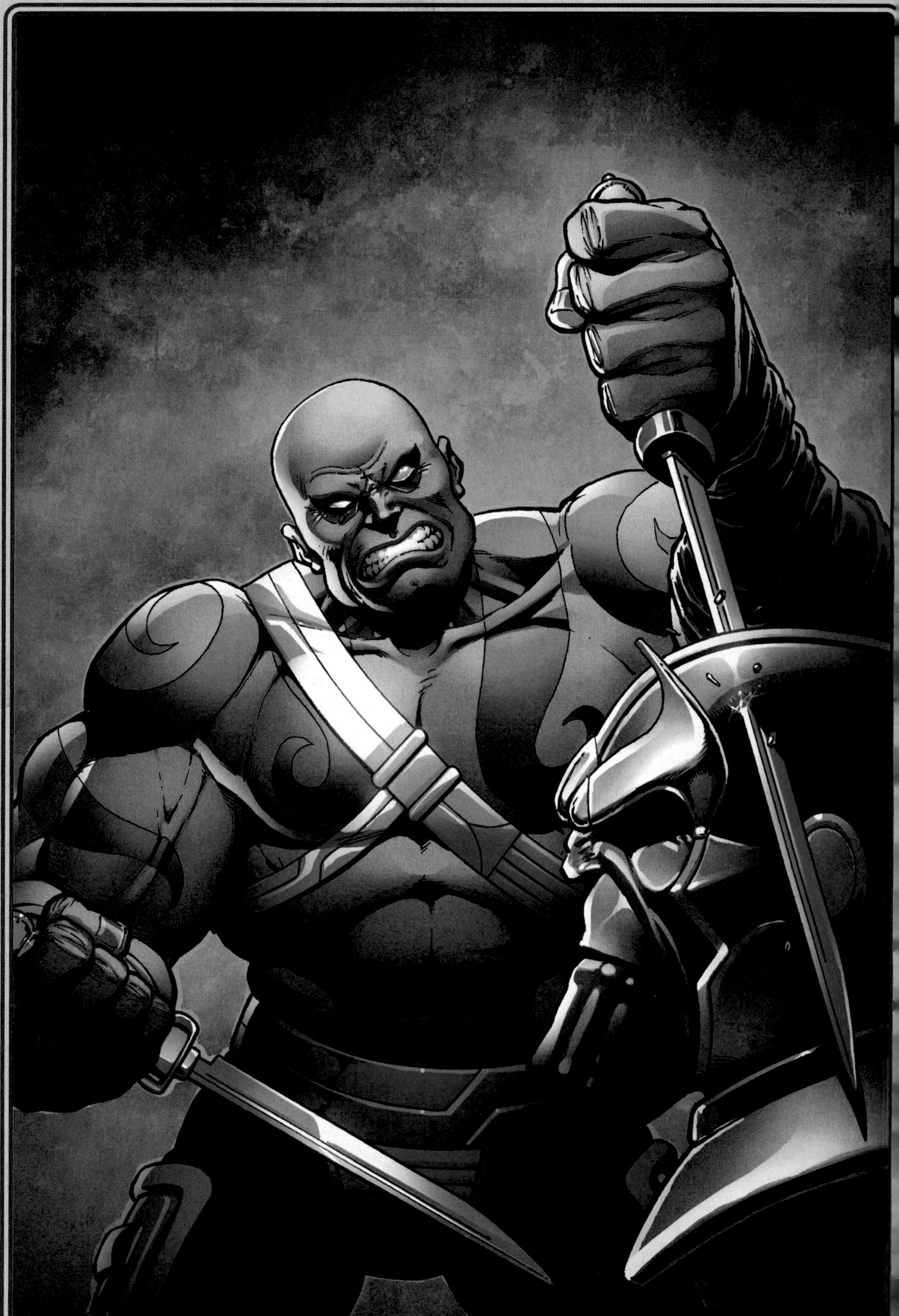

#6 CLASSIC VARIANT
JIM STARLIN & FRANK D'ARMATA

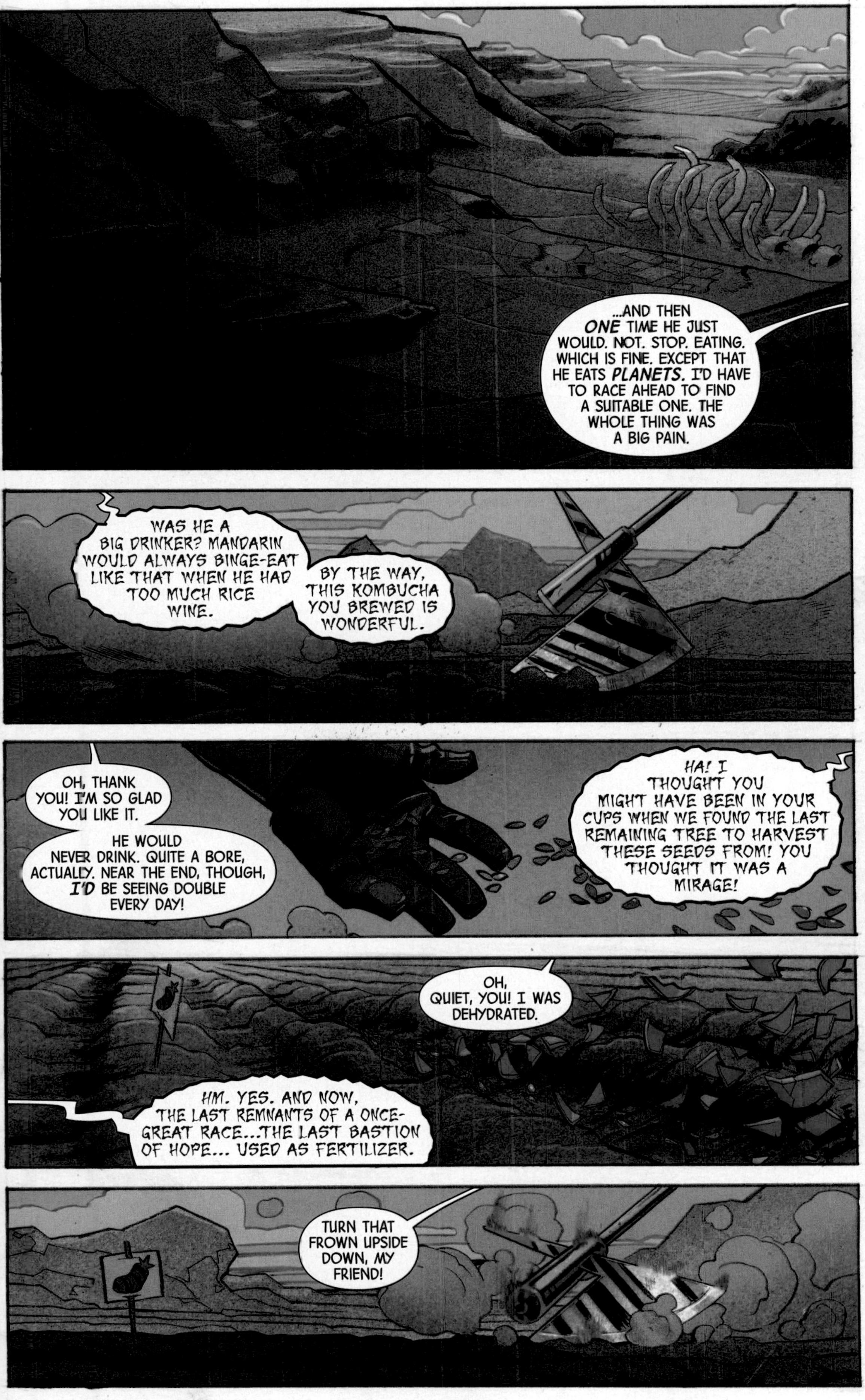
...AND THEN ONE TIME HE JUST WOULD. NOT. STOP. EATING. WHICH IS FINE. EXCEPT THAT HE EATS PLANETS. I'D HAVE TO RACE AHEAD TO FIND A SUITABLE ONE. THE WHOLE THING WAS A BIG PAIN.
WAS HE A BIG DRINKER? MANDARIN WOULD ALWAYS BINGE-EAT LIKE THAT WHEN HE HAD TOO MUCH RICE WINE.
BY THE WAY, THIS KOMBUCHA YOU BREWED IS WONDERFUL.
OH, THANK YOU! I'M SO GLAD YOU LIKE IT.
HE WOULD NEVER DRINK. QUITE A BORE, ACTUALLY. NEAR THE END, THOUGH, I'D BE SEEING DOUBLE EVERY DAY!
HA! I THOUGHT YOU MIGHT HAVE BEEN IN YOUR CUPS WHEN WE FOUND THE LAST REMAINING TREE TO HARVEST THESE SEEDS FROM! YOU THOUGHT IT WAS A MIRAGE!
OH, QUIET, YOU! I WAS DEHYDRATED.
HM. YES. AND NOW, THE LAST REMNANTS OF A ONCE-GREAT RACE...THE LAST BASTION OF HOPE... USED AS FERTILIZER.
TURN THAT FROWN UPSIDE DOWN, MY FRIEND!

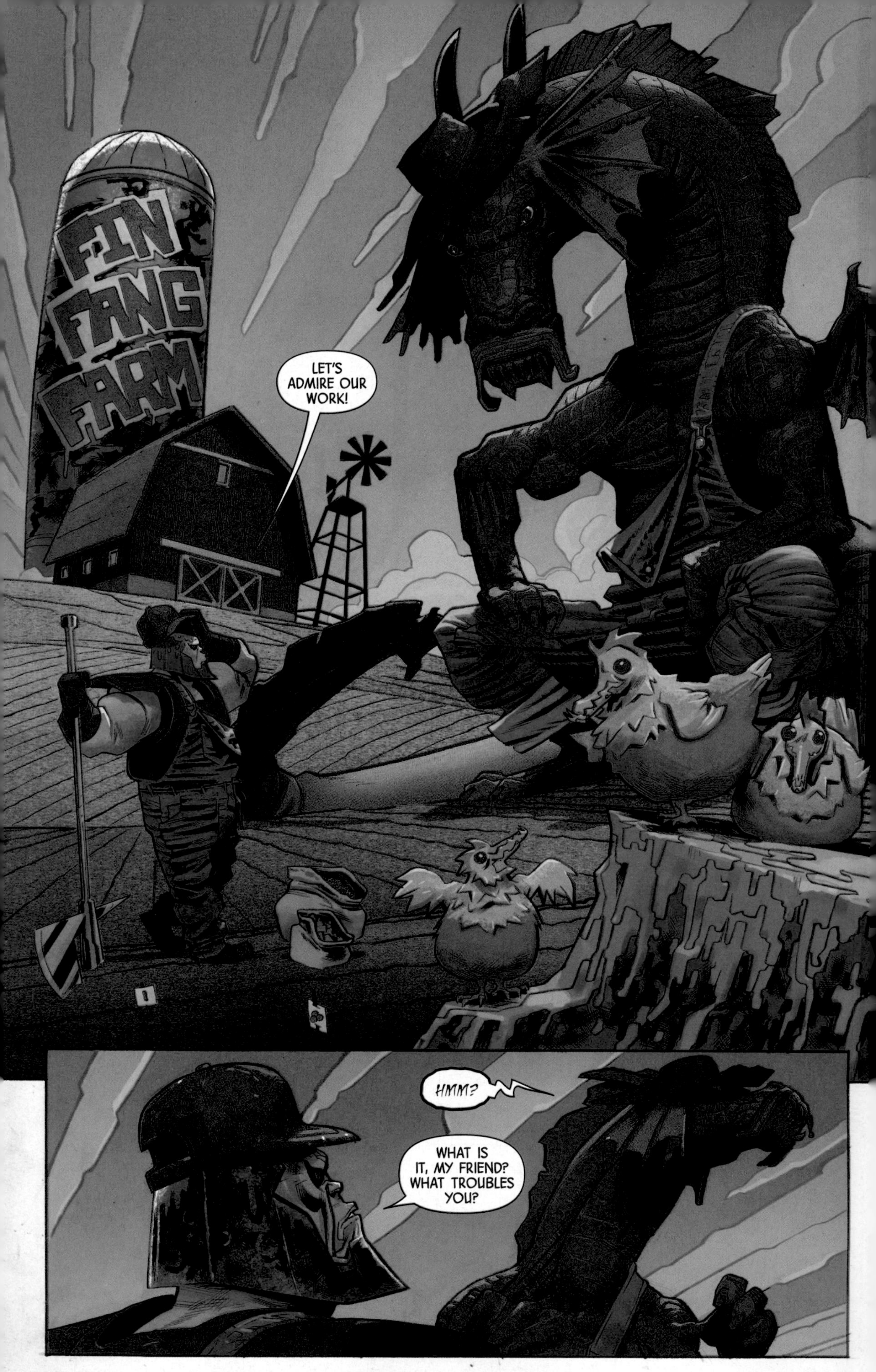
FIN FANG FARM
LET'S ADMIRE OUR WORK!
HMM?
WHAT IS IT, MY FRIEND? WHAT TROUBLES YOU?

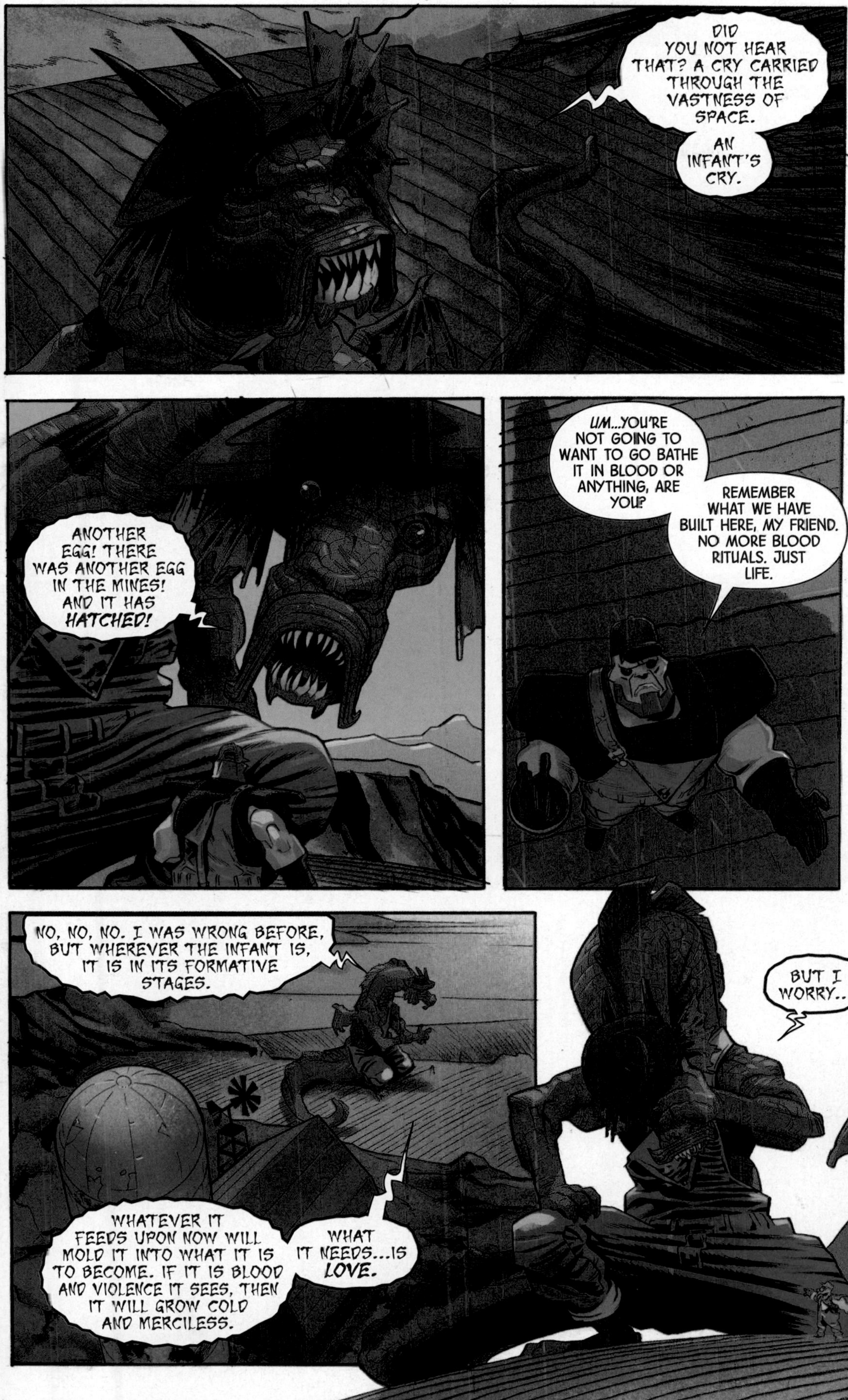
DID YOU NOT HEAR THAT? A CRY CARRIED THROUGH THE VASTNESS OF SPACE.
AN INFANT'S CRY.
ANOTHER EGG! THERE WAS ANOTHER EGG IN THE MINES! AND IT HAS *HATCHED!*
UM...YOU'RE NOT GOING TO WANT TO GO BATHE IT IN BLOOD OR ANYTHING, ARE YOU?
REMEMBER WHAT WE HAVE BUILT HERE, MY FRIEND. NO MORE BLOOD RITUALS. JUST LIFE.
NO, NO, NO. I WAS WRONG BEFORE, BUT WHEREVER THE INFANT IS, IT IS IN ITS FORMATIVE STAGES.
BUT I WORRY...
WHATEVER IT FEEDS UPON NOW WILL MOLD IT INTO WHAT IT IS TO BECOME. IF IT IS BLOOD AND VIOLENCE IT SEES, THEN IT WILL GROW COLD AND MERCILESS.
WHAT IT NEEDS...IS *LOVE.*

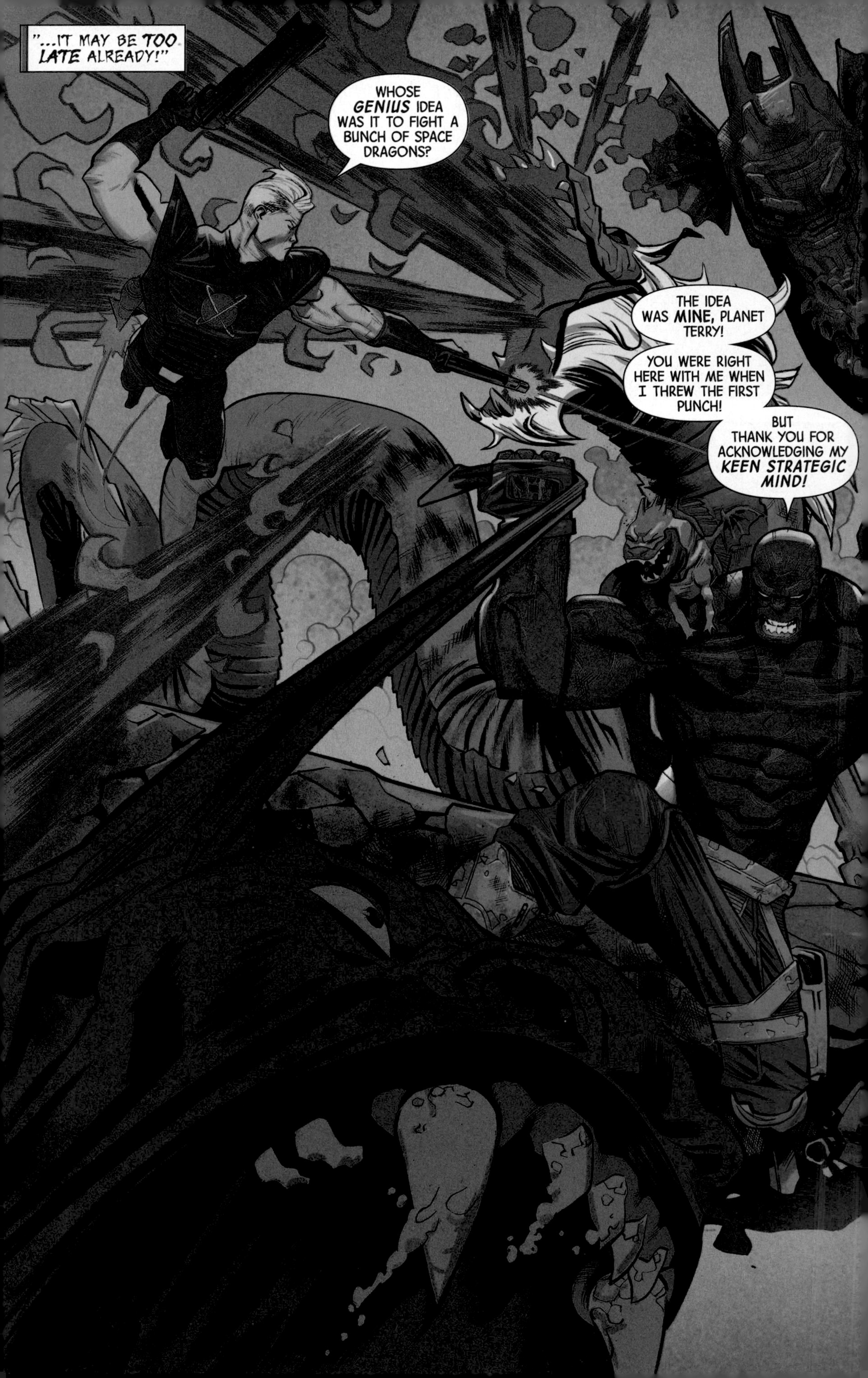
"...IT MAY BE TOO LATE ALREADY!"
WHOSE GENIUS IDEA WAS IT TO FIGHT A BUNCH OF SPACE DRAGONS?
THE IDEA WAS MINE, PLANET TERRY!
YOU WERE RIGHT HERE WITH ME WHEN I THREW THE FIRST PUNCH!
BUT THANK YOU FOR ACKNOWLEDGING MY KEEN STRATEGIC MIND!

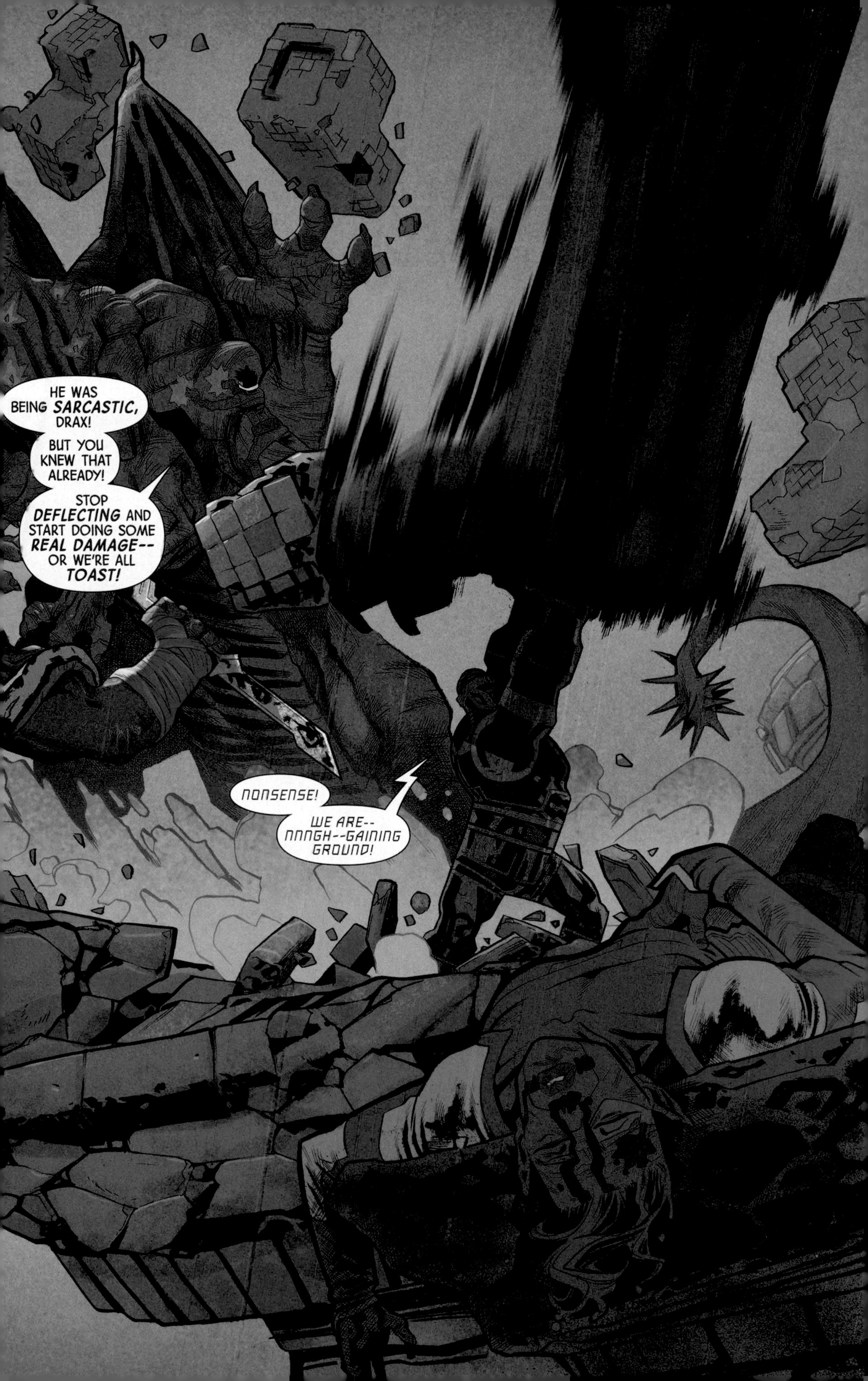
HE WAS BEING SARCASTIC, DRAX!
BUT YOU KNEW THAT ALREADY!
STOP DEFLECTING AND START DOING SOME REAL DAMAGE-- OR WE'RE ALL TOAST!
NONSENSE!
WE ARE-- NNNGH--GAINING GROUND!

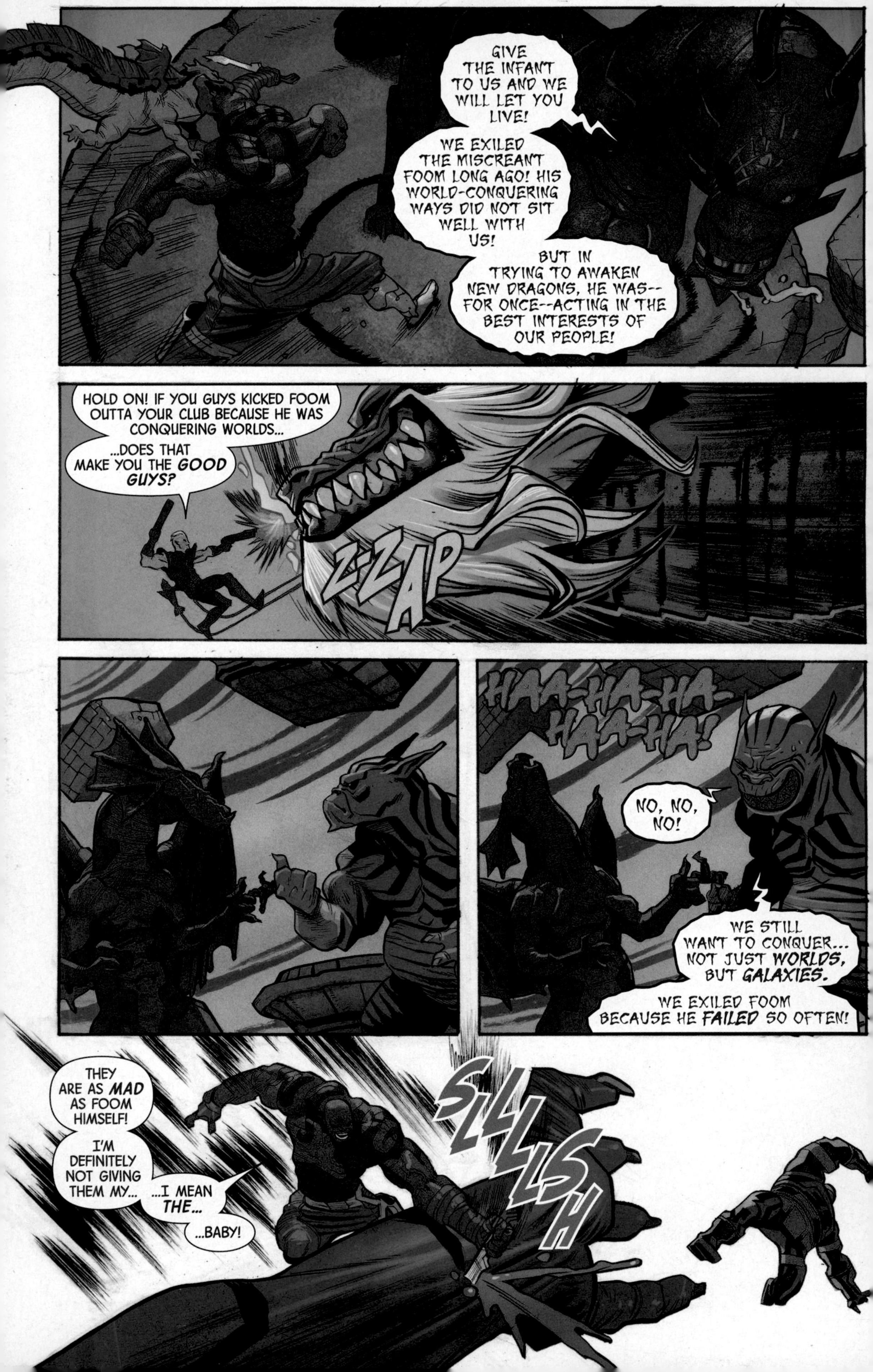
GIVE THE INFANT TO US AND WE WILL LET YOU LIVE!
WE EXILED THE MISCREANT FOOM LONG AGO! HIS WORLD-CONQUERING WAYS DID NOT SIT WELL WITH US!
BUT IN TRYING TO AWAKEN NEW DRAGONS, HE WAS--FOR ONCE--ACTING IN THE BEST INTERESTS OF OUR PEOPLE!
HOLD ON! IF YOU GUYS KICKED FOOM OUTTA YOUR CLUB BECAUSE HE WAS CONQUERING WORLDS...
...DOES THAT MAKE YOU THE GOOD GUYS?
Z-ZAP
HAA-HA-HA-HAA-HA!
NO, NO, NO!
WE STILL WANT TO CONQUER... NOT JUST WORLDS, BUT GALAXIES.
WE EXILED FOOM BECAUSE HE FAILED SO OFTEN!
THEY ARE AS MAD AS FOOM HIMSELF!
I'M DEFINITELY NOT GIVING THEM MY...
...I MEAN THE...
...BABY!
SLLLSH

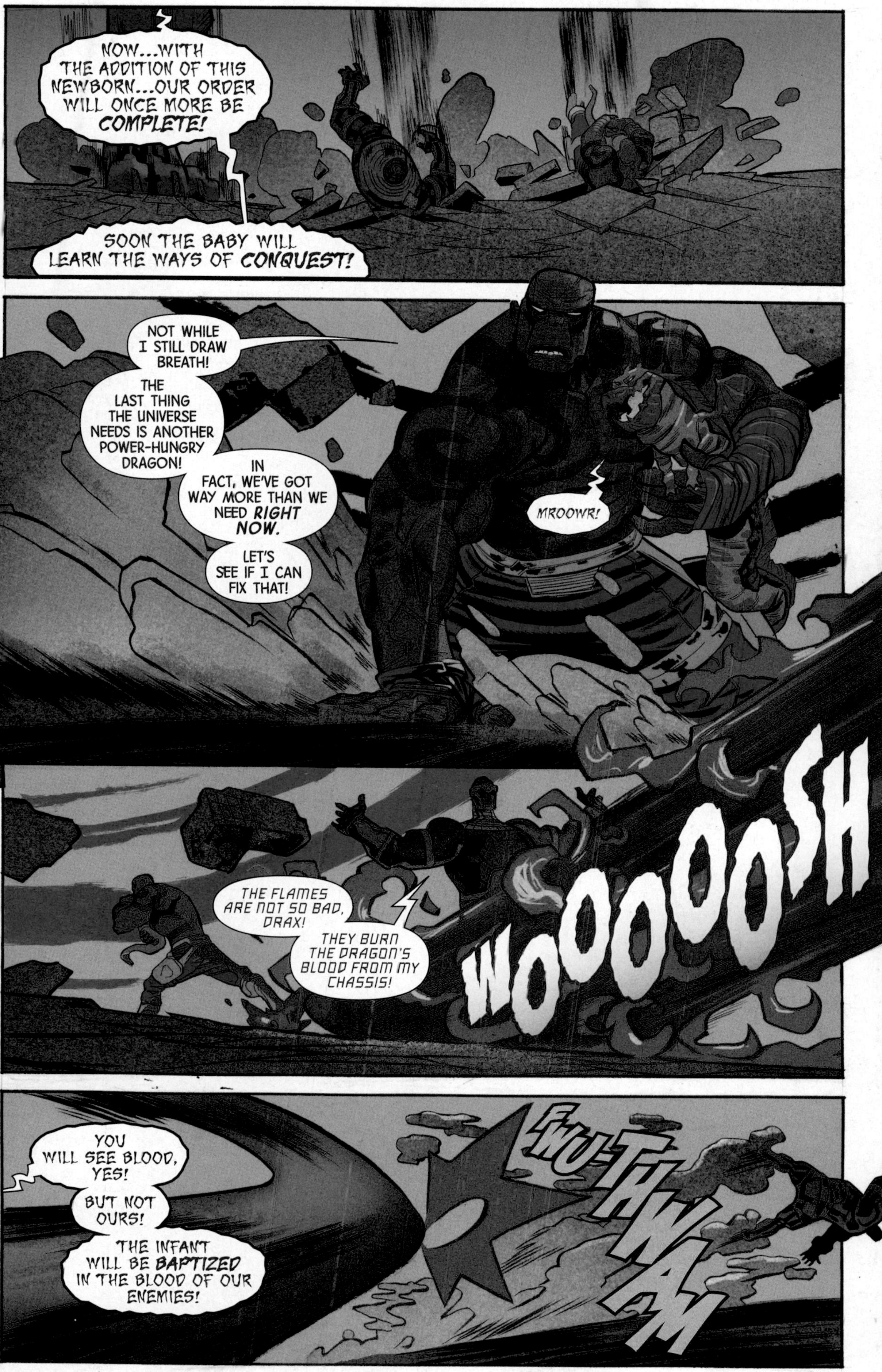
NOW...WITH THE ADDITION OF THIS NEWBORN...OUR ORDER WILL ONCE MORE BE COMPLETE!
SOON THE BABY WILL LEARN THE WAYS OF CONQUEST!
NOT WHILE I STILL DRAW BREATH!
THE LAST THING THE UNIVERSE NEEDS IS ANOTHER POWER-HUNGRY DRAGON!
IN FACT, WE'VE GOT WAY MORE THAN WE NEED RIGHT NOW.
LET'S SEE IF I CAN FIX THAT!
MROOWR!
WOOOOOOSH
THE FLAMES ARE NOT SO BAD, DRAX!
THEY BURN THE DRAGON'S BLOOD FROM MY CHASSIS!
YOU WILL SEE BLOOD, YES!
BUT NOT OURS!
THE INFANT WILL BE BAPTIZED IN THE BLOOD OF OUR ENEMIES!
FWU-THWAM

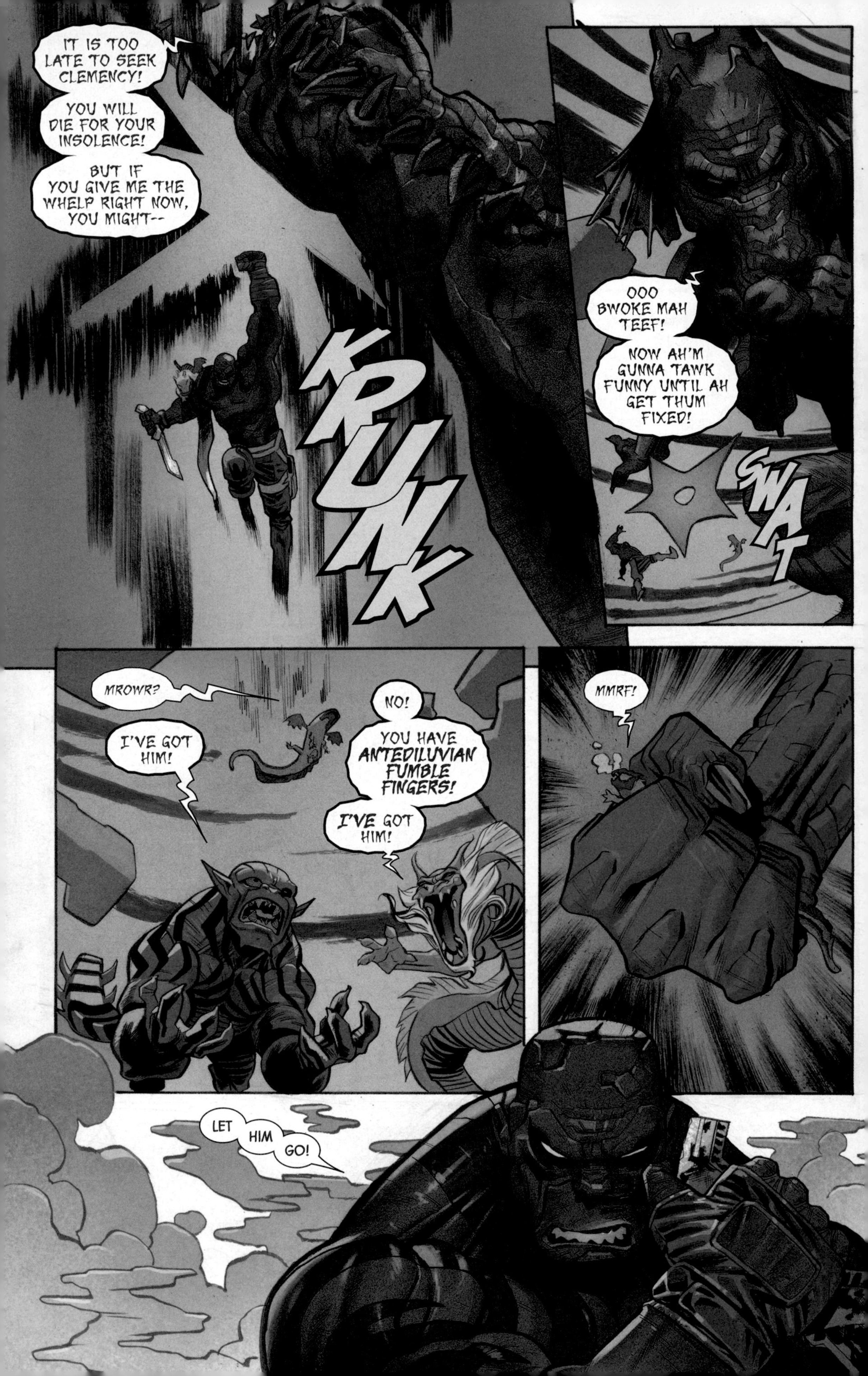
IT IS TOO LATE TO SEEK CLEMENCY!
YOU WILL DIE FOR YOUR INSOLENCE!
BUT IF YOU GIVE ME THE WHELP RIGHT NOW, YOU MIGHT--
KRUNK
OOO BWOKE MAH TEEF!
NOW AH'M GUNNA TAWK FUNNY UNTIL AH GET THUM FIXED!
SWAT
MROWR?
I'VE GOT HIM!
NO!
YOU HAVE ANTEDILUVIAN FUMBLE FINGERS!
I'VE GOT HIM!
MMRF!
LET HIM GO!

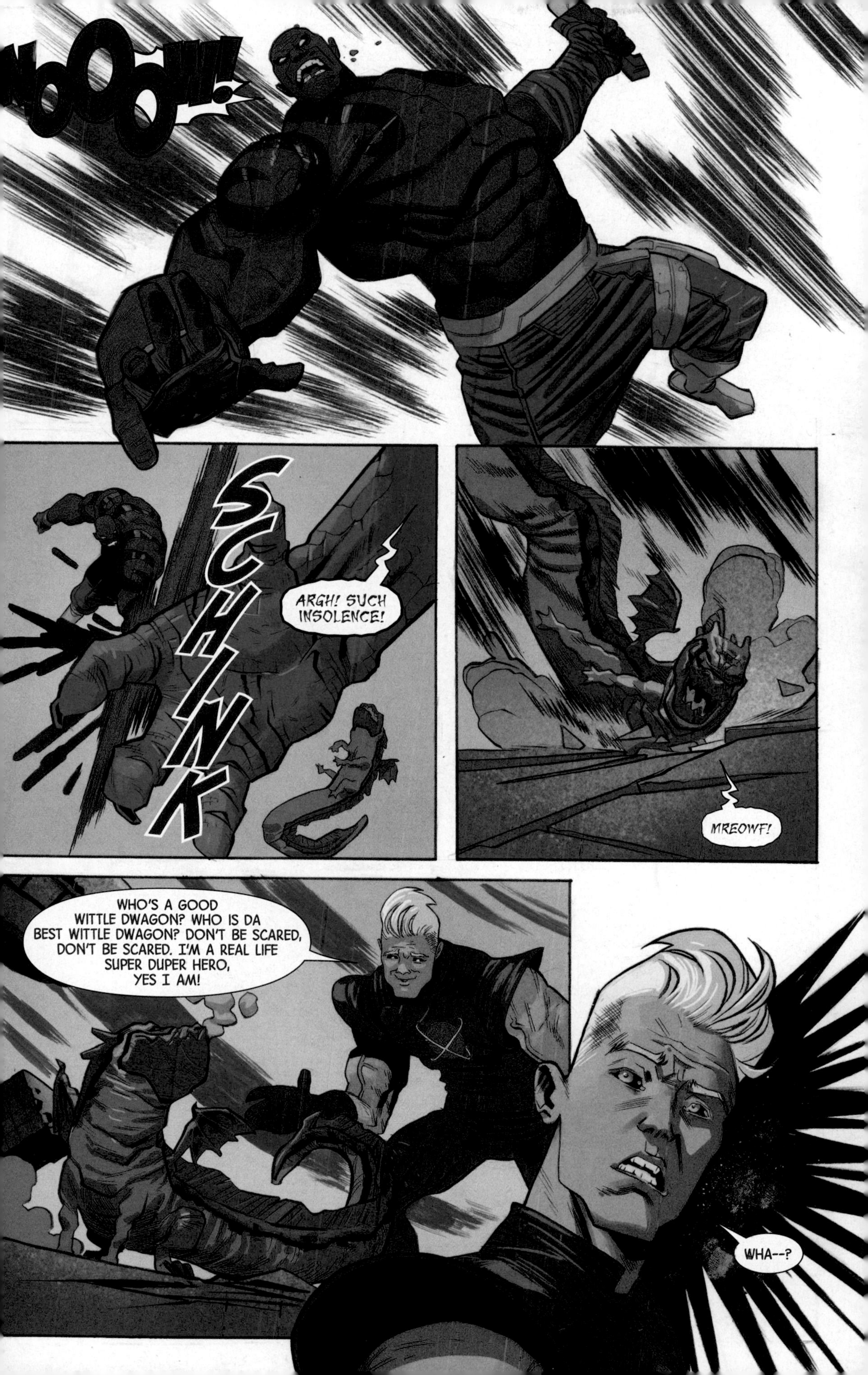
WOOOOH!!
SCHHINK
ARGH! SUCH INSOLENCE!
MREOWF!
WHO'S A GOOD WITTLE DWAGON? WHO IS DA BEST WITTLE DWAGON? DON'T BE SCARED, DON'T BE SCARED. I'M A REAL LIFE SUPER DUPER HERO, YES I AM!
WHA--?

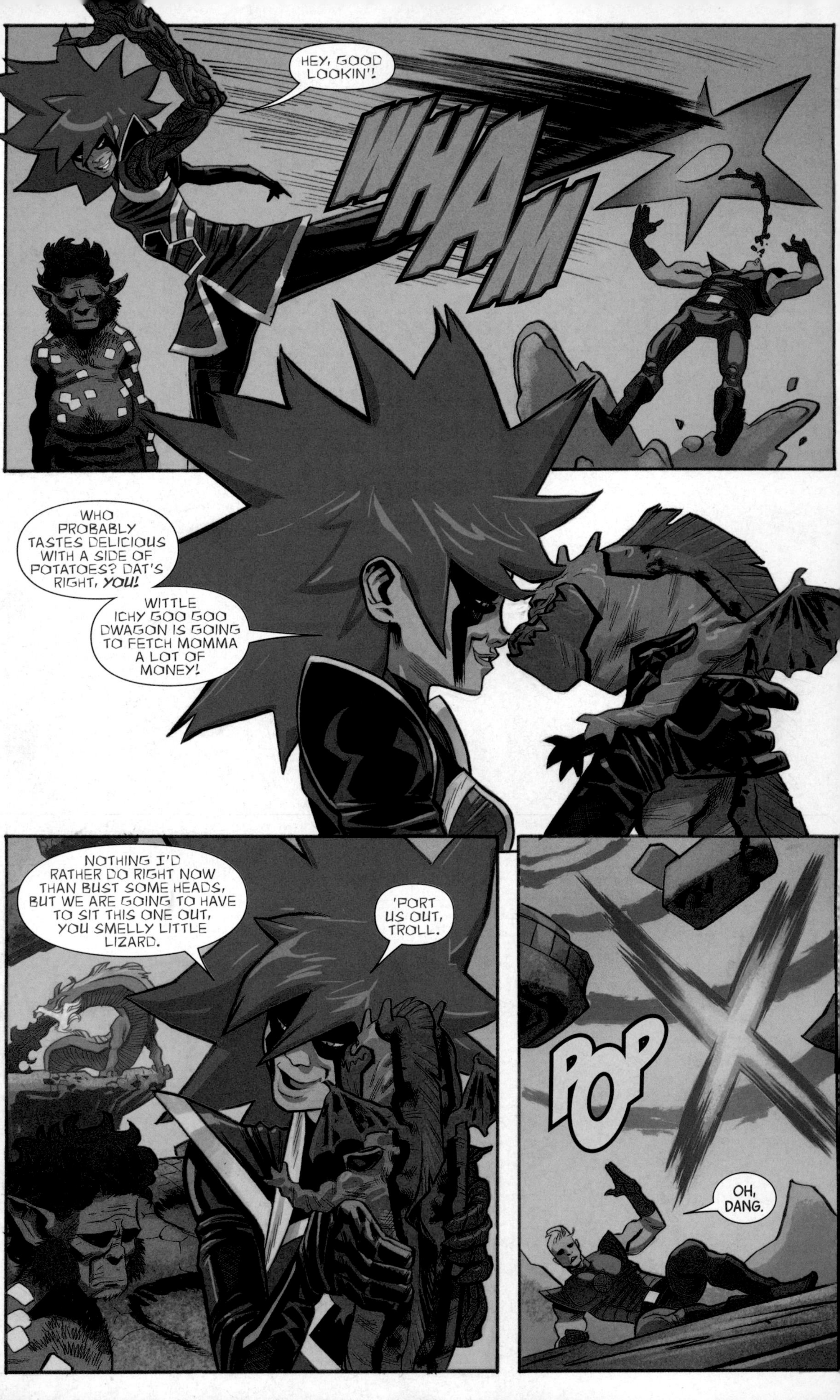
HEY, GOOD LOOKIN'!
WHAM
WHO PROBABLY TASTES DELICIOUS WITH A SIDE OF POTATOES? DAT'S RIGHT, *YOU!*
WITTLE ICHY GOO GOO DWAGON IS GOING TO FETCH MOMMA A LOT OF MONEY!
NOTHING I'D RATHER DO RIGHT NOW THAN BUST SOME HEADS, BUT WE ARE GOING TO HAVE TO SIT THIS ONE OUT, YOU SMELLY LITTLE LIZARD.
'PORT US OUT, TROLL.
POP
OH, DANG.

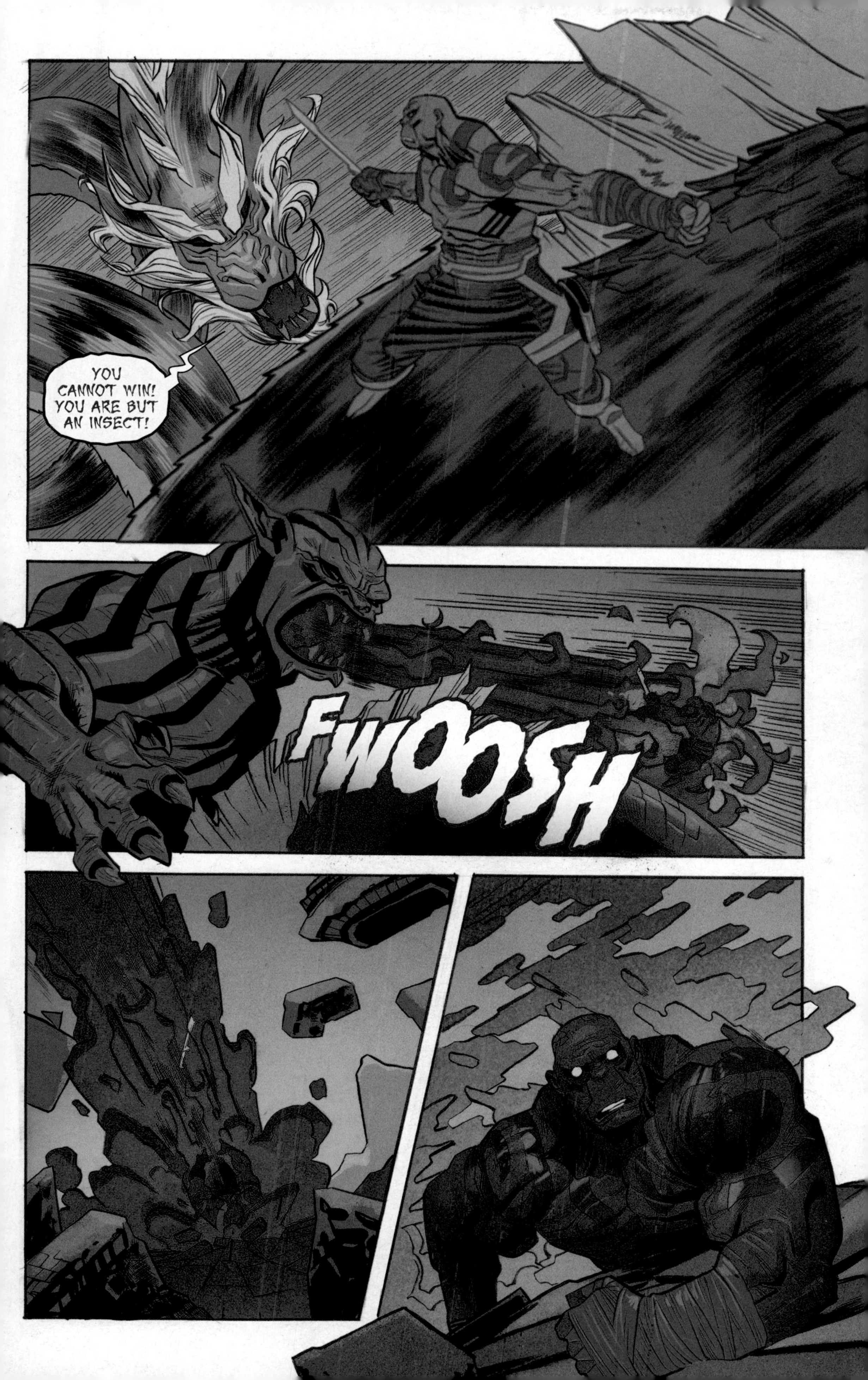
YOU CANNOT WIN! YOU ARE BUT AN INSECT!
FWOOSH

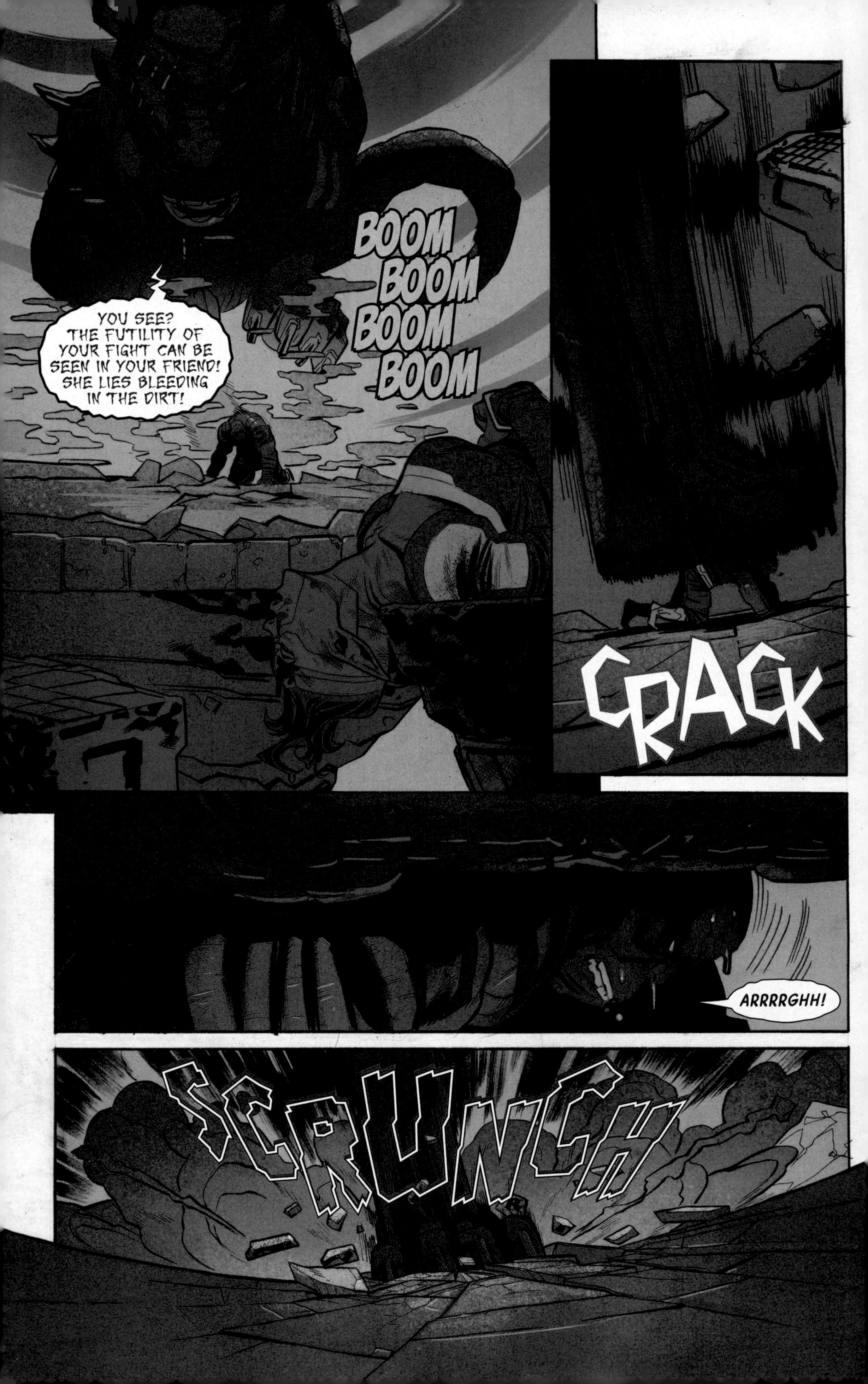
YOU SEE? THE FUTILITY OF YOUR FIGHT CAN BE SEEN IN YOUR FRIEND! SHE LIES BLEEDING IN THE DIRT!
BOOM BOOM BOOM BOOM
CRACK
ARRRRGHH!
SCRUNCH

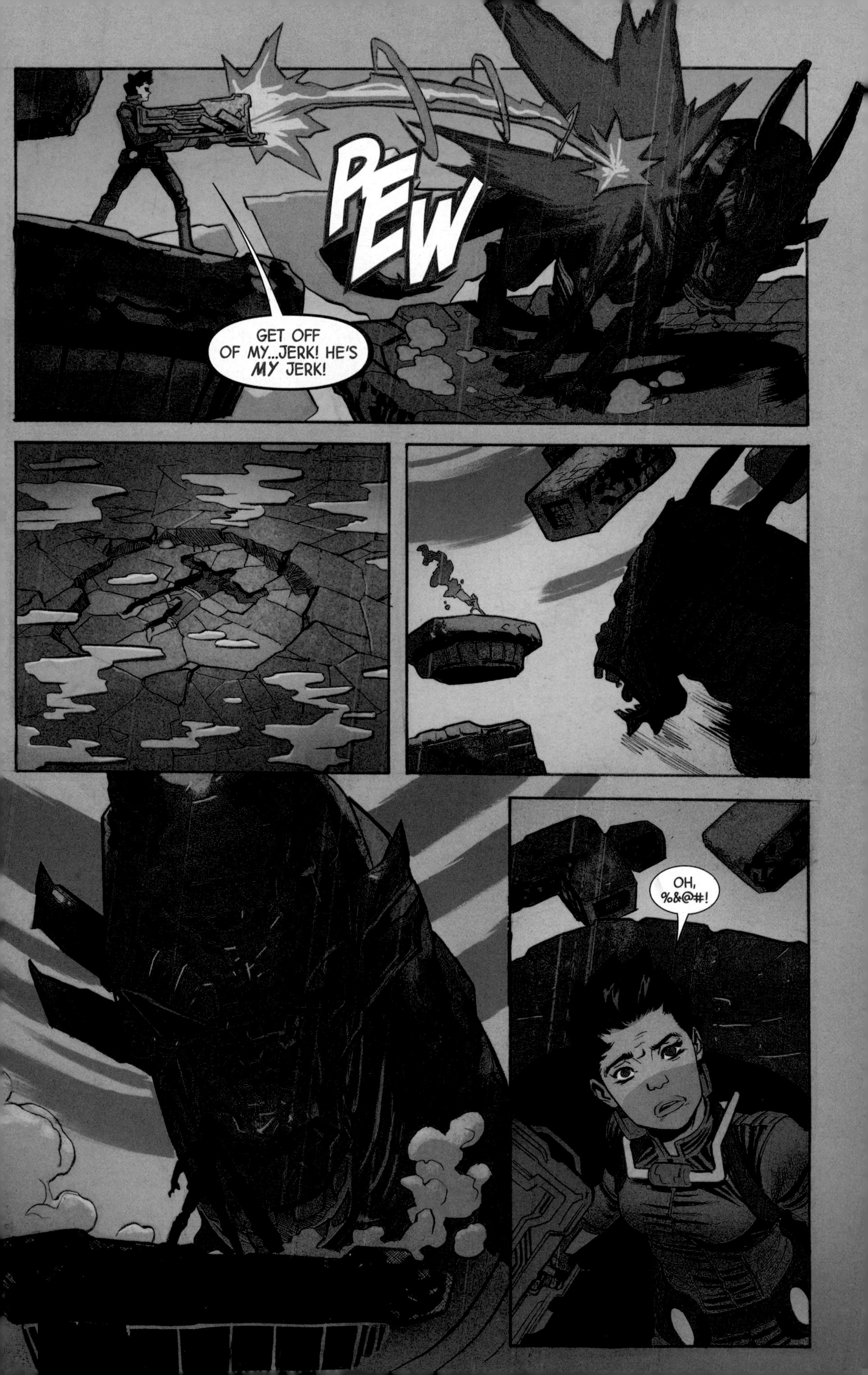
PEW
GET OFF OF MY...JERK! HE'S MY JERK!
OH, %&@#!

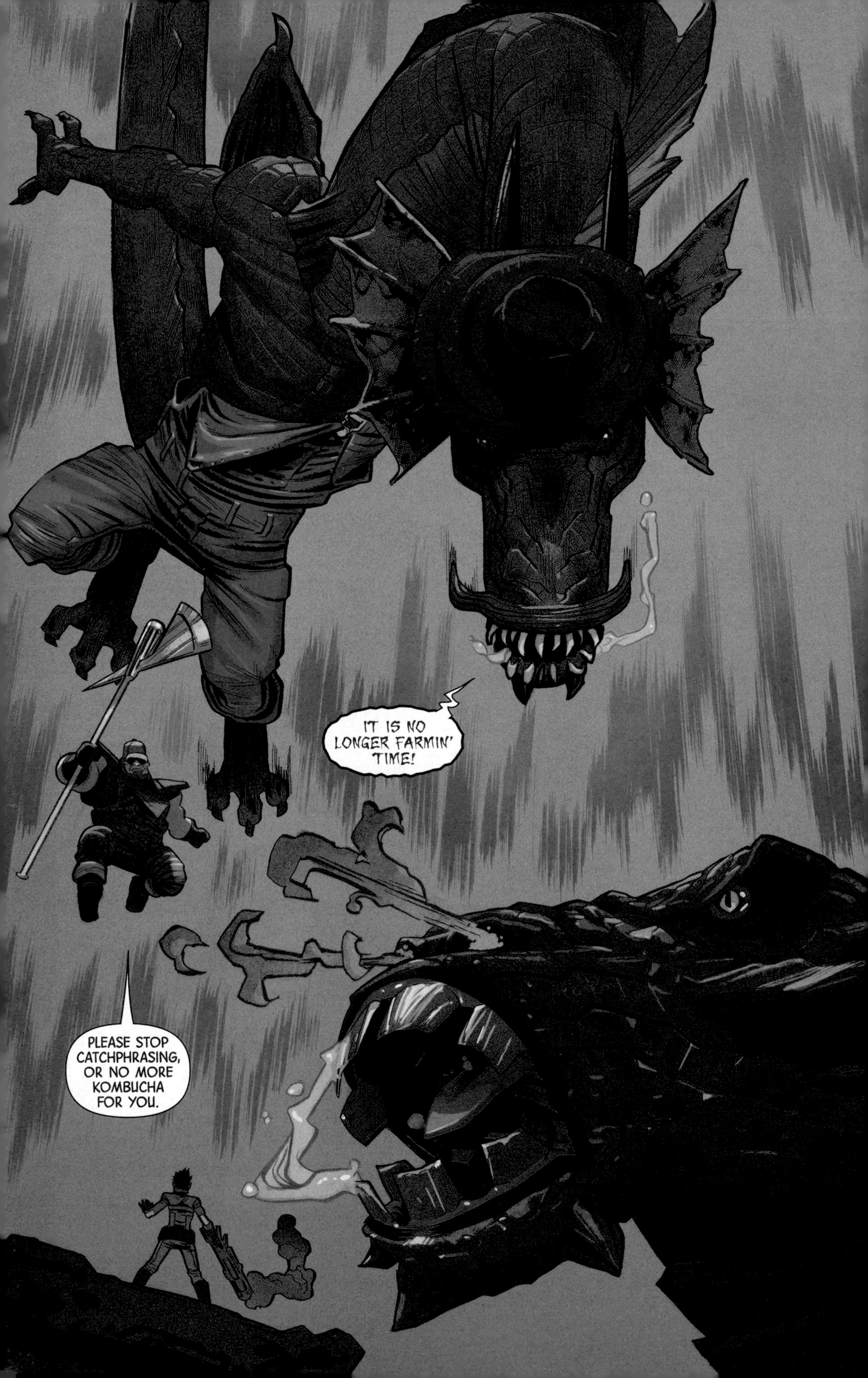
IT IS NO LONGER FARMIN' TIME!
PLEASE STOP CATCHPHRASING, OR NO MORE KOMBUCHA FOR YOU.

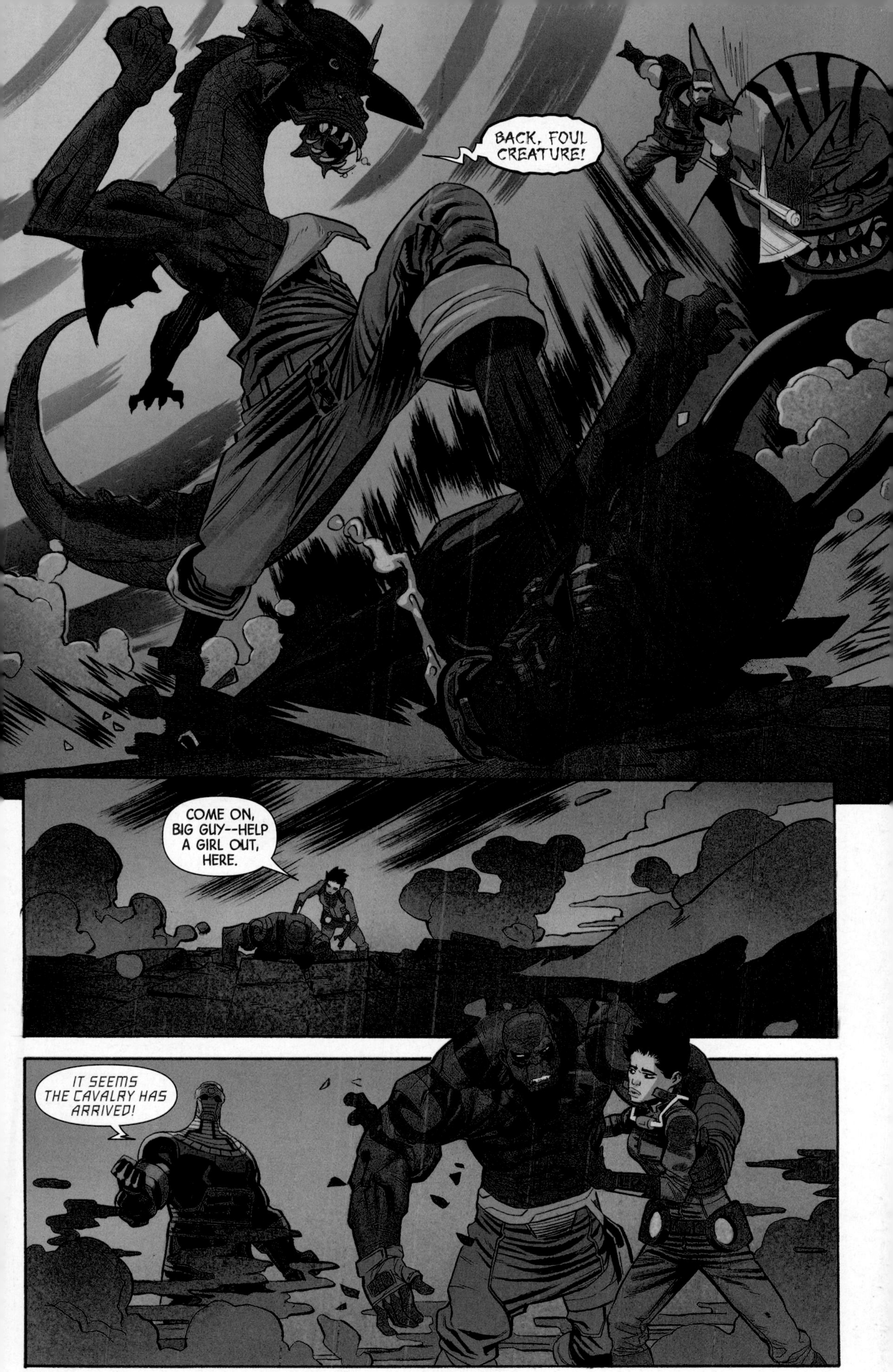
BACK, FOUL CREATURE!
COME ON, BIG GUY--HELP A GIRL OUT, HERE.
IT SEEMS THE CAVALRY HAS ARRIVED!

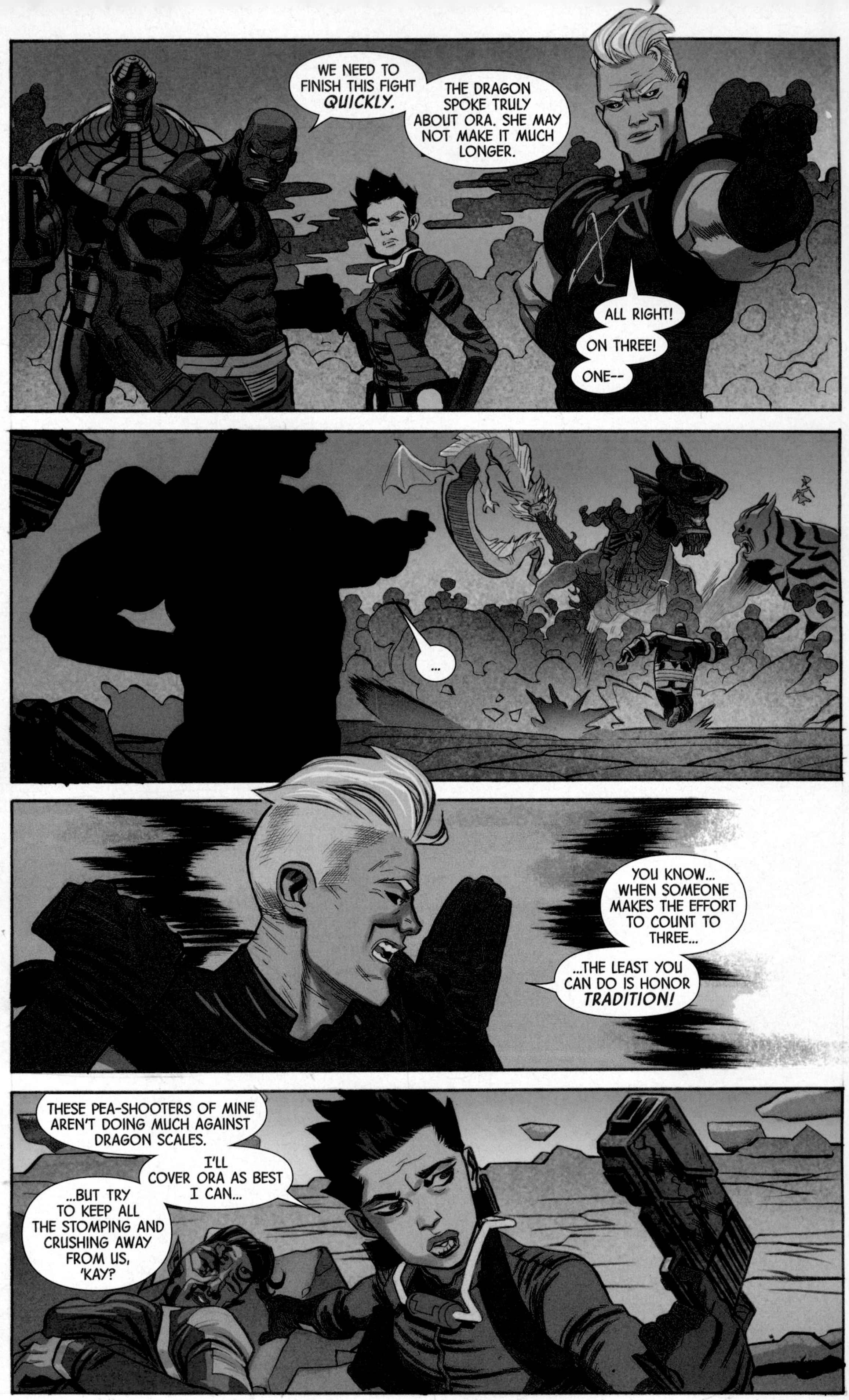
WE NEED TO FINISH THIS FIGHT QUICKLY.
THE DRAGON SPOKE TRULY ABOUT ORA. SHE MAY NOT MAKE IT MUCH LONGER.
ALL RIGHT!
ON THREE!
ONE--
...
YOU KNOW... WHEN SOMEONE MAKES THE EFFORT TO COUNT TO THREE...
...THE LEAST YOU CAN DO IS HONOR TRADITION!
THESE PEA-SHOOTERS OF MINE AREN'T DOING MUCH AGAINST DRAGON SCALES.
I'LL COVER ORA AS BEST I CAN...
...BUT TRY TO KEEP ALL THE STOMPING AND CRUSHING AWAY FROM US, 'KAY?

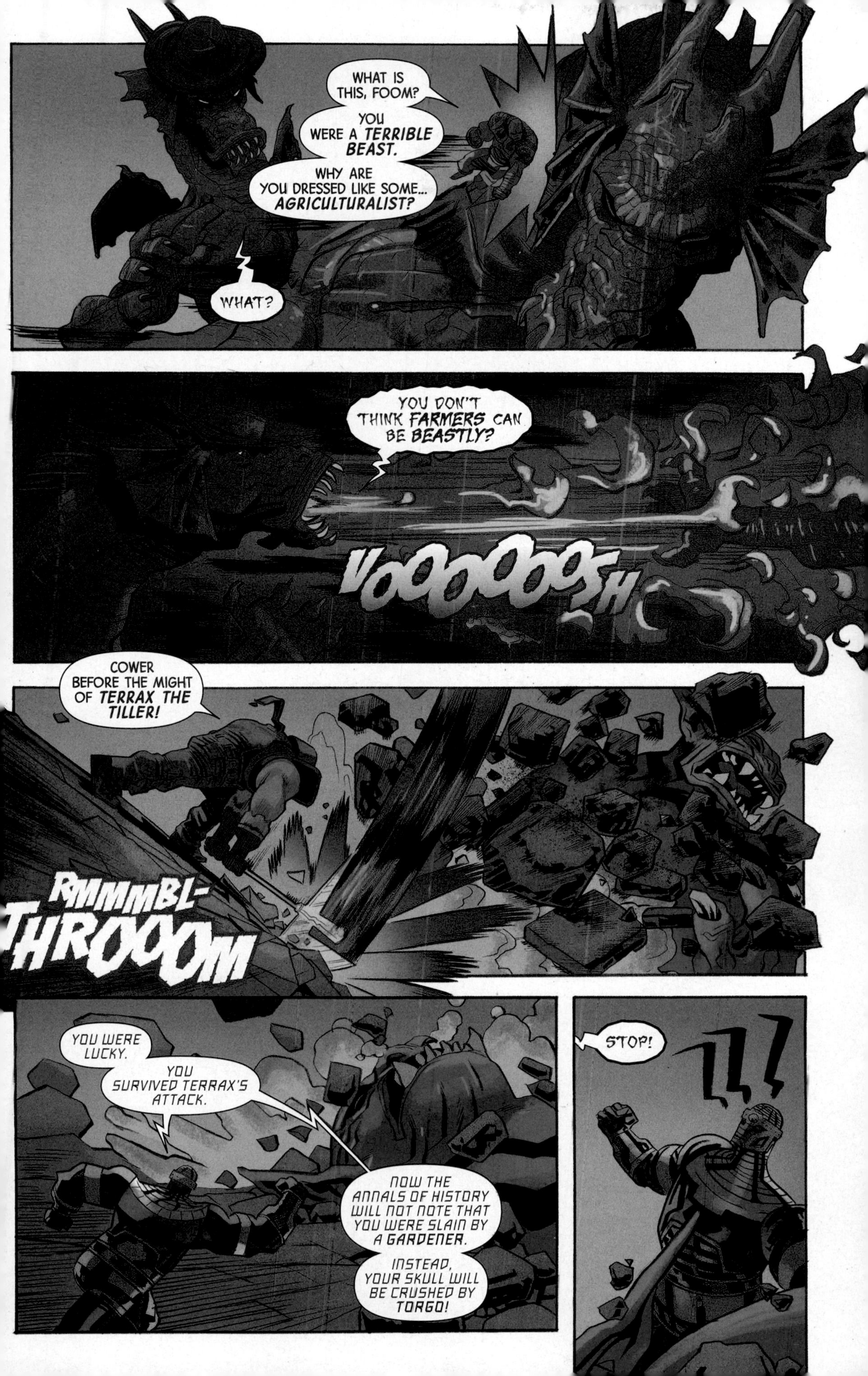
WHAT IS THIS, FOOM?
YOU WERE A TERRIBLE BEAST.
WHY ARE YOU DRESSED LIKE SOME... AGRICULTURALIST?
WHAT?
YOU DON'T THINK FARMERS CAN BE BEASTLY?
VOOOOOOOSH
COWER BEFORE THE MIGHT OF TERRAX THE TILLER!
RMMMBL-THROOOM
YOU WERE LUCKY.
YOU SURVIVED TERRAX'S ATTACK.
NOW THE ANNALS OF HISTORY WILL NOT NOTE THAT YOU WERE SLAIN BY A GARDENER.
INSTEAD, YOUR SKULL WILL BE CRUSHED BY TORGO!
STOP!

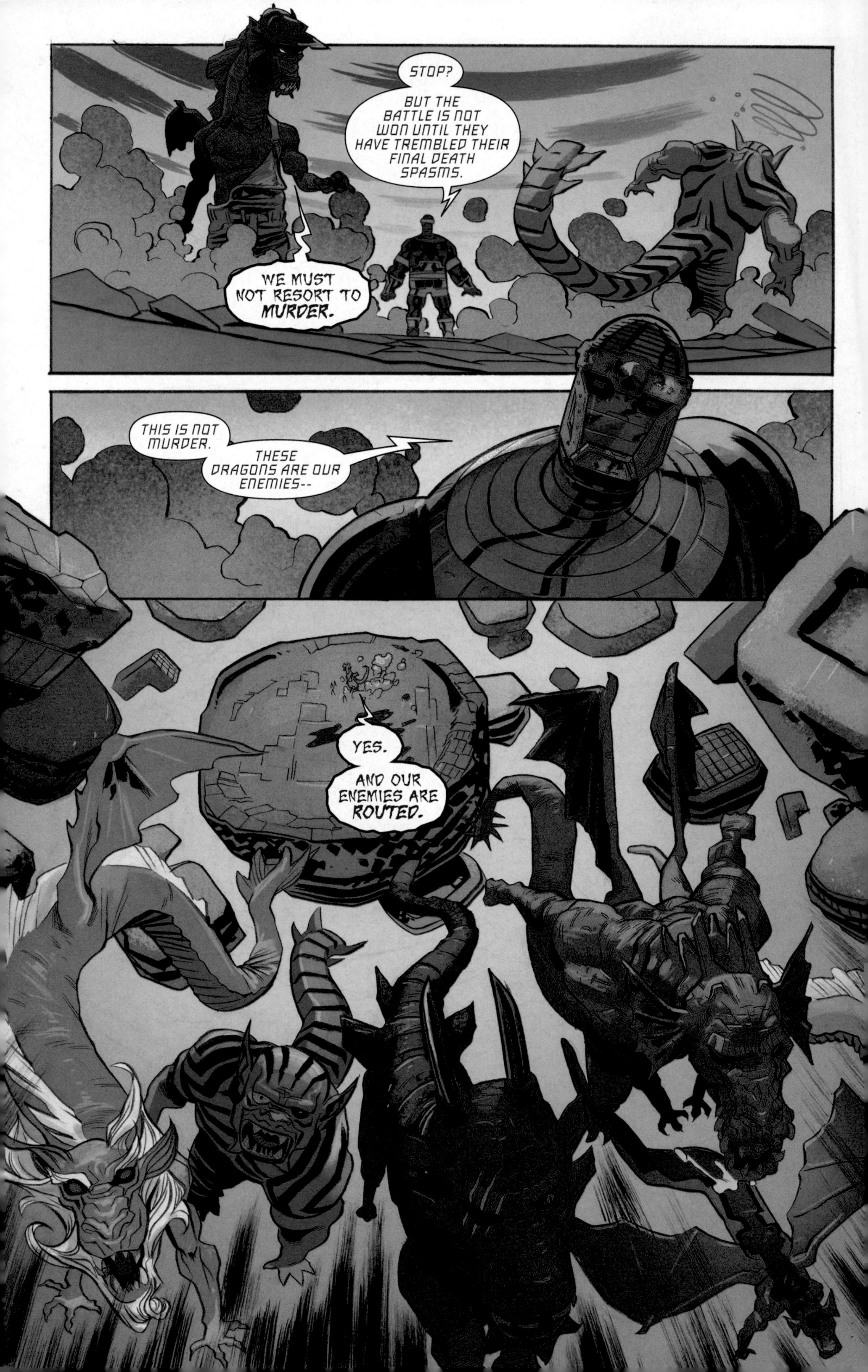
STOP?
BUT THE BATTLE IS NOT WON UNTIL THEY HAVE TREMBLED THEIR FINAL DEATH SPASMS.
WE MUST NOT RESORT TO MURDER.
THIS IS NOT MURDER.
THESE DRAGONS ARE OUR ENEMIES--
YES.
AND OUR ENEMIES ARE ROUTED.

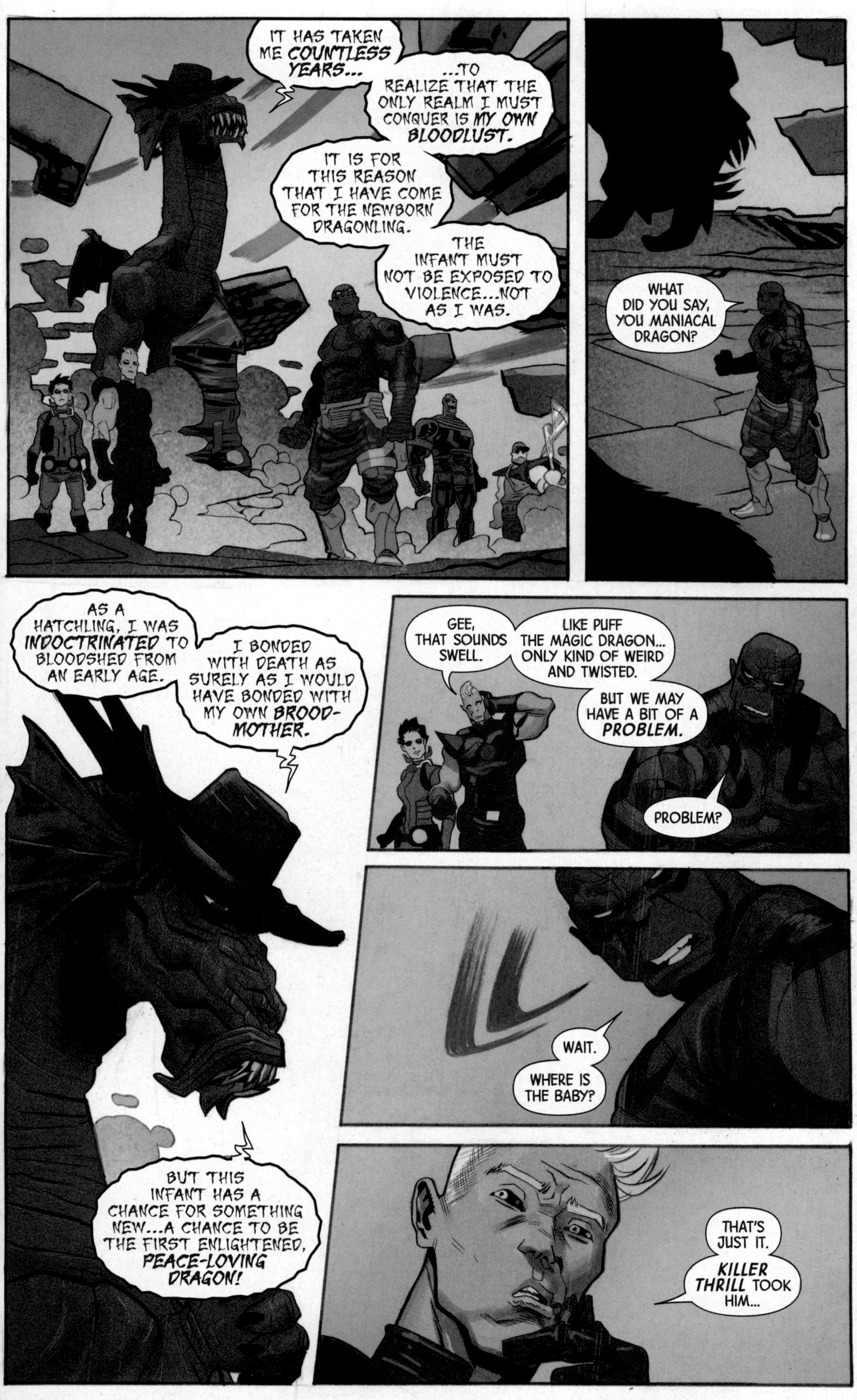
IT HAS TAKEN ME COUNTLESS YEARS...
...TO REALIZE THAT THE ONLY REALM I MUST CONQUER IS MY OWN BLOODLUST.
IT IS FOR THIS REASON THAT I HAVE COME FOR THE NEWBORN DRAGONLING.
THE INFANT MUST NOT BE EXPOSED TO VIOLENCE...NOT AS I WAS.
WHAT DID YOU SAY, YOU MANIACAL DRAGON?
AS A HATCHLING, I WAS INDOCTRINATED TO BLOODSHED FROM AN EARLY AGE.
I BONDED WITH DEATH AS SURELY AS I WOULD HAVE BONDED WITH MY OWN BROOD-MOTHER.
BUT THIS INFANT HAS A CHANCE FOR SOMETHING NEW...A CHANCE TO BE THE FIRST ENLIGHTENED, PEACE-LOVING DRAGON!
GEE, THAT SOUNDS SWELL.
LIKE PUFF THE MAGIC DRAGON... ONLY KIND OF WEIRD AND TWISTED.
BUT WE MAY HAVE A BIT OF A PROBLEM.
PROBLEM?
WAIT.
WHERE IS THE BABY?
THAT'S JUST IT. KILLER THRILL TOOK HIM...

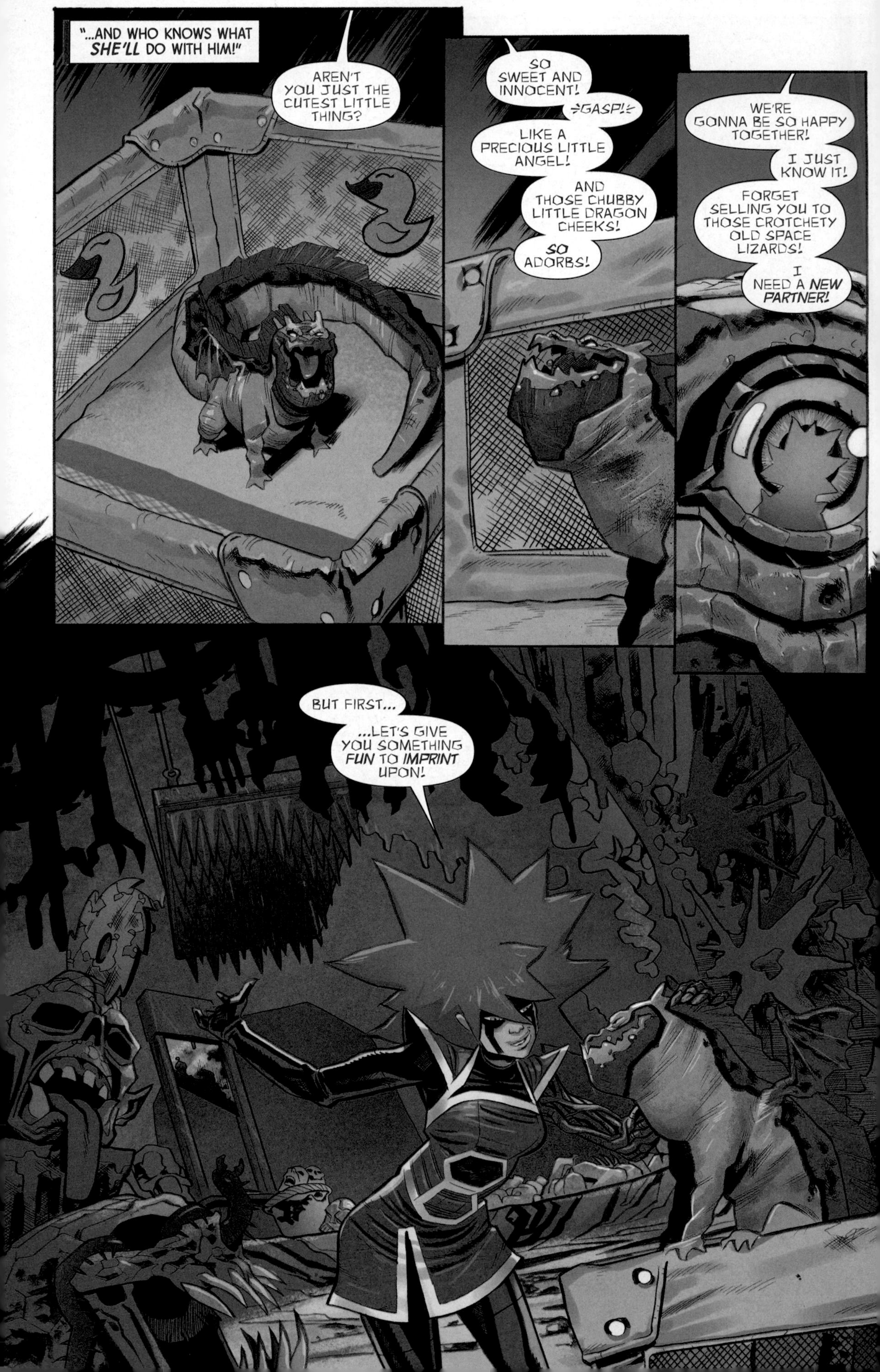

"...AND WHO KNOWS WHAT SHE'LL DO WITH HIM!"
AREN'T YOU JUST THE CUTEST LITTLE THING?
SO SWEET AND INNOCENT!
GASP!
LIKE A PRECIOUS LITTLE ANGEL!
AND THOSE CHUBBY LITTLE DRAGON CHEEKS!
SO ADORBS!
WE'RE GONNA BE SO HAPPY TOGETHER!
I JUST KNOW IT!
FORGET SELLING YOU TO THOSE CROTCHETY OLD SPACE LIZARDS!
I NEED A NEW PARTNER!
BUT FIRST...
...LET'S GIVE YOU SOMETHING FUN TO IMPRINT UPON!

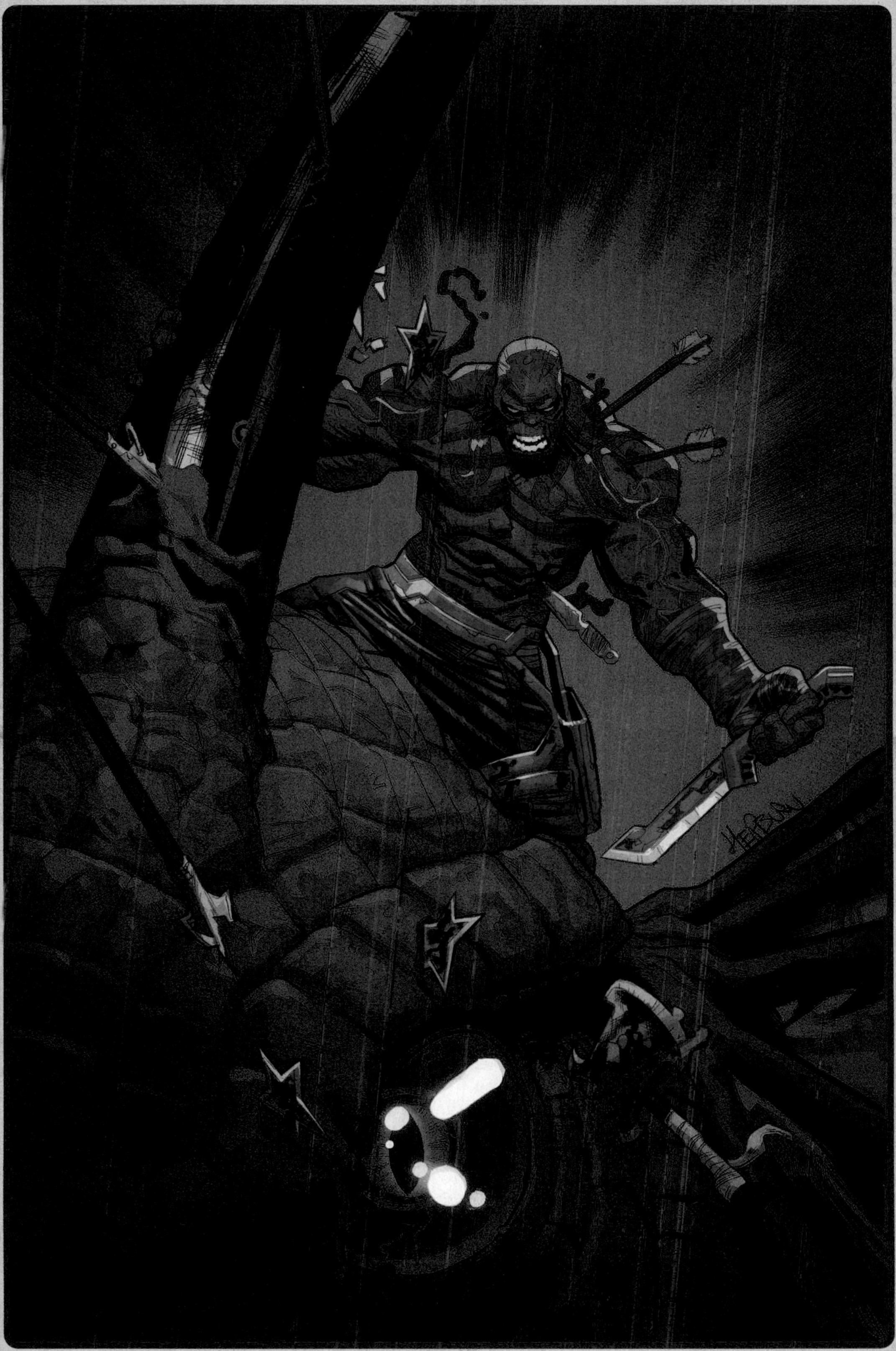

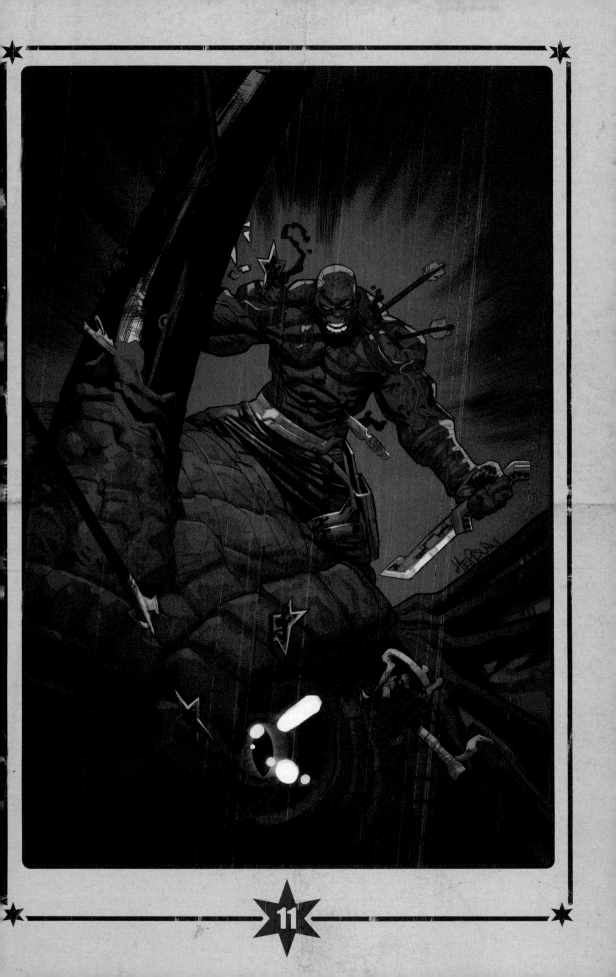

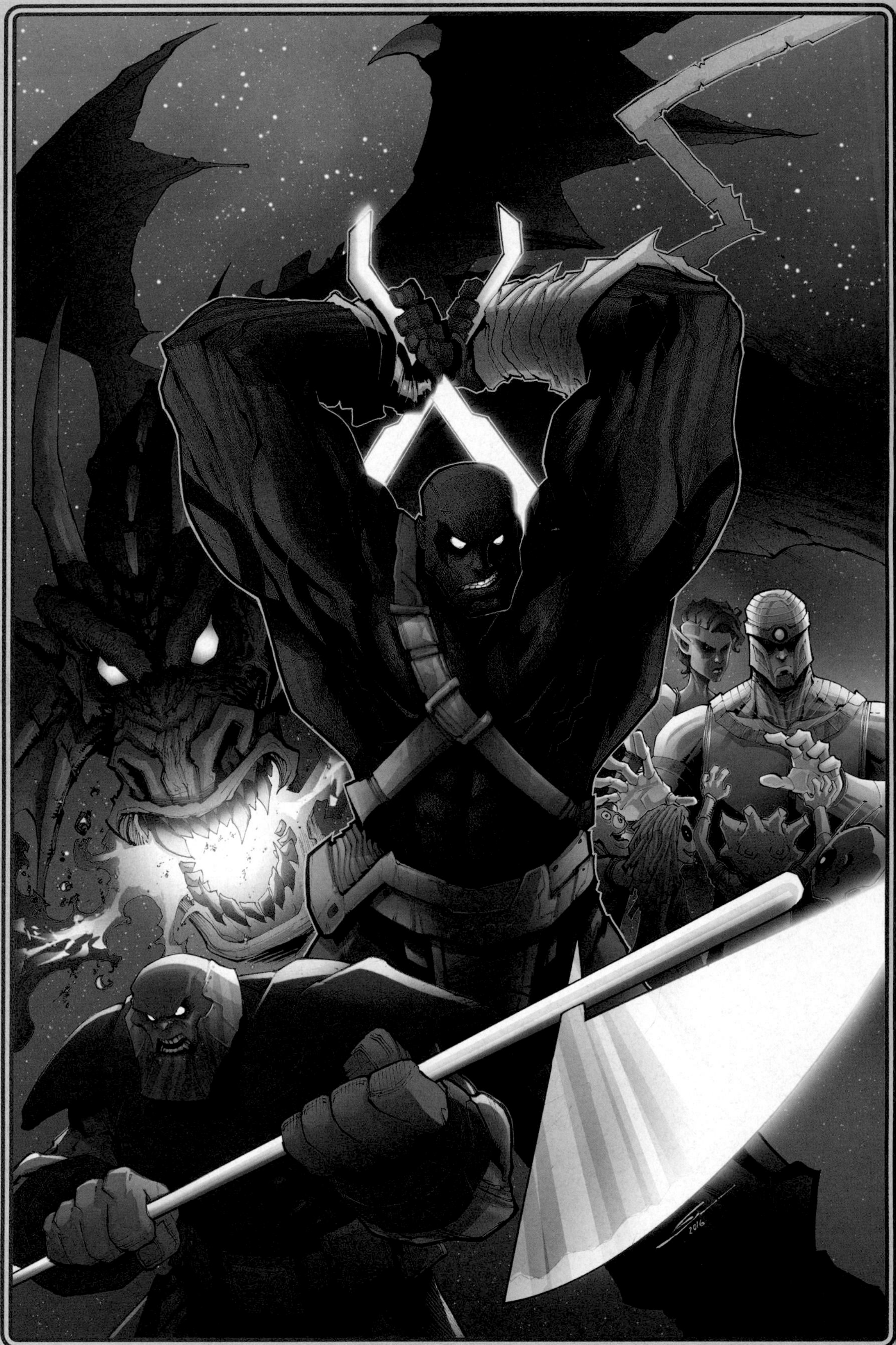

#6 STORY THUS FAR VARIANT

GERARDO SANDOVAL

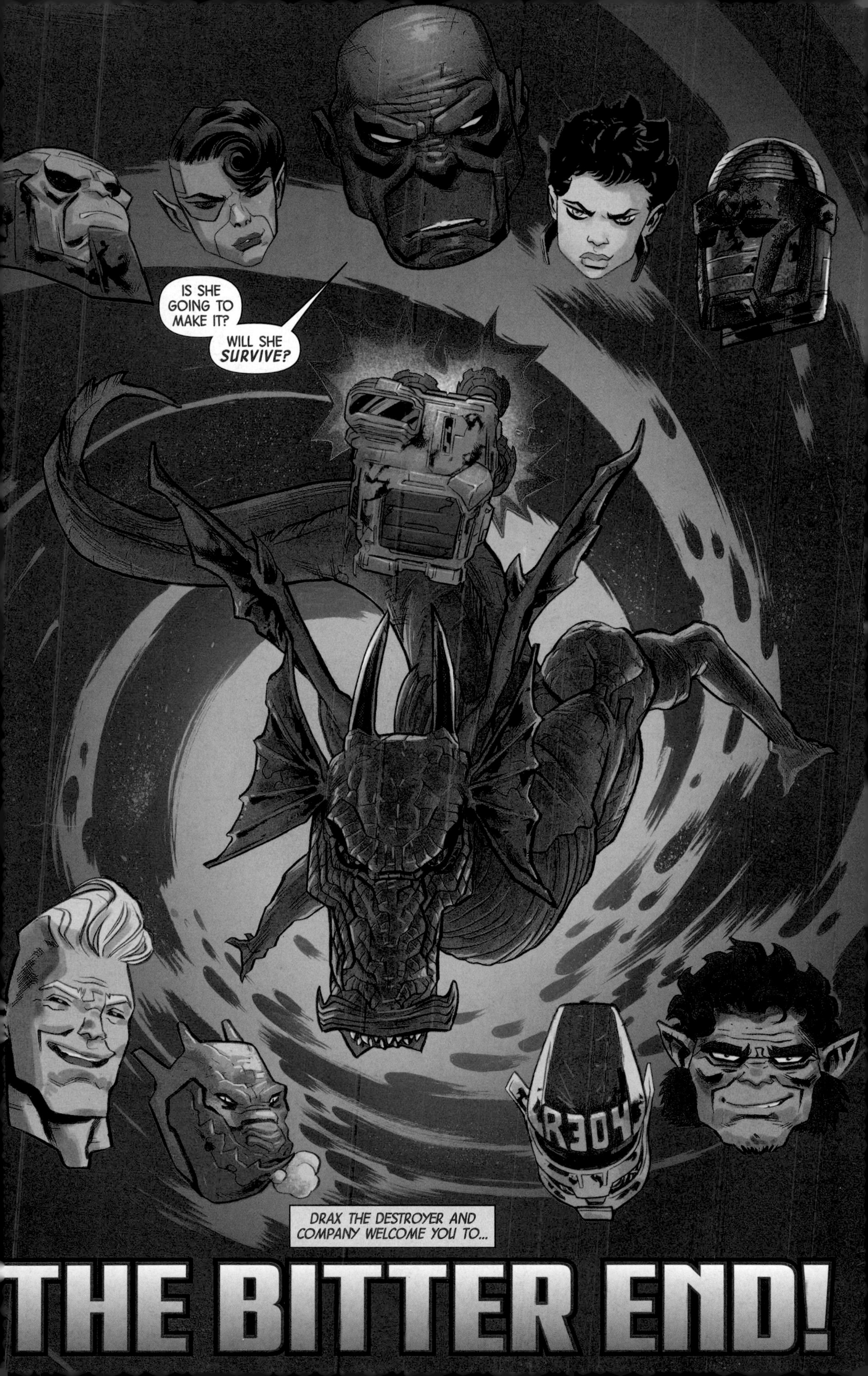
IS SHE GOING TO MAKE IT?
WILL SHE SURVIVE?
DRAX THE DESTROYER AND COMPANY WELCOME YOU TO...
THE BITTER END!

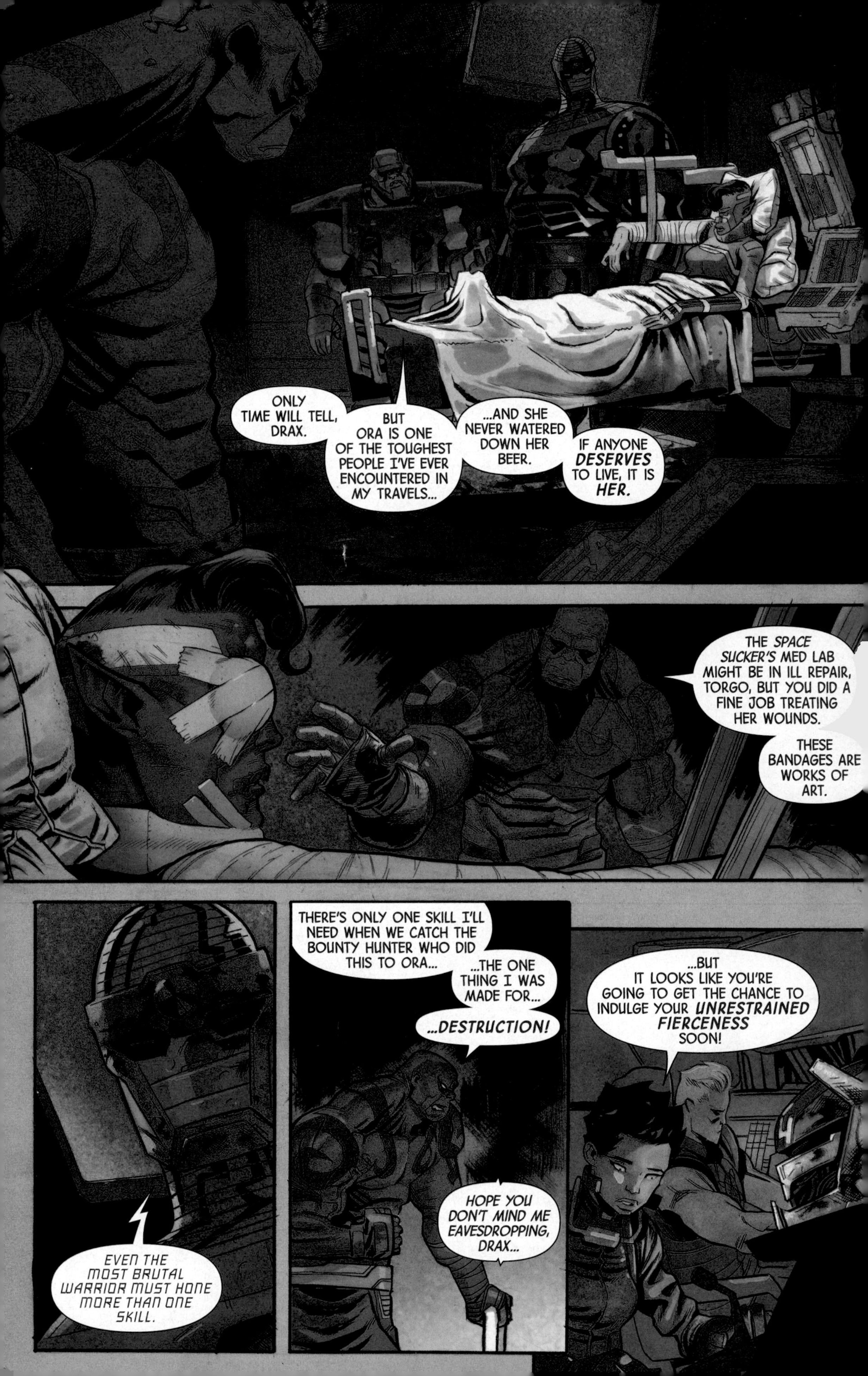

ONLY TIME WILL TELL, DRAX.
BUT ORA IS ONE OF THE TOUGHEST PEOPLE I'VE EVER ENCOUNTERED IN MY TRAVELS...
...AND SHE NEVER WATERED DOWN HER BEER.
IF ANYONE DESERVES TO LIVE, IT IS HER.
THE SPACE SUCKER'S MED LAB MIGHT BE IN ILL REPAIR, TORGO, BUT YOU DID A FINE JOB TREATING HER WOUNDS.
THESE BANDAGES ARE WORKS OF ART.
EVEN THE MOST BRUTAL WARRIOR MUST HONE MORE THAN ONE SKILL.
THERE'S ONLY ONE SKILL I'LL NEED WHEN WE CATCH THE BOUNTY HUNTER WHO DID THIS TO ORA...
...THE ONE THING I WAS MADE FOR...
...DESTRUCTION!
HOPE YOU DON'T MIND ME EAVESDROPPING, DRAX...
...BUT IT LOOKS LIKE YOU'RE GOING TO GET THE CHANCE TO INDULGE YOUR UNRESTRAINED FIERCENESS SOON!

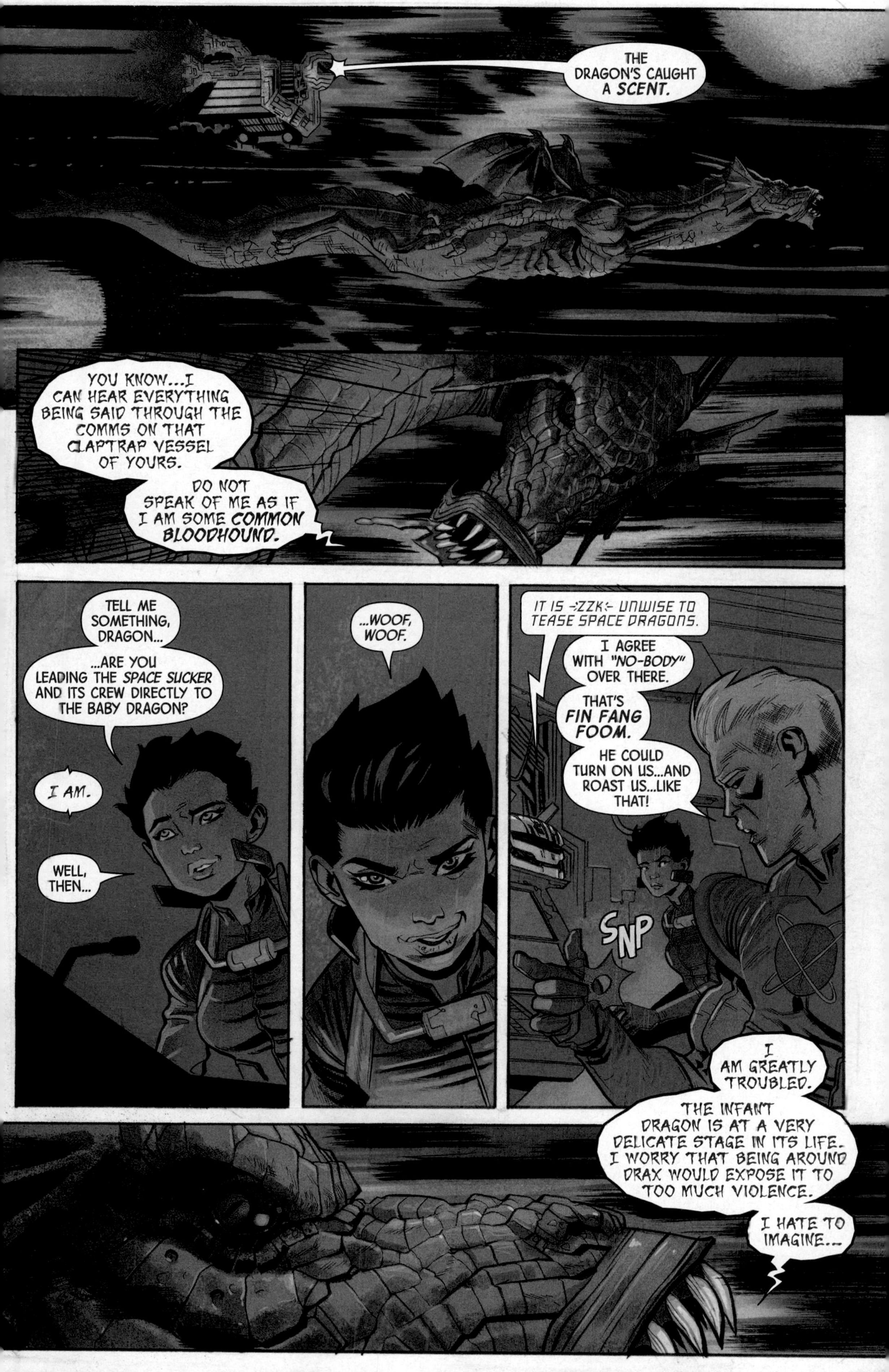
THE DRAGON'S CAUGHT A SCENT.
YOU KNOW...I CAN HEAR EVERYTHING BEING SAID THROUGH THE COMMS ON THAT CLAPTRAP VESSEL OF YOURS.
DO NOT SPEAK OF ME AS IF I AM SOME COMMON BLOODHOUND.
TELL ME SOMETHING, DRAGON...
...ARE YOU LEADING THE SPACE SUCKER AND ITS CREW DIRECTLY TO THE BABY DRAGON?
I AM.
WELL, THEN...
...WOOF, WOOF.
IT IS -ZZK- UNWISE TO TEASE SPACE DRAGONS.
I AGREE WITH "NO-BODY" OVER THERE.
THAT'S FIN FANG FOOM.
HE COULD TURN ON US...AND ROAST US...LIKE THAT!
SNP
I AM GREATLY TROUBLED.
THE INFANT DRAGON IS AT A VERY DELICATE STAGE IN ITS LIFE. I WORRY THAT BEING AROUND DRAX WOULD EXPOSE IT TO TOO MUCH VIOLENCE.
I HATE TO IMAGINE...

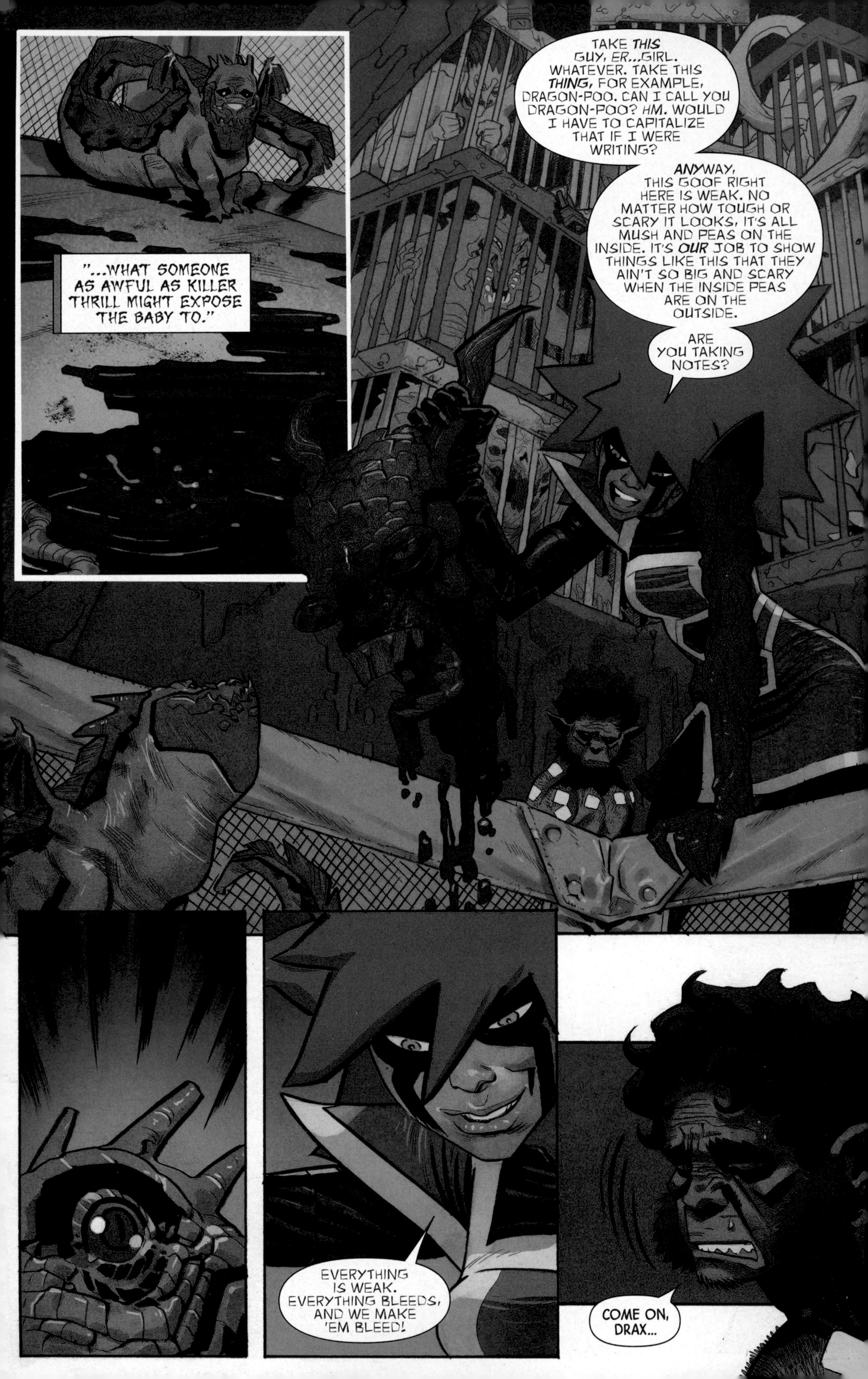
"...WHAT SOMEONE AS AWFUL AS KILLER THRILL MIGHT EXPOSE THE BABY TO."
TAKE *THIS* GUY, *ER*...GIRL. WHATEVER. TAKE THIS *THING*, FOR EXAMPLE, DRAGON-POO. CAN I CALL YOU DRAGON-POO? *HM.* WOULD I HAVE TO CAPITALIZE THAT IF I WERE WRITING?
ANYWAY, THIS GOOF RIGHT HERE IS WEAK. NO MATTER HOW TOUGH OR SCARY IT LOOKS, IT'S ALL MUSH AND PEAS ON THE INSIDE. IT'S *OUR* JOB TO SHOW THINGS LIKE THIS THAT THEY AIN'T SO BIG AND SCARY WHEN THE INSIDE PEAS ARE ON THE OUTSIDE.
ARE YOU TAKING NOTES?
EVERYTHING IS WEAK. EVERYTHING BLEEDS, AND WE MAKE 'EM BLEED!
COME ON, DRAX...

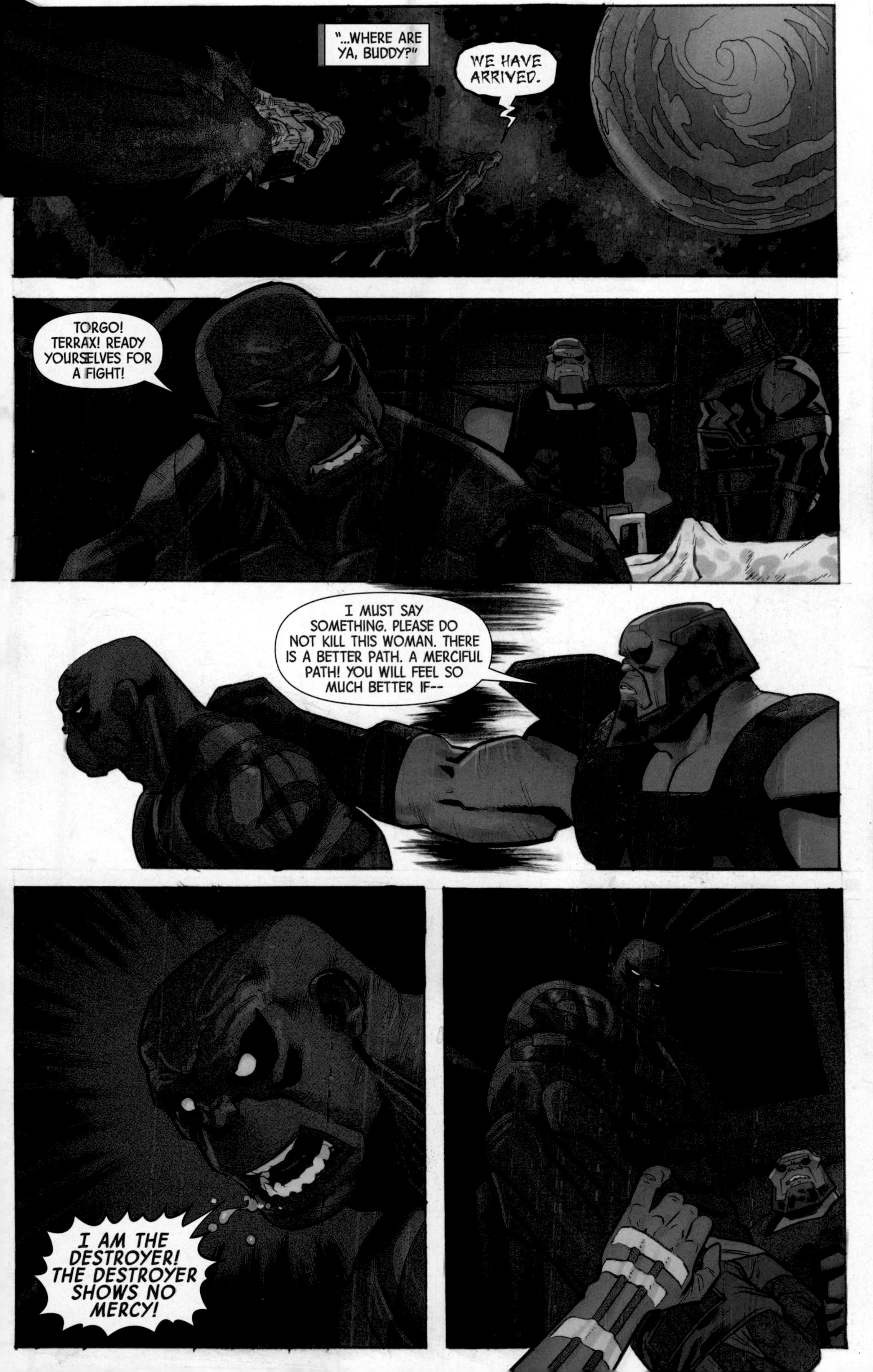
"...WHERE ARE YA, BUDDY?"
WE HAVE ARRIVED.
TORGO! TERRAX! READY YOURSELVES FOR A FIGHT!
I MUST SAY SOMETHING. PLEASE DO NOT KILL THIS WOMAN. THERE IS A BETTER PATH. A MERCIFUL PATH! YOU WILL FEEL SO MUCH BETTER IF--
I AM THE DESTROYER! THE DESTROYER SHOWS NO MERCY!

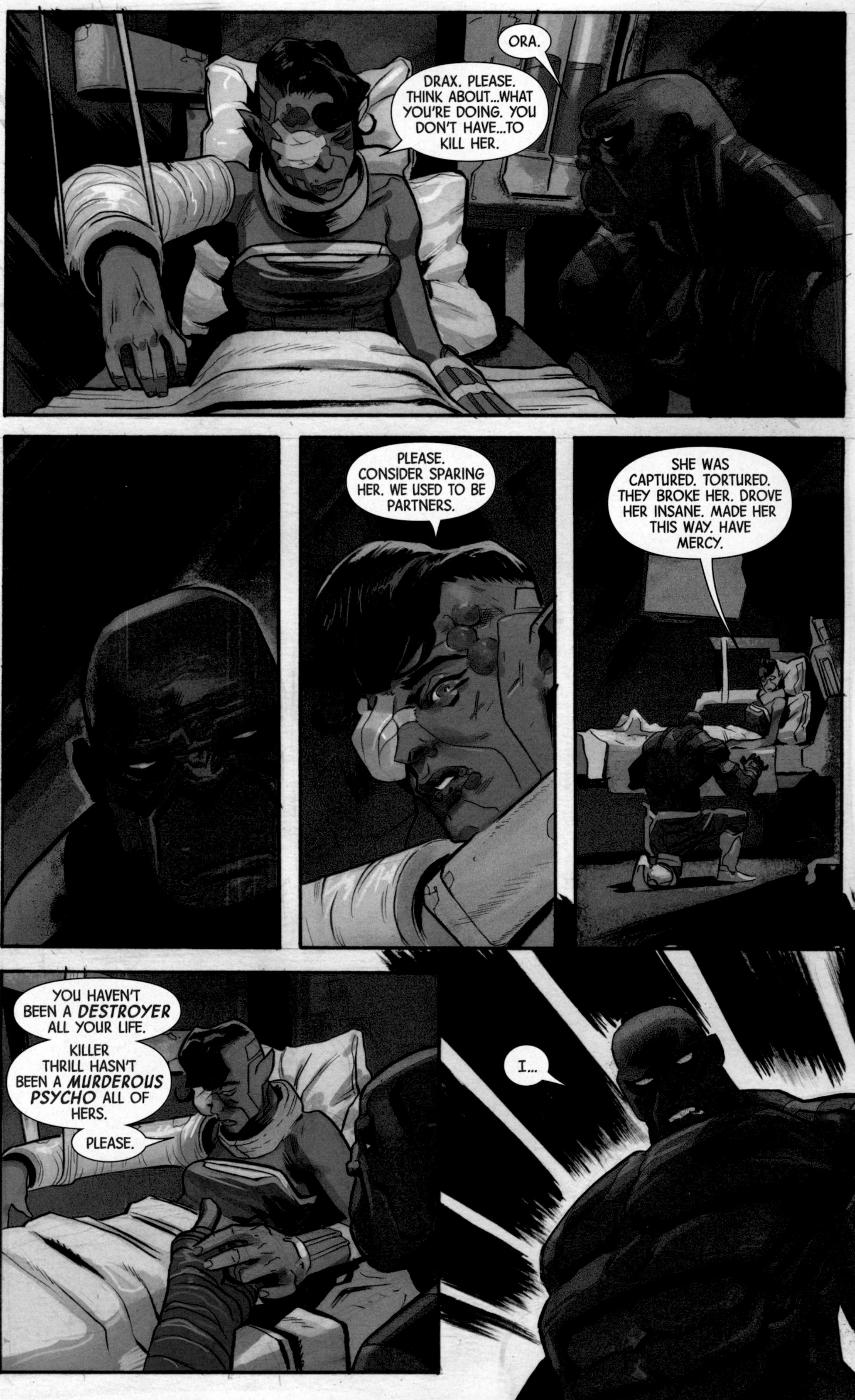
ORA.
DRAX. PLEASE. THINK ABOUT...WHAT YOU'RE DOING. YOU DON'T HAVE...TO KILL HER.
PLEASE. CONSIDER SPARING HER. WE USED TO BE PARTNERS.
SHE WAS CAPTURED. TORTURED. THEY BROKE HER. DROVE HER INSANE. MADE HER THIS WAY. HAVE MERCY.
YOU HAVEN'T BEEN A DESTROYER ALL YOUR LIFE.
KILLER THRILL HASN'T BEEN A MURDEROUS PSYCHO ALL OF HERS.
PLEASE.
I...

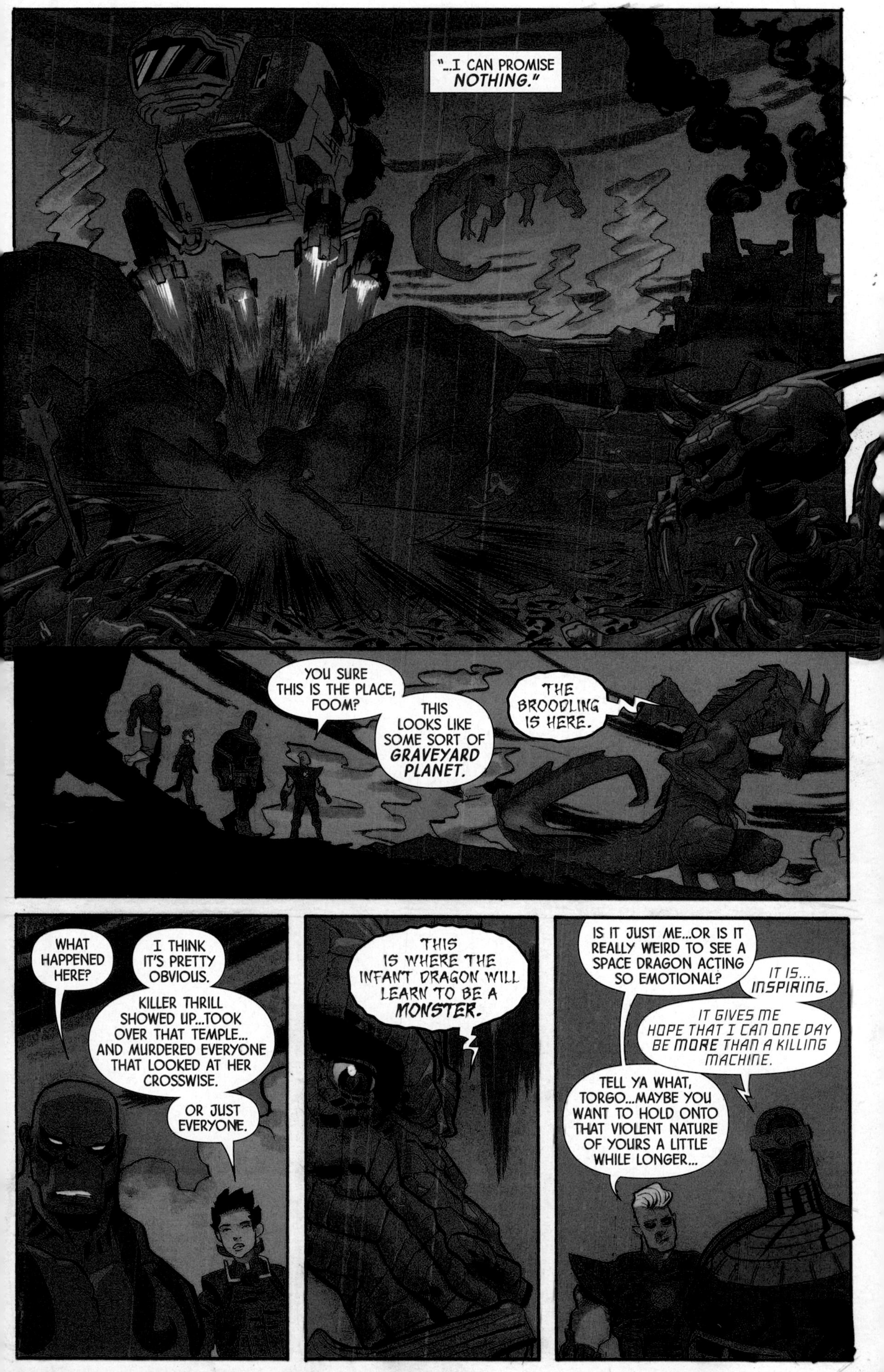
"...I CAN PROMISE NOTHING."
YOU SURE THIS IS THE PLACE, FOOM?
THIS LOOKS LIKE SOME SORT OF GRAVEYARD PLANET.
THE BROODLING IS HERE.
WHAT HAPPENED HERE?
I THINK IT'S PRETTY OBVIOUS.
KILLER THRILL SHOWED UP...TOOK OVER THAT TEMPLE... AND MURDERED EVERYONE THAT LOOKED AT HER CROSSWISE.
OR JUST EVERYONE.
THIS IS WHERE THE INFANT DRAGON WILL LEARN TO BE A MONSTER.
IS IT JUST ME...OR IS IT REALLY WEIRD TO SEE A SPACE DRAGON ACTING SO EMOTIONAL?
IT IS... INSPIRING.
IT GIVES ME HOPE THAT I CAN ONE DAY BE MORE THAN A KILLING MACHINE.
TELL YA WHAT, TORGO...MAYBE YOU WANT TO HOLD ONTO THAT VIOLENT NATURE OF YOURS A LITTLE WHILE LONGER...

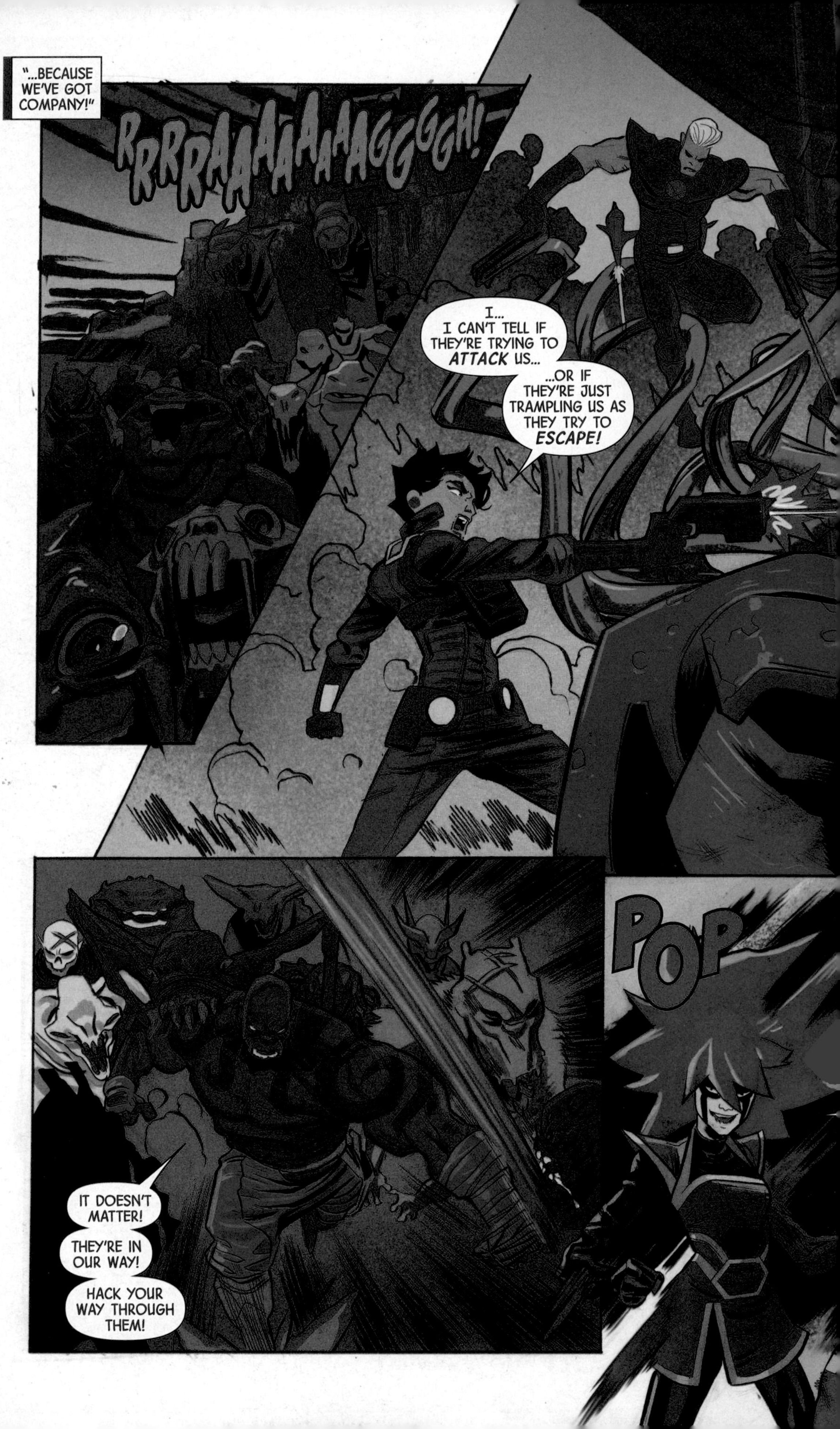
"...BECAUSE WE'VE GOT COMPANY!"
RRRRAAAAAAAAGGGGH!
I... I CAN'T TELL IF THEY'RE TRYING TO ATTACK US...
...OR IF THEY'RE JUST TRAMPLING US AS THEY TRY TO ESCAPE!
IT DOESN'T MATTER!
THEY'RE IN OUR WAY!
HACK YOUR WAY THROUGH THEM!
POP

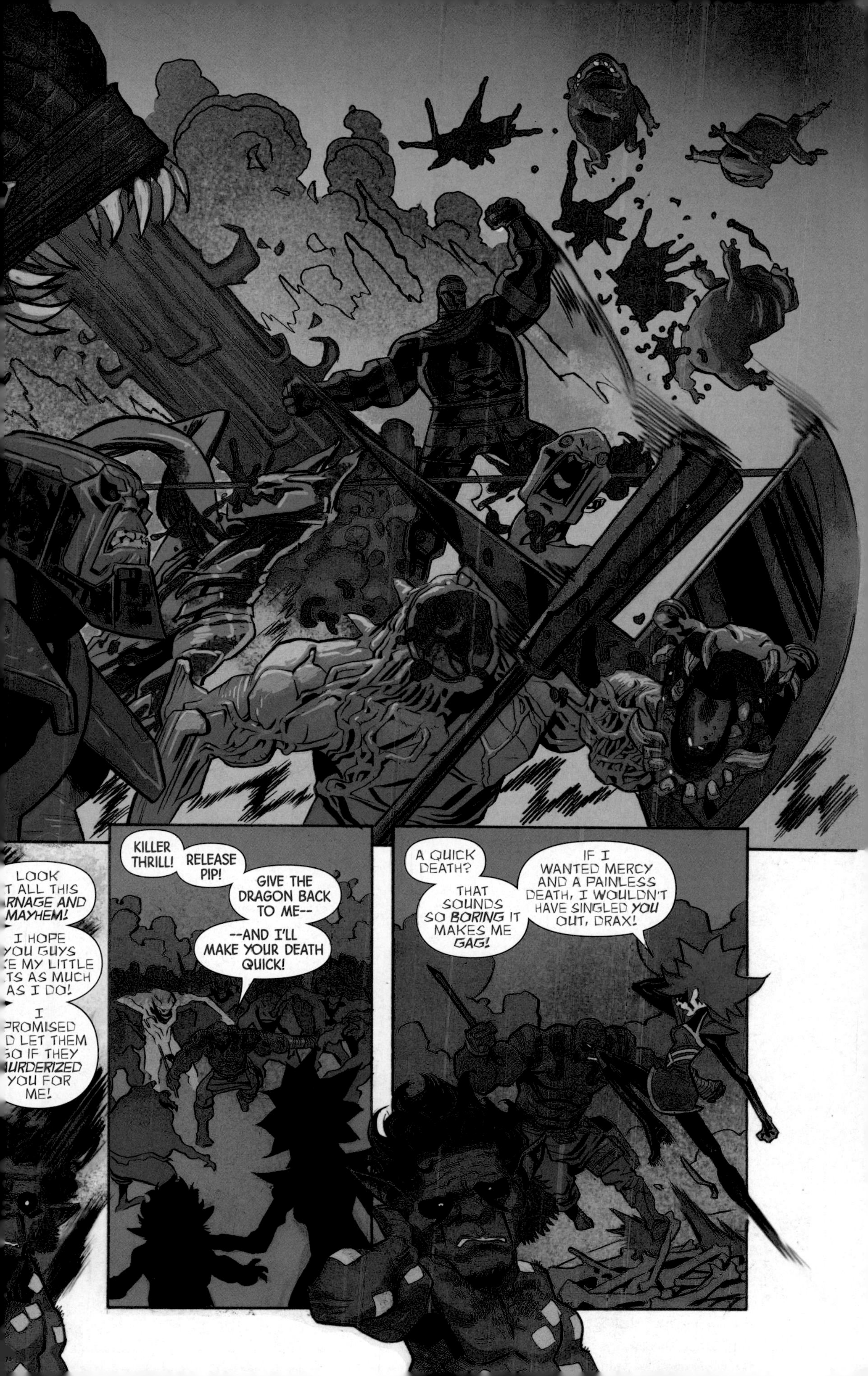
LOOK
T ALL THIS
ARNAGE AND
MAYHEM!
I HOPE
YOU GUYS
E MY LITTLE
TS AS MUCH
AS I DO!
I
PROMISED
D LET THEM
GO IF THEY
URDERIZED
YOU FOR
ME!
KILLER THRILL!
RELEASE PIP!
GIVE THE DRAGON BACK TO ME--
--AND I'LL MAKE YOUR DEATH QUICK!
A QUICK DEATH?
THAT SOUNDS SO BORING IT MAKES ME GAG!
IF I WANTED MERCY AND A PAINLESS DEATH, I WOULDN'T HAVE SINGLED YOU OUT, DRAX!

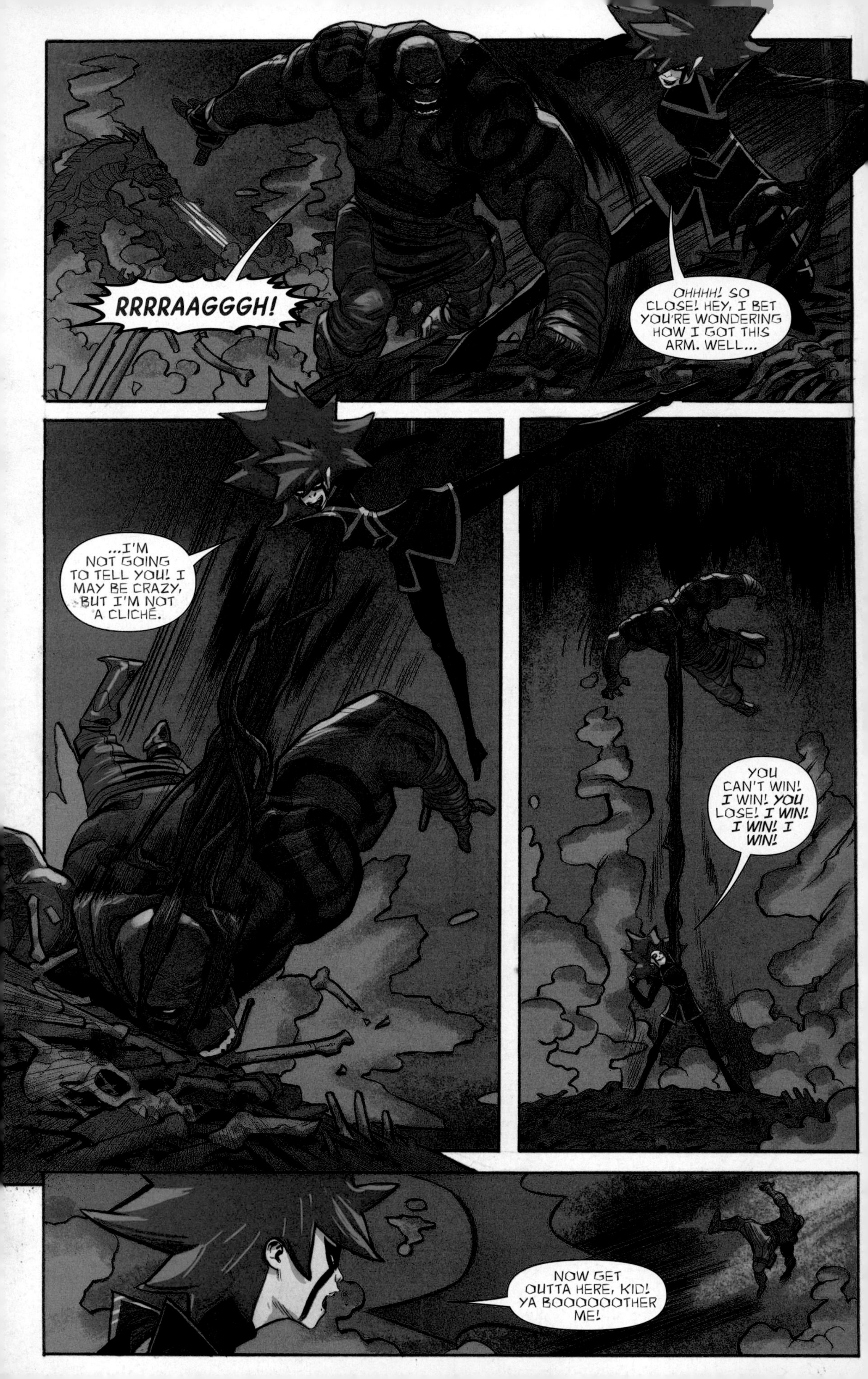
RRRRAAGGGH!
OHHHH! SO CLOSE! HEY, I BET YOU'RE WONDERING HOW I GOT THIS ARM. WELL...
...I'M NOT GOING TO TELL YOU! I MAY BE CRAZY, BUT I'M NOT A CLICHÉ.
YOU CAN'T WIN! I WIN! YOU LOSE! I WIN! I WIN! I WIN!
NOW GET OUTTA HERE, KID! YA BOOOOOOOTHER ME!

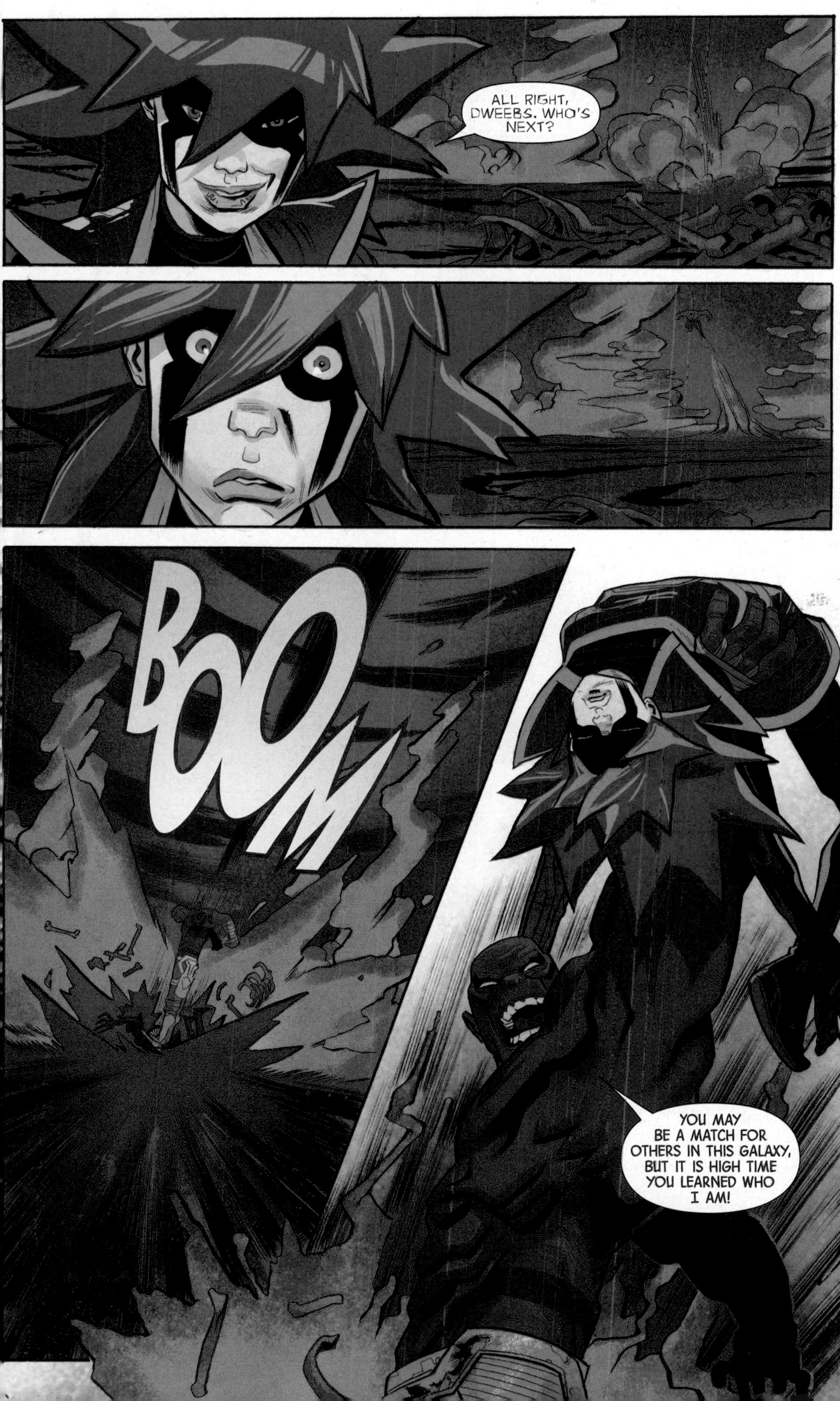
ALL RIGHT, DWEEBS. WHO'S NEXT?
BOOM
YOU MAY BE A MATCH FOR OTHERS IN THIS GALAXY, BUT IT IS HIGH TIME YOU LEARNED WHO I AM!

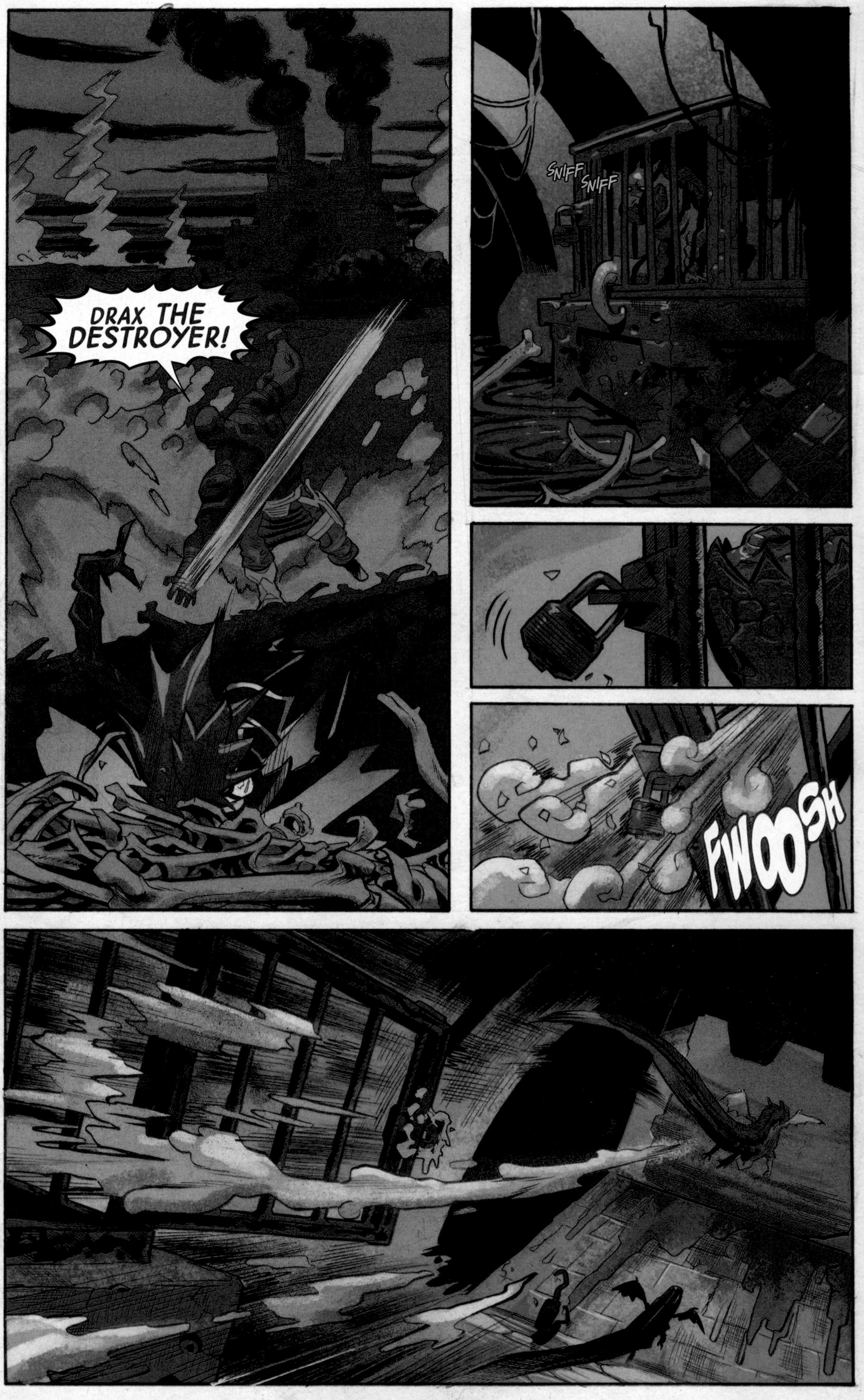
DRAX THE DESTROYER!
SNIFF SNIFF
FWOOSH

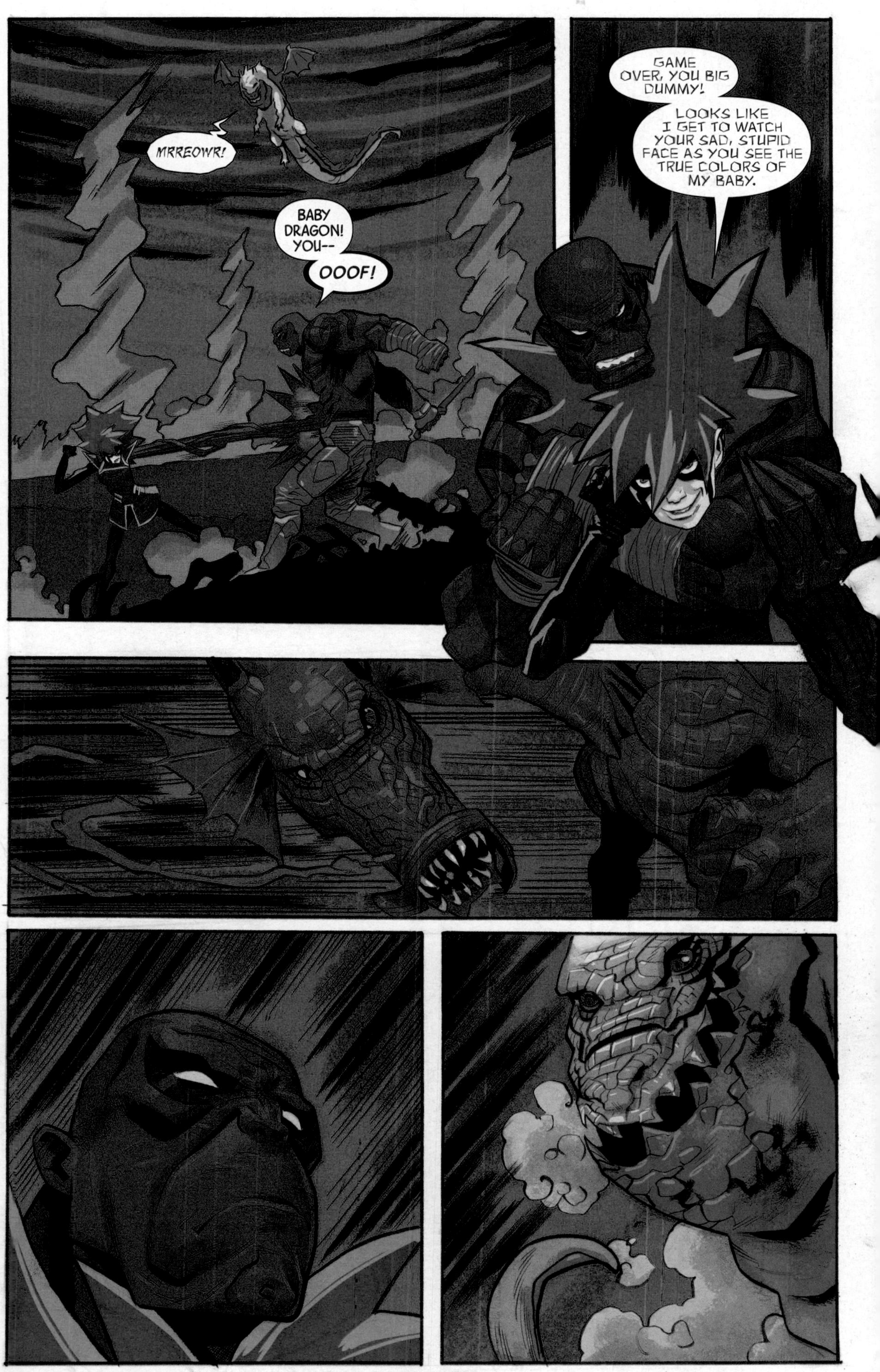

MRREOWR!
BABY DRAGON! YOU--
OOOF!
GAME OVER, YOU BIG DUMMY!
LOOKS LIKE I GET TO WATCH YOUR SAD, STUPID FACE AS YOU SEE THE TRUE COLORS OF MY BABY.

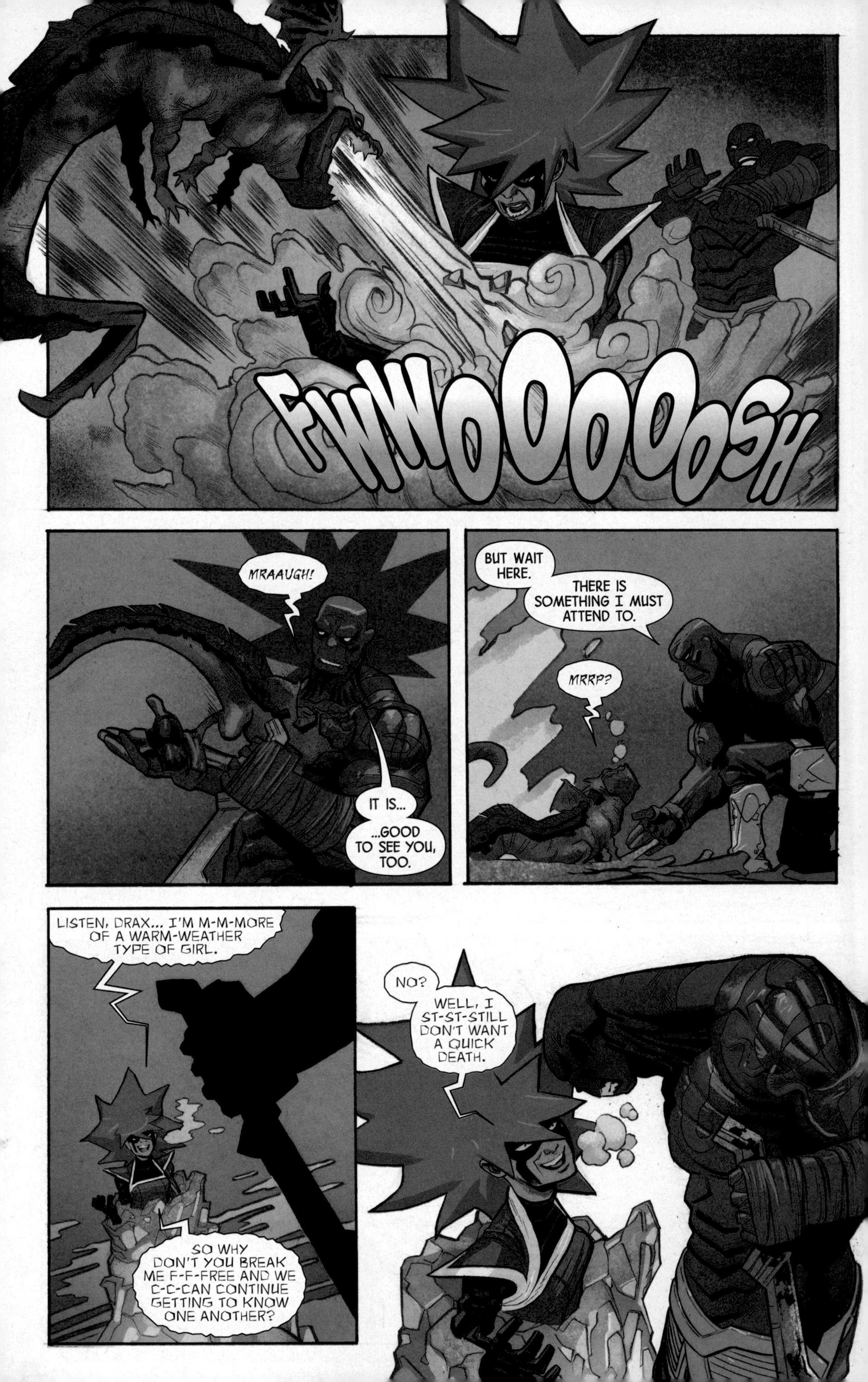
FWWOOOOOSH
MRAAUGH!
IT IS...
...GOOD TO SEE YOU, TOO.
BUT WAIT HERE.
THERE IS SOMETHING I MUST ATTEND TO.
MRRP?
LISTEN, DRAX... I'M M-M-MORE OF A WARM-WEATHER TYPE OF GIRL.
NO?
WELL, I ST-ST-STILL DON'T WANT A QUICK DEATH.
SO WHY DON'T YOU BREAK ME F-F-FREE AND WE C-C-CAN CONTINUE GETTING TO KNOW ONE ANOTHER?

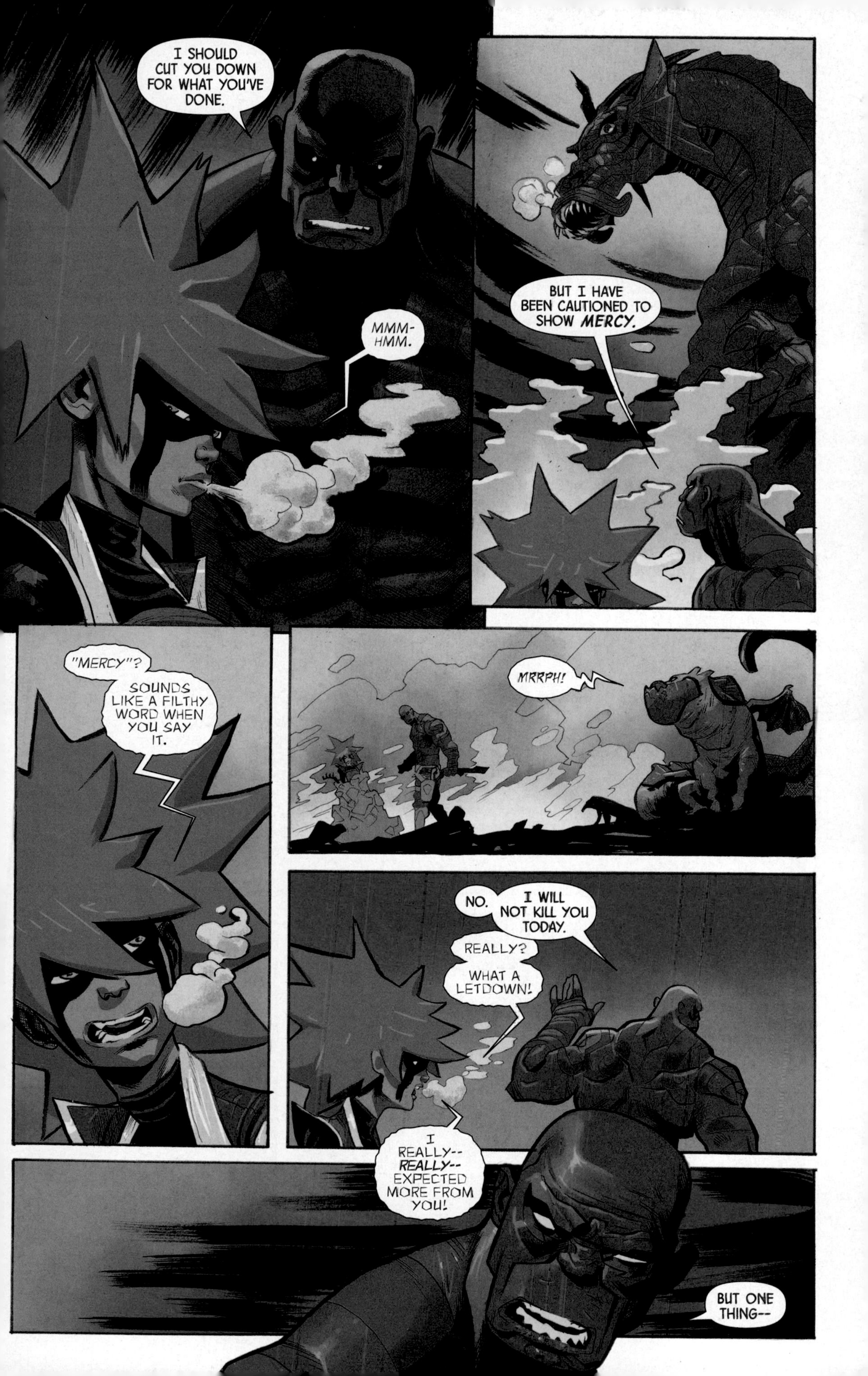
I SHOULD CUT YOU DOWN FOR WHAT YOU'VE DONE.
MMM-HMM.
BUT I HAVE BEEN CAUTIONED TO SHOW *MERCY*.
"MERCY"?
SOUNDS LIKE A FILTHY WORD WHEN YOU SAY IT.
MRRPH!
NO.
I WILL NOT KILL YOU TODAY.
REALLY?
WHAT A LETDOWN!
I REALLY-- *REALLY--* EXPECTED MORE FROM YOU!
BUT ONE THING--

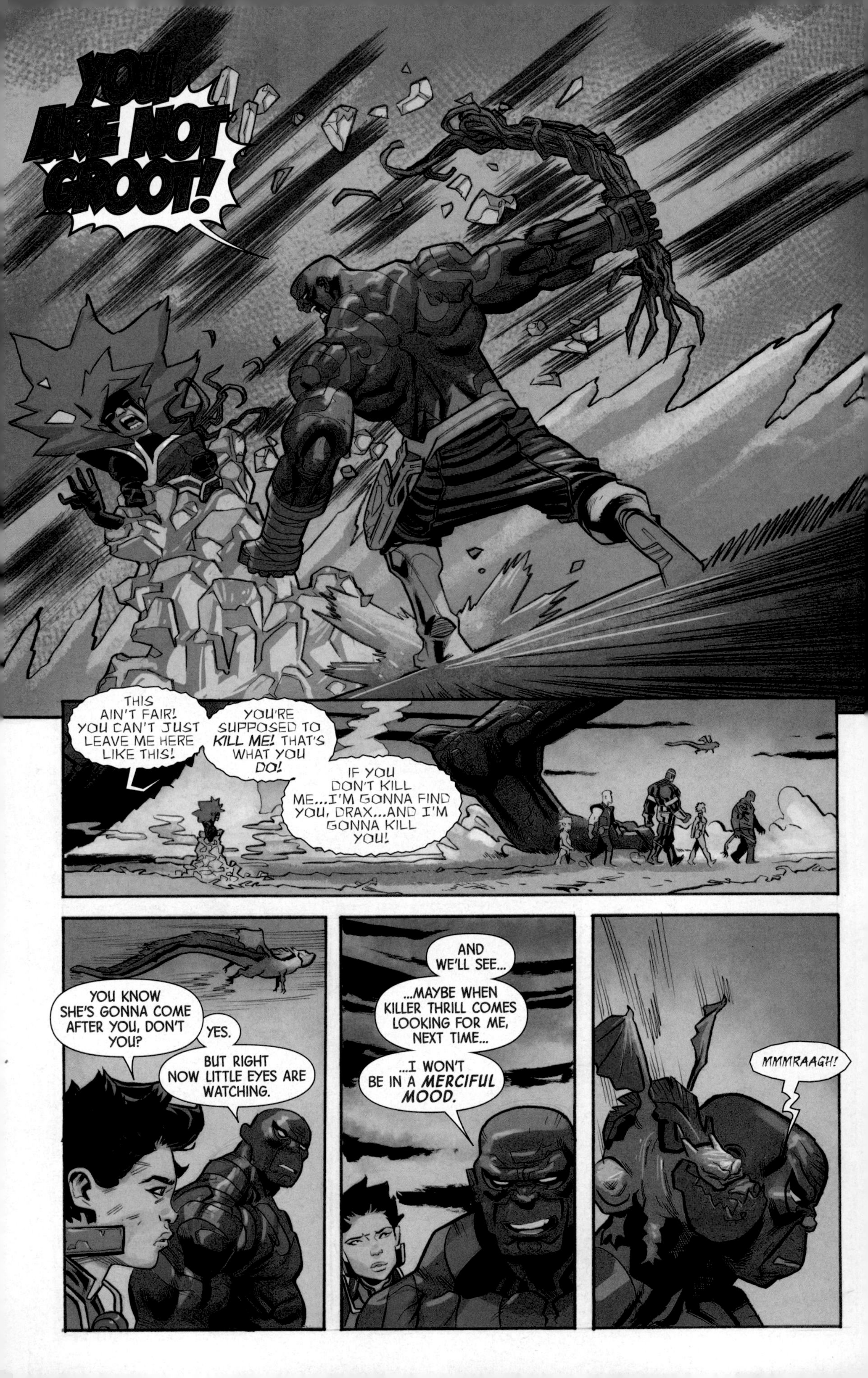
YOU! YOU ARE NOT GROOT!
THIS AIN'T FAIR! YOU CAN'T JUST LEAVE ME HERE LIKE THIS!
YOU'RE SUPPOSED TO KILL ME! THAT'S WHAT YOU DO!
IF YOU DON'T KILL ME...I'M GONNA FIND YOU, DRAX...AND I'M GONNA KILL YOU!
YOU KNOW SHE'S GONNA COME AFTER YOU, DON'T YOU?
YES.
BUT RIGHT NOW LITTLE EYES ARE WATCHING.
AND WE'LL SEE...
...MAYBE WHEN KILLER THRILL COMES LOOKING FOR ME, NEXT TIME...
...I WON'T BE IN A MERCIFUL MOOD.
MMMRAAGH!

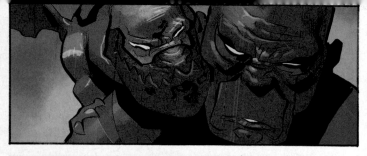

YOU KNOW YOU CANNOT KEEP THE BROODLING, YES?

IF THE BABY STAYS WITH YOU...IT WILL LEARN TO BE LIKE YOU.

IT WILL BE A *MENACE.*

YOU'RE RIGHT, FOOM.

HE CANNOT STAY WITH ME.

BUT HE CANNOT GO WITH YOU, EITHER.

WHAT? WHAT IS THIS YOU ARE SAYING?

THE INFANT IS MY *KIN!*

I CAN PROTECT IT LIKE NO OTHER!

I HAVE NO DOUBT YOU *CAN*--AND *WOULD*-- DEFEND THE BABY.

BUT YOU CANNOT PROTECT IT FROM YOUR OWN NATURE, AND YOU KNOW IT.

IT IS A PAINFUL LESSON, BUT ONE YOU AND I MUST *BOTH* ACCEPT.

DRAX IS RIGHT.

SOONER OR LATER, WE WILL BOTH TIRE OF FARMING.

WHEN THAT HAPPENS, WE'LL RETURN TO WHAT WE KNOW BEST-- *CONQUEST.*

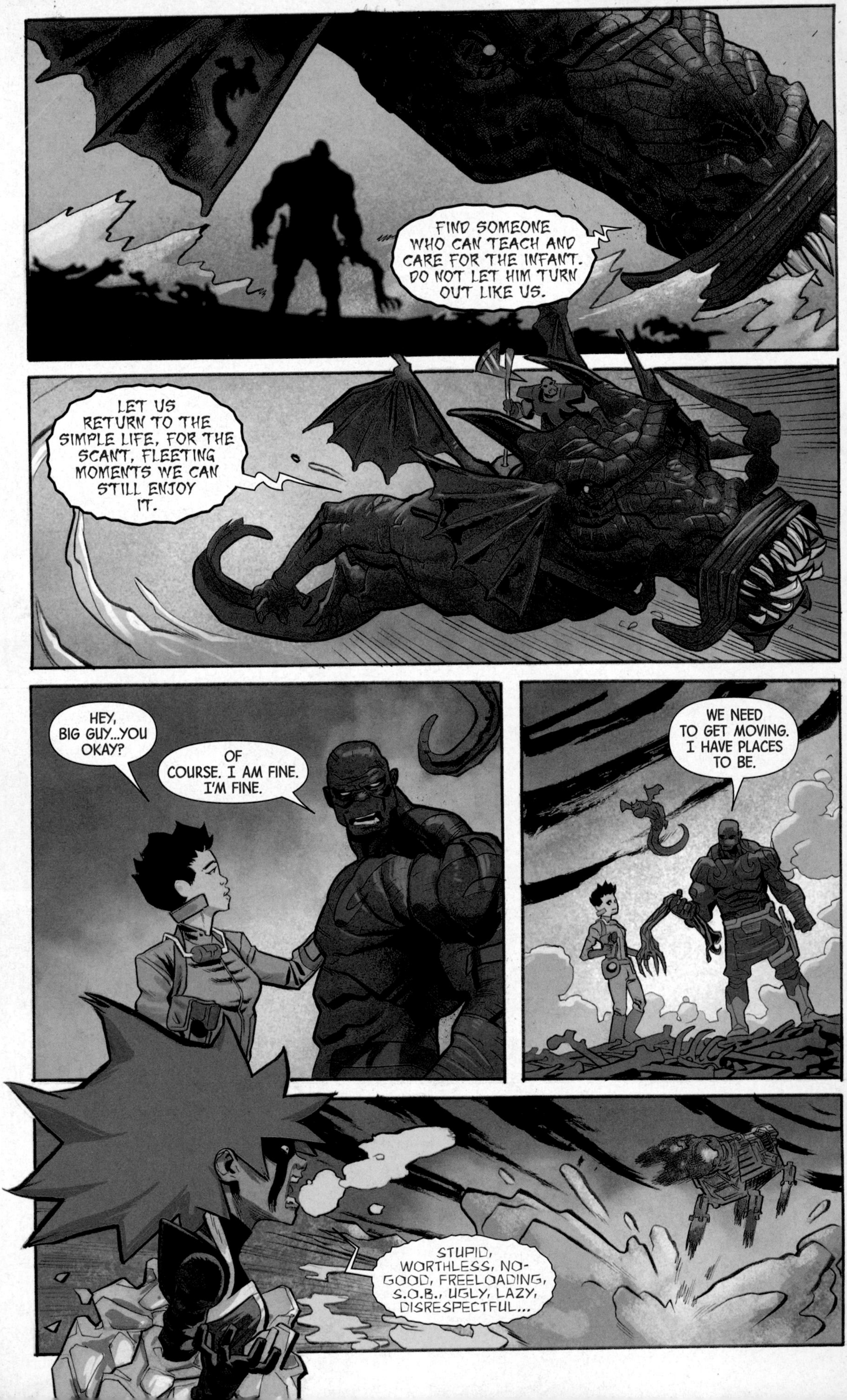
FIND SOMEONE WHO CAN TEACH AND CARE FOR THE INFANT. DO NOT LET HIM TURN OUT LIKE US.
LET US RETURN TO THE SIMPLE LIFE, FOR THE SCANT, FLEETING MOMENTS WE CAN STILL ENJOY IT.
HEY, BIG GUY...YOU OKAY?
OF COURSE. I AM FINE. I'M FINE.
WE NEED TO GET MOVING. I HAVE PLACES TO BE.
STUPID, WORTHLESS, NO-GOOD, FREELOADING, S.O.B., UGLY, LAZY, DISRESPECTFUL...

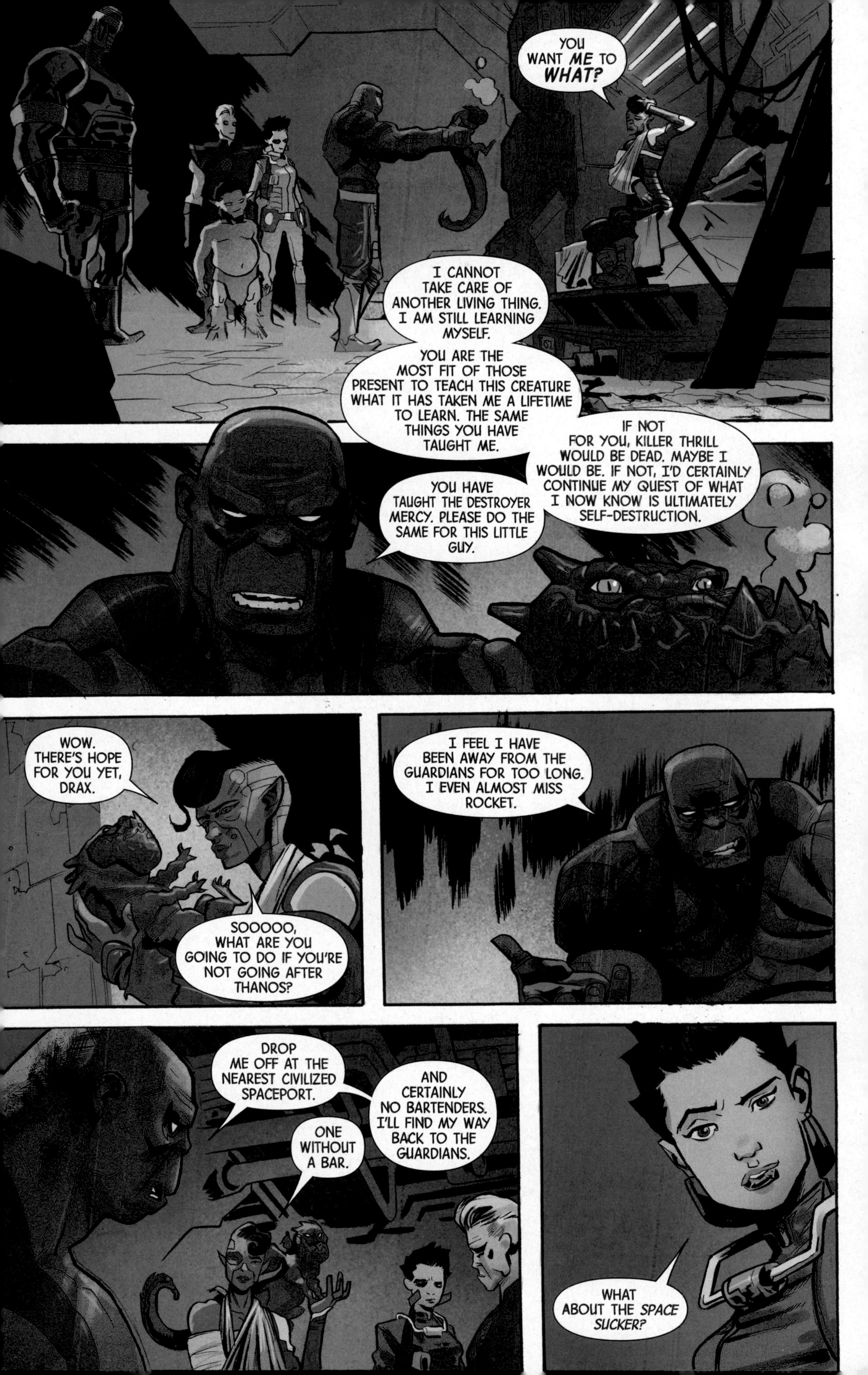
YOU WANT *ME* TO *WHAT?*
I CANNOT TAKE CARE OF ANOTHER LIVING THING. I AM STILL LEARNING MYSELF.
YOU ARE THE MOST FIT OF THOSE PRESENT TO TEACH THIS CREATURE WHAT IT HAS TAKEN ME A LIFETIME TO LEARN. THE SAME THINGS YOU HAVE TAUGHT ME.
IF NOT FOR YOU, KILLER THRILL WOULD BE DEAD. MAYBE I WOULD BE. IF NOT, I'D CERTAINLY CONTINUE MY QUEST OF WHAT I NOW KNOW IS ULTIMATELY SELF-DESTRUCTION.
YOU HAVE TAUGHT THE DESTROYER MERCY. PLEASE DO THE SAME FOR THIS LITTLE GUY.
WOW. THERE'S HOPE FOR YOU YET, DRAX.
SOOOOO, WHAT ARE YOU GOING TO DO IF YOU'RE NOT GOING AFTER THANOS?
I FEEL I HAVE BEEN AWAY FROM THE GUARDIANS FOR TOO LONG. I EVEN ALMOST MISS ROCKET.
DROP ME OFF AT THE NEAREST CIVILIZED SPACEPORT.
ONE WITHOUT A BAR.
AND CERTAINLY NO BARTENDERS. I'LL FIND MY WAY BACK TO THE GUARDIANS.
WHAT ABOUT THE *SPACE SUCKER?*

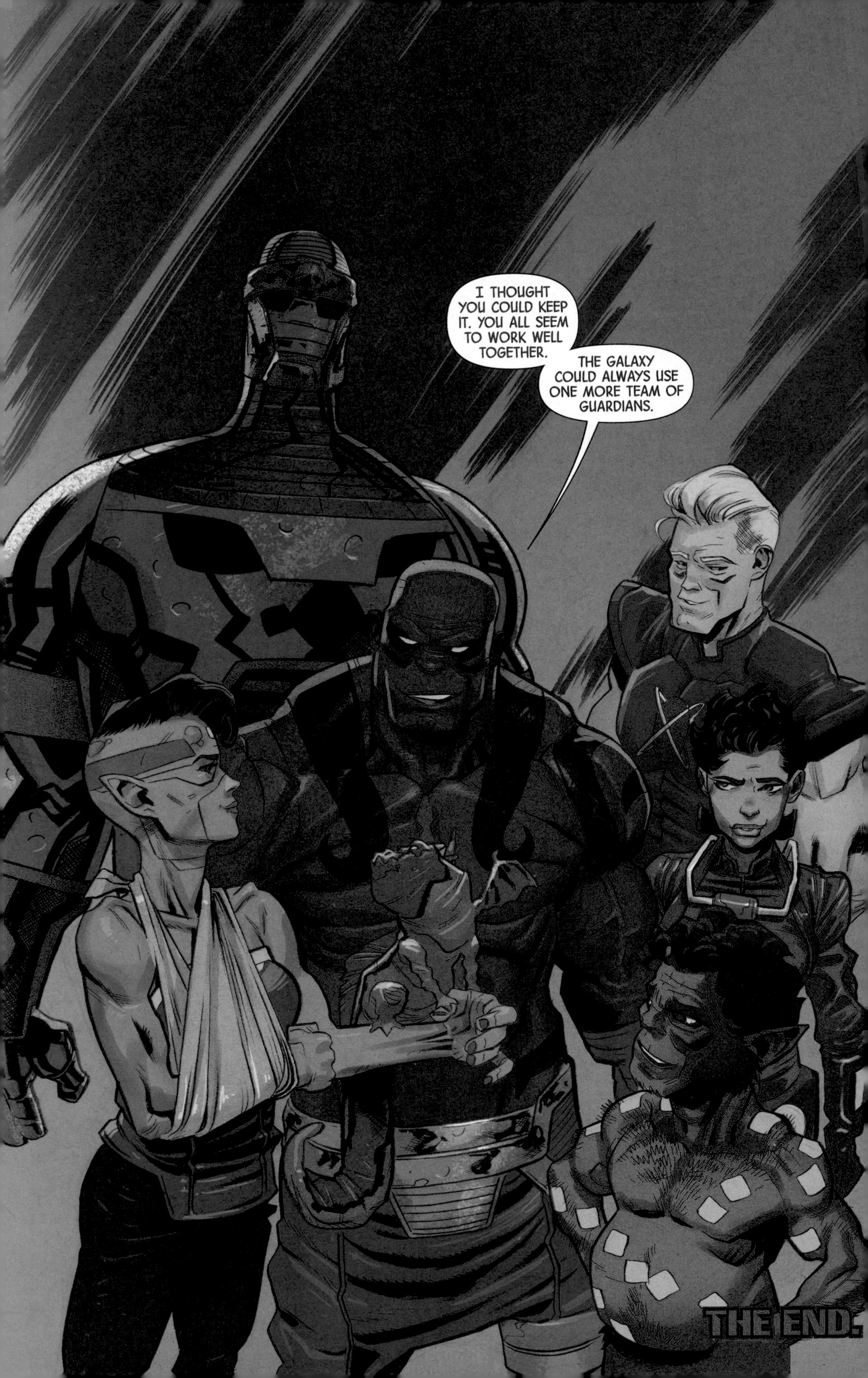
I THOUGHT YOU COULD KEEP IT. YOU ALL SEEM TO WORK WELL TOGETHER.
THE GALAXY COULD ALWAYS USE ONE MORE TEAM OF GUARDIANS.
THE END.

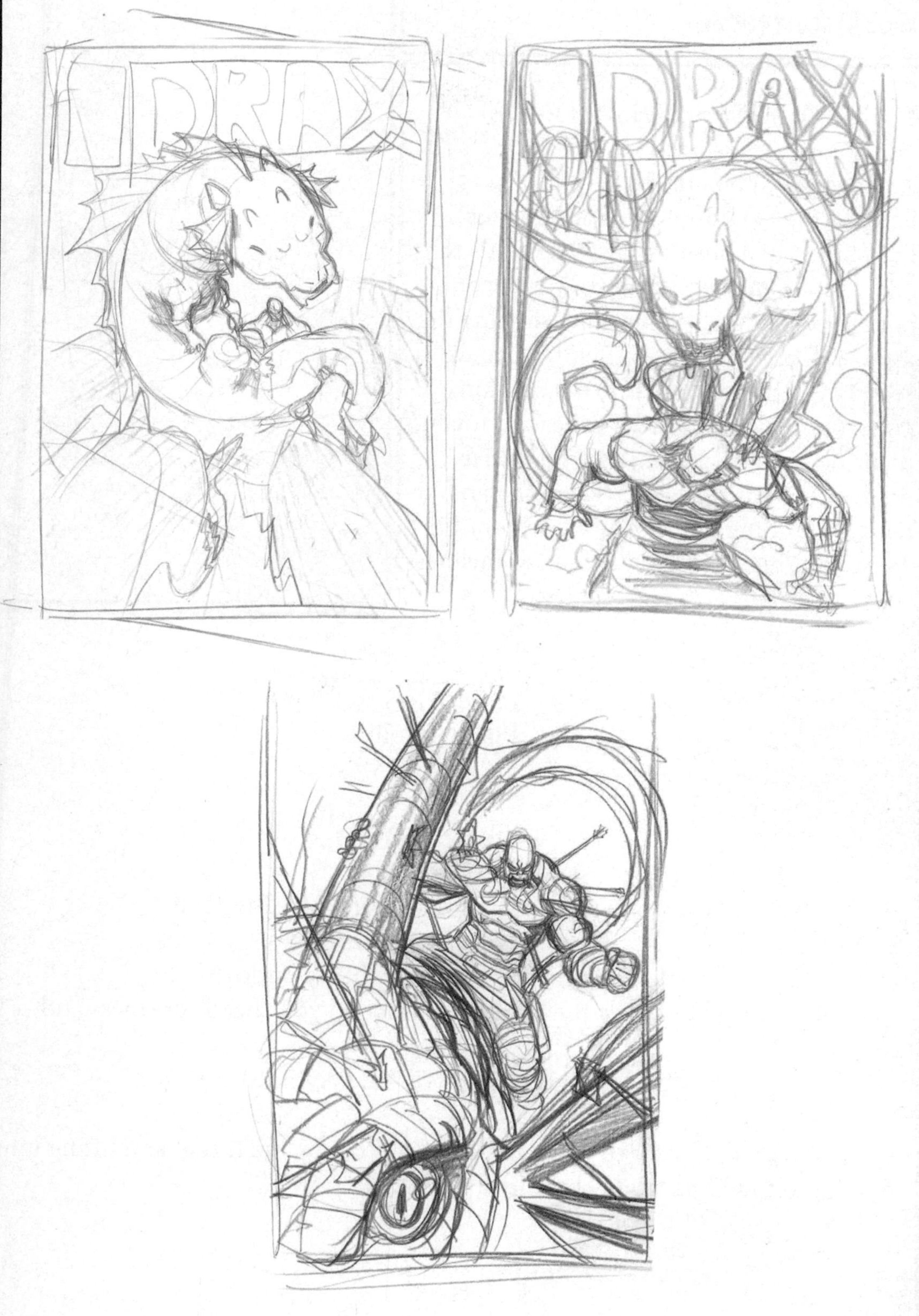
DRAX
DRAX

#10 AND #11 COVER ROUGHS

DRAX #7, PAGES 14-15
SCRIPT BY CM PUNK & CULLEN BUNN
PENCILS BY SCOTT HEPBURN

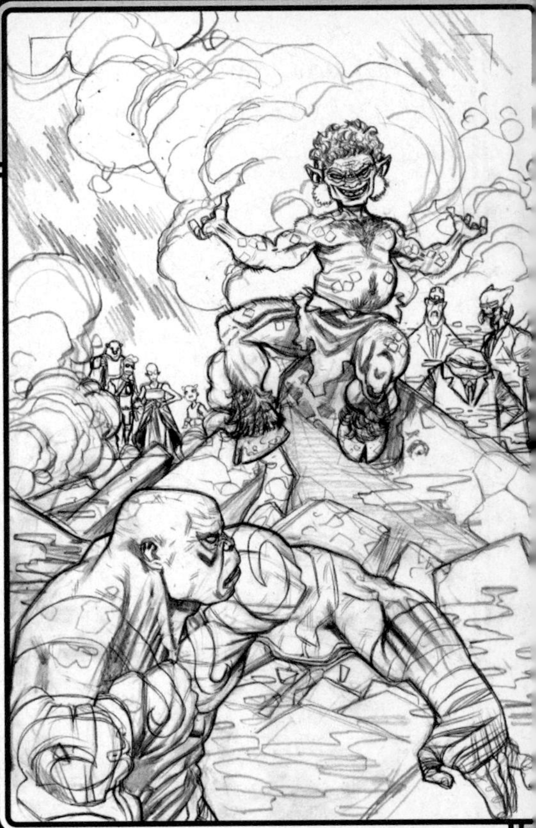

PAGE FOURTEEN (SPLASH PAGE)

1- Angle from behind Drax (still smoldering from multiple blaster shots). He has landed in a business district of this sci-fi city. We should see citizens (a variety of alien races) in the background, skirting the area, watching nervously. Before him, we see PIP THE TROLL! He is not smoking a cigar, but he is covered from head to toe in nicotine patches. He smiles broadly. He holds his hands out, as if welcoming an old friend. Standing not too far away from Pip are several big, bruiser aliens, all in business suits. These are Pip's bodyguards.

DRAX:
Pip the Troll!

PIP:
That's right, Drax!
Yer ol' pal Pip!
Only in these parts I'm known as "Mr. The Troll."
I'm kind of a mogul these days.
It's good to see you, though, big buddy!
I hope we can look past the whole "contract on your head" business and—

PAGE FIFTEEN (FIVE PANELS)

1- Still smoking, Drax steps forward, grabbing Pip by the throat and lifting him off the ground. Pip's smile becomes a grimace.

PIP:
Hrrk!

2 – Cammi and Planet Terry react. Cammi steps forward, reaching out (she still has the egg in one hand). Planet Terry draws his laser pistol. Cammi is in the way of his shot.

CAMMI:
Drax—don't!

TERRY:
Step aside, Cammi. Let me rotisserate him!

3 – Drax holds Pip up. He looks at him coldly.

DRAX:
You put a bounty on my head!
You must be out of your mind!

PIP (Small, weak):
Drahhhxx… lemme… ehhxplain…

4 – As Drax holds Pip up, the Bodyguards start to move forward. They are reaching into their jackets, drawing weapons.

BODYGUARD:
You've got about two seconds to let him go, meathead!

5 – Past some of the Bodyguards as Pip raises a hand, telling them to stand down.

PIP (Weak, small):
It's ahhhll right, fellahhhs!
Thhhis is juussst a misunderstanding…
…thaat's all.

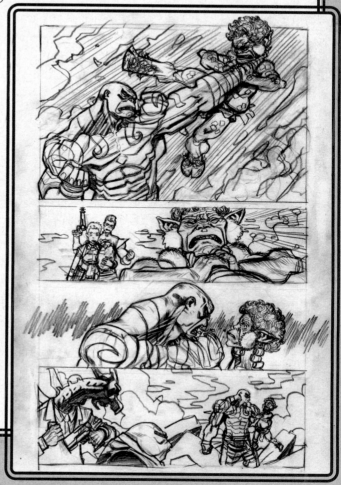

DRAX'S DICTATION MACHINE

Drax,

I am enjoying your adventures in babysitting, errr, I mean, journey to kill Thanos! I can't help but think that Fin Fang Foom's offspring may be of some assistance to you. You could adopt it and call it Larry! I do have a question, what are the meanings behind your tattoos? And do you have plans for any more after ending Thanos? Keep fighting the good fight!

Chad McDaniel

HAHAHAH! I KNEW that was Chad! I was in the *Space Sucker's* waste reclamation center/ sleeping quarters, packing my knives for my journey back, when I heard a sound coming from the command console. Naturally, the pocket calculator that passes for a computer had started reading out correspondence. Though I had no plans to dictate a log. Chad has written in before, I couldn't help but recognize his syntax.

Chab, I — Chab, computer, I'm saying Chab. WITH A 'B,' COMPUTER, CHAB WITH A 'B'! IT WAS TRANSCRIBEB CORRECTLY JUST AAARRRGGGGHHH! [Inaudible] HOW?! [Inaudible]

Mister McBaniel, if you've been following my journey closely, you unberstanb that I wish I coulb take your abvice regarbing the baby, but it's not meant to be. Your question about my tattoos is a goob one, I — no. NO! Goob is UNACCEPTABLE [Inaudible] [Incorrect input] [ERROR]

...My tattoos are my memories. Next, I think I will get some blue mist. To Chad and everyone who — oh! I hit the computer and it's working again! Readers, violence is not always the answer, but it often works with computer problems. There is some good advice in exchange for that which you've given me. I also advise you to listen to others. Here, I'll leave the receiver on as I finish packing. Maybe some more pleasant messages will come in. Brax out.

Well, there it is. The last DRAX. Oh, don't cry, you'll be able to read about his adventures in various other Marvel books. You may never see hippy Terrax or Farmer Foom ever again, though. Thinking about it, I'm not sure exactly who allowed us to do that. You should see the stuff they said "NO!" to!

Writing this book has been an amazing time. Well, it's been half amazing. The other half is Cullen Bunn. Couldn't have done it without him. Really. Imagine writing over sixty monthly titles (most of which are really, really good...okay, they're all good), then being asked to co-write something with me. Not sure why he said yes. Really not sure why he agreed after I told him I wanted it to be a "weird space opera." I guess he's as sick as I am. Good luck finding another two guys who "just get" Planet Terry!

Then there's Scott Hepburn, who "just got" what Cullen and I were putting down on paper. I've read a lot of these farewells, and my fair share of forwards. I feel fortunate to be writing one now, knowing what other writers mean when they say nice things about an artist. Nobody else could've done what Scott did with DRAX. I love the emotion in his art, along with his subtlety.

I'd like to take the time right now to thank my editors. All of 'em! Jonathan, Jacob, and Kathleen. Let it be known that I was always on time. They never once had to send multiple emails to check on pages. Yes, always on time. It was a fun crash course learning from you all!

Don't be sad, True Believer! These characters live on in the trades. I'm happy we got to wrap it up our own way, and we never had creator changes. Because nobody wants to see what anyone else would do with a nicotine-starved Pip the Troll!

Until next time!

CM Punk

There you have it. Drax's adventures continue, of course, but this series has reached its conclusion.

When the idea of this book was first presented to me, I had no idea what to expect. I've been a Drax fan — in all of his incarnations — for many years. But every co-writing situation is different, and I had no idea what my esteemed colleague might have in mind. As soon as Punk and I hopped on the phone to talk about the book, though, I knew this was going to be something special. The book we ended up talking about was something unlike any other space adventure book on the shelves.

It's easy for someone who sees a Drax book on those shelves to assume what the book might be. I mean, the guy's the Destroyer, after all. He destroys things! And, sure, there's plenty of destruction. But I doubt anyone would have expected an ensemble book featuring such an oddball cast. I doubt anyone expected this much fun from a brute like Drax. What I think makes this book so different is that it was so fun and it goes in directions readers would never really expect. I'm writing half of every issue, and I still find myself laughing and being surprised as the scripts come in... and that's before Scott Hepburn works his wonderful brand of magic insanity on the page.

So, I think a lot of people — incorrectly assuming they knew what a Drax book was all about — have yet to discover Terrax the Tiller, or the endearing death-driven Torgo, or Ora, the Galaxy's deadliest bartender. They missed out on Killer Thrill's first appearance (but not her last)... and Pip the Troll covered in Nicotine patches... and the triumphant return of Cammi... and the even more unexpected return of Planet %#$@ Terry! And let's not forget Fin Fang Farm.

Never, ever forget.

But maybe they'll discover these stories in the trades. And they will weep that they did not read them sooner! Weep, I say! Weep!

Whenever a book comes to an end, there's a sense of sadness. With DRAX, I feel it all the more acutely. I'm really proud of the book that we put together. And who knows? Maybe we'll get a chance to return to these characters again. I'm pretty sure Punk, Hepburn, and I would jump at the chance to tell more stories featuring any or all of these characters.

Thanks for coming along for the ride!

CB Punk

DRAX #11 FAREWELL LETTER